Canadian Centre for Architecture
Sternberg Press

When Is the Digital in Architecture?

Canadian Centre for Architecture
Sternberg Press

WHEN IS THE DIGITAL IN ARCHITECTURE?

Edited by Andrew Goodhouse

Mirko Zardini	Eight Million Stories	9
Marco Frascari	1521 An Age of Paper	23
Mario Carpo	1570 Building with Geometry, Drawing with Numbers	33
Wolfgang Ernst	1837 Toward a Museology of Algorithmic Architectures from Within	45
Antoine Picon	1884 Histories of the Digital: Information, Computer and Communication	79
Peter Galison	1895 Epistemic Machines: Image and Logic	99
Orit Halpern	1943 Architecture as Machine: The Smart City Deconstructed	121

Contents

Mark Wigley	**1963** Black Screens: The Architect's Vision in a Digital Age	177
Molly Wright Steenson	**1964** Information Archaeologies	193
Andrew Witt	**1970** The Machinic Animal: Autonomic Networks and Behavioural Computation	213
Greg Lynn	**1987** Going Native: Notes on Selected Artifacts from Digital Architecture at the End of the Twentieth Century	279
Nathalie Bredella	**1991** In the Midst of Things: Architecture's Encounter with Digital Technology, Media Theory and Material Culture	335
Stan Allen	**1992** The Paperless Studios in Context	383

Bernard Tschumi	1992 The Making of a Generation: How the Paperless Studios Came About	405
Phil Bernstein	2002 Sound Advice and Clear Drawings: Design and Computation in the Second Machine Age	421
	Notes	439
	Bibliography	447
	Projects selected as part of the Archaeology of the Digital research program	452
	Index	454
	Biographies	457
	Image and copyright credits	459
	Credits	463

EIGHT MILLION STORIES

Mirko Zardini

There can be no doubt that there is a digital moment in architecture practice, a moment at which a certain set of tools allowed architects to realize ideas that they could not have realized before and to develop new approaches to projects at a range of scales and in a variety of contexts. Certainly the experimentation that took place so widely in the period between the late 1980s and the early 2000s was prompted by the articulation of problems before the adoption of tools. This is the moment that the CCA

Mirko Zardini

chose to address with Greg Lynn through the Archaeology of the Digital research program, begun in 2011 and developed through the acquisition of twenty-five pivotal projects and the production of three exhibitions, two print publications and a series of digital monographs, which concern each of the projects. Taken as a whole, this body of work addresses how architecture began to engage with digital tools during a specific period. There was a sense of urgency in trying to capture this period, particularly because digital materials produced as part of the twenty-five projects were growing increasingly difficult to access as older forms of software became incompatible with new machines.

But if we take care to identify the digital as a condition that is made possible by the conceptual foundations of digital media and not necessarily by digital media itself, the boundaries of the digital moment—when it began and under what circumstances—

become less clear. There are eight million stories of the origins of the digital in architecture, and this book brings together fourteen of them in a chronology of responses to the question of when the digital is in architecture. The arguments here address specific changes in ways of thinking about architecture, building and cities, as well as the shifts in technology that resulted from these changes, marking both a capstone to Archaeology of the Digital and the beginning of an investigation of other beginnings of the digital in architecture. Some of the stories presented here were originally formed through the CCA's earlier investigations of the topic.

In 2004, the CCA organized a seminar entitled *Devices of Design* in collaboration with the Daniel Langlois Foundation, inviting historians and architects to discuss the ways technologies were used in new approaches to designing and building. The seminar was prompted by the increasingly

Mirko Zardini

widespread use of digital tools in architecture, and it was the CCA's first attempt to understand the implications of this shift for the construction, conservation and accessibility of an architecture archive. Four of the arguments from *Devices of Design* are included here. Marco Frascari shows how paper in the sixteenth century relates to architectural thinking, and how this tool responded to the architect's concern with articulating distinct ways of interpreting the design. So maybe the digital begins there. Or maybe it begins with the invention of printing, a new information technology in the sixteenth century that, according to Mario Carpo, allowed Palladio to develop a numerical approach to architecture. Although design software seems to reify a design and therefore to return to a geometry without measurements, the digits in the digital are read by a computer today in the same way that human eyes scanned the printed page five centuries ago. And according to Peter Galison, we should look for the origins of the digital in moments like the period of intense, productive collaboration between theoreticians and experimentalists in science in the early years of the twentieth century. This point defined a new mode of collaboration across intellectual traditions that indirectly informs an interest in addressing architectural problems with new digital tools. It could be that a specific change in the support used for the representation of architectural concepts is the starting point for a history of the digital. Mark Wigley identifies one such point: the shift from the white page to the black screen in the mid-1960s. The implications of this representational shift are clearly shown in projects by Cedric Price and David Greene, neither of whom had access to a computer at the time.

The seminar *Toolkit for Today: Archaeology of the Digital*, held at the CCA in 2013, introduced other archaeological and his-

Mirko Zardini

torical perspectives by scholars, students and practitioners in the context of the first Archaeology of the Digital exhibition. This book includes four arguments that were originally presented in this seminar. According to Antoine Picon, the management of data in the city and the development of urbanism in the late nineteenth century form a starting point for a history of the digital. He argues that the invention of the tabulating machine to address the need to process an otherwise overwhelming quantity of census data is essential to understanding the digital today. Molly Wright Steenson discusses the way Christopher Alexander, Cedric Price and Nicholas Negroponte formatted information to organize activities in space, structure urban planning scenarios and create a data-rich virtual reality. The work of these three architects, in her view, defines a beginning for contemporary approaches to spatializing data. The paperless studios at Columbia University's

Graduate School of Architecture, Planning and Preservation (GSAPP) have been widely described as incubators of the avant-garde in relation to digital tools in architectural production. But Stan Allen shows how these studios emerged from a wider cultural context and emphasizes the intellectual, theoretical interest in the digital over technical or aesthetic experimentation. And former GSAPP dean Bernard Tschumi insists that the studios allowed a younger generation to take control of a discourse that became widely influential in the following years.

Perhaps the pre-digital age continued long after architects began using computers. In a position originally articulated at the CCA in 2016, Phil Bernstein suggests that technological developments in architecture practice that seem radical at first glance —particularly the adoption of computer-aided design software—are just more efficient ways of communicating the same information that is contained in a drawing

Mirko Zardini

done by hand five hundred years ago. Only with the introduction of building information modelling in the early twenty-first century, and the new possibilities for collaboration in the design process that it implies, does the story of the digital really begin.

This book presents five new essays commissioned from researchers, Greg Lynn among them, whose work opens other lines of investigation into the digital in architecture. Media archaeology offers one way into this topic. Wolfgang Ernst insists that a media-archaeological approach to the digital in architecture is not based on historical continuity but rather on flashes of insight that illuminate certain symbolic logic systems and physical analytical machines. Examining material and theoretical media and machines from the past allows for an archaeological understanding of the digital present. Starting from the machine, whether on paper, in hardware or in virtual space, Ernst reveals a fractured lineage that includes

[17] Ramon Llull's fourteenth-century combinatorial system, Charles Babbage's analytical engine, the room-size UNIVAC I Factronic computer and Asymptote Architecture's navigable New York Stock Exchange Virtual Trading Floor. Orit Halpern hints at how fragile an apparently definitive point of origin in any history of the digital can be, showing that the cybernetic character of the contemporary smart city inherits the work on responsive environments carried out by Nicholas Negroponte and the Architecture Machine Group, and later the Media Lab, at the Massachusetts Institute of Technology from the 1960s through the 1980s. Negroponte's approach was shaped by earlier models of cybernetics and computer programming that defined responsive networks of information. Halpern's argument seems to suggest that it is often possible to cut the pages on the left side of the book, to find an earlier chapter that we hadn't noticed before.

Mirko Zardini

According to Andrew Witt, design through quantification and computation intensified in the 1950s and 1960s and reached a kind of apex at Expo '70. Beyond the contemporary relevance of certain projects developed around 1970, the exposition itself can be seen as a point of origin for a specific kind of environmental, network-based understanding of the digital in architecture, as Expo '70's Festival Plaza was meant to enact Arata Isozaki's concept of a soft architecture of information technology and software dispersed throughout space.[1] The argument of the Archaeology of the Digital research program is that architects incorporated digital tools as creative extensions of their practices and gave these new technologies carefully defined roles within a working process. Greg Lynn presents this argument here, and claims that any history of the digital must draw from an archaeology. Interactive environments, both virtual and physical, and the easy movement of images across media and even into physical reality are characteristics of contemporary society.[2] Nathalie Bredella implies a genealogy of this condition in her description of the dialogue between artists and architects at media art institutes, particularly in Europe in the early 1990s, which produced spaces and networks through interaction between humans and digital technology.

In his narrative of the paperless studios, Bernard Tschumi asks: did the digital allow for the development of new concepts, or just a new way of expressing the concerns that a new generation of architects was defining? This is the kind of question that a question like When is the digital in architecture? uncovers. And if asking a question like this can produce eight million stories in response, then it is easy to see how it could lead to eight million digressions and redirections that narrow in focus and change geographies, producing a *Tristram Shandy* of the digital as the CCA continues to build

Mirko Zardini

[20] its digital archive and makes it increasingly accessible to researchers. If this novel of digressions is distributed across future research projects and extended with studies of new archival material, so much the better for the reader.

1   Thomas Daniell, "Bug Eyes and Blockhead," *Log* 36 (Winter 2016): 47.

2   Hito Steyerl, "Too Much World: Is the Internet Dead?," in *The Internet Does Not Exist*, eds. Julieta Aranda, Brian Kuan Wood and Anton Vidokle (Berlin: Sternberg Press, 2015), 18.

Marco Frascari

In <u>1521</u>, Cesare Cesariano's Italian-language translation of Vitruvius was published. The translation includes the duomo in Milan as a contemporary visual example and, specifically, a plan of the cathedral that occupies a full page gives the page's material an active role. More than just working as an allegory for the ground on which the building is built, paper in this case gives form to a design concept; the cathedral exists in a certain sense on the paper. This is the anagogic sense, and it is one of the conditions of digital material now.

This text is the transcription of a presentation that was given at the CCA in 2004.

MARCO FRASCARI

1 Sheet music for "The Age of Paper." Music and lyrics by Henry Walker, lithography by Concanen and Lee, 1862. The Lester S. Levy Collection of Sheet Music, The Sheridan Libraries, The Johns Hopkins University

AN AGE OF PAPER

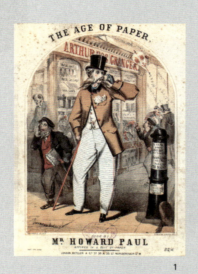

1

We often talk about paper as a support for writing, but it is really a dominant part of clothing manufacturing, to the point that, for instance, in 1870, one Boston manufacturer produced seventy-five thousand paper cuffs. A song from 1860s London has the refrain, "For paper now is all the rage, and nothing else will suit the age." It was sung by a man called Howard Paul, who was dressed entirely in paper (fig. 1).

An English newspaper once asked Clifford Pickover, who worked at IBM's Thomas J. Watson Research Center, what the most famous invention was. Pickover said it was the invention of paper, and he compared paper to the Internet because both paper and the Internet break the barriers of time and distance. And really, architecture entered the age of paper in the fourteenth century. Paper was invented by the Chinese, and moved along the Silk Road to the Arabs. There is an eleventh-century treatise in Arabic called "The Writing Base of Scribes and the Instruments of Their Intelligence," and it was about how to make paper. So paper

Marco Frascari

2

came, of course, from the Arabs, to Europe. In the beginning paper was condemned; the Church forbade scribes to write the Word of God on paper because paper was a "pagan art." But slowly, paper landed on the table of the architect, and played a major role in the transformation of architecture. You can see, for instance, in a painting by Lorenzo Lotto, an architect holding a compass, and touching the top of a roll of paper with his index finger (fig. 2). Unfortunately, in modern times, there has been a misunderstanding of the nature of paper in relation to architecture, caused by the profession on the one hand and Cartesian thinking on the other.

    I was quite surprised when I came to the United States and learned that yellow, light tracing paper is called "trash." Then I learned the term *bumwad*. I was told not to use this term in front of clients. But if you search for "bumwad" on the Internet, you find it for sale under this name. Paper became something without value. Of course there are exceptions. People can use tracing paper properly, like Venturi. But because of the way the profession billed the client and because of Descartes's description of an image as a bit of ink thrown here and there on paper, as is now done with an ink-jet printer —basically, Descartes invented the ink-jet print—it became a convention that paper doesn't interact with what you are designing. And in 1992, with the invention of the so-called "paperless" studios, there was a pushing out of paper. Moving from the analog to the digital mode was a way of privileging the environment over paper.

    But in reality, to understand what's going on with paper, we have to go back in time and use the following distich,

2   Lorenzo Lotto. *Portrait of an Architect*, sixteenth century. Oil on canvas, 86 x 108.5 cm. Gemäldegalerie, Staatliche Museen Berlin

3   Cesare Cesariano. Plan of Milan Cathedral, in *Di Lucio Vitruuio Pollione De architectura libri dece…* (Como: Gotardus de Ponte, 1521), liber primus, p. XIIII. CCA. NA44.V848 (0006180)

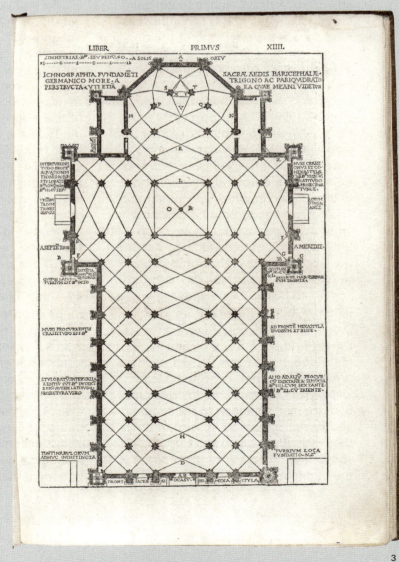

Marco Frascari

which was a tool for analyzing text in the Middle Ages: *Littera gesta docet, quid credas allegoria. Moralis quid agas, quo tendas anagogia.* [The literal interpretation teaches the acts, the allegorical what you should believe. The moral teaches what you should do, the anagogic what you should seek.] Basically, these are the four senses of a text: the literal, the allegorical, the moral and the anagogic. A drawing has these four conditions as well. It is literal because it describes the envelope of the building; allegorical because you have to rely on a modification of representation; moral because it has to respect the building code; and the anagogic is what gestures to something else, a form or an iconography. When we transfer the idea from analog to digital, we lose *anagogia*, and that, I think, is the key issue: we should be able to understand how anagogy works in the drawing, or on the paper.

To try to understand a bit better what *anagogy* means, I have to do a little bit of etymology. *Anagogy* comes from the Greek, and it is the combination of two words, *ana*, "above, high," and *agein*, "to lead." The proper Latin translation, which was done immediately, is *sursumductio*, and it can be found in the writings of Isidore of Seville, Bede and Rabanus Maurus. In architectural drawings, the literal and the allegorical senses refer strictly to analogical constructs that speak to the tectonic and formal imagination. And of course they are didascalic in the tropological sense, the moral sense that speaks to the intellect free from the imagination.

But what is most important is *anagogia*, which speaks to the *telos* of the drawing and demonstrates that, basically, the future is in front of the past. And it is very important to understand, especially in the distich, that *anagogia* is the last sense in writing or drawing. There are many ways in which the distich is memorized for teaching, but there is always this condition: anagogy is the last sense.

So it is in this formal and qualitative condition that architecture is drawn to anagogy. Of course, architecture started paperless; a paperless studio was nothing new. To build a paperless building, one went to the site marked with pegs and then looked at the location of the woods, the city and the river. One made all the connections necessary to build a building, and that was the first step. Then the second step was the use of the tracing floor. There was drawing, but it took place on-site, and was done in large dimensions. The next step is the analogical step, and it is beautifully described by Cesare Cesariano (fig. 3). He shows the *iconographia* that is the plan of Milan's cathedral, and he says that *iconographia* is an impression made over the ground or on dust—he is referring to the traditional abacus, which was a tray full of sand—or on *pasta*, a kind of dough. I can imagine someone rolling the *pasta* to make a large sheet, and making the impression on that—or even on snow—just as one draws on paper. This operation on paper is done with the compass—which is clearly analogical, as the leg of the compass becomes the leg of the architect on the

4 Carlo Scarpa. Brion family tomb, overall plan with studies for the water pavilion (*lower right*) and other elements, c. 1970–1974. Reprographic print with coloured pencil on drafting film overlay, 98.3 x 82.5 cm. Collection Archivio Carlo Scarpa, Trevignano

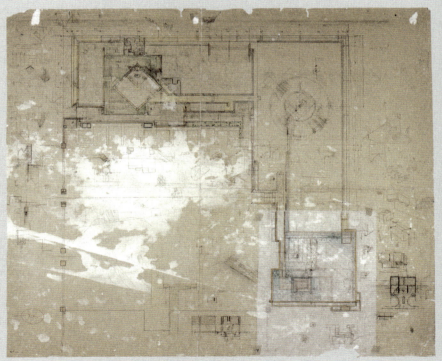

Marco Frascari

site—and with the *lituus*, the device that the Roman augur used to describe the temple. The temple is something that was in the sky, not on the ground, so you had to draw with a stick of wood, the *lituus*, which was supposed to not burn, and wait for the flight of birds. Then you have the projection down on the ground, made by crossing the two lines, and that is the sketch.

I'll move from Cesariano to Vincenzo Scamozzi, who has a very long chapter in which he says, "I have been asked too many times how you prepare paper." He gives a complicated description of how he prepares paper, how he makes it very nice by using sheets, one on top of the other, pushing, pulling and making the surface completely in support of the paper. He talks about tracing the cross on the paper, but in this case, paper becomes another tool; it's not only the support. He takes a piece of paper and folds it in four, and it becomes a square. He is performing a transformation of the design and there is a change of material. Paper is no longer the support; it becomes an active part of the game.

Now I have to talk about ink, because through ink we understand something peculiar. All of Scamozzi's descriptions about how you draw on paper—you make a groove on the paper, you run ink on top of it—give us the normal understanding of the use of paper. But Scamozzi has a completely different understanding of it, and this comes through when he talks about how you make ink. He says, you get some gall, you put it in wine—of course it has to be Romanian wine because it is very dry, and the gall is from Istria. Then you put this in a big jar in the sun for thirty days. By the way, this is the same technique used to prepare *nocino*: you take a big jar, you fill it up with walnuts and you put it in the sun for thirty days. Scamozzi says that this is very good ink because it works beautifully on the surface. He says that the ink has to be prepared, modified and adjusted, and that the quality of the paper is shown by the purple colour that comes out from the washes and from the light markings that appear on the back of the paper in the same colour. He is thinking about the percolating of the ink through the paper; when the ink goes through, you can draw on the other side. Paper takes on a completely different nature because of this percolating quality, and it is really the power of the paper that allows for another understanding of the surface.

Now let's move to *carta da lucido*, which is heavy tracing paper. Cennino Cennini describes how to make it: you run linseed oil on top of the paper, and it becomes transparent. But the paper is very greasy; you can do a few things with it, but you can't use it in architecture. It wasn't until the mid-nineteenth century that good tracing paper was invented. There are great inventions to reproduce drawings on tracing paper, including the now-obsolete heliographic copier.

With the invention of tracing paper, the architect prepared a *sotto lucido*, an underdrawing, and then someone else could draw the *lucido* on top. In drawing in the *lucido*, you lost the anagogic dimension of the drawing. A *sotto lucido* by Carlo Scarpa was conceived as such, and a second person would draw on top of it, understanding all the notations that are around it (fig. 4). He would prepare the *lucido* to be printed and then sent for production. The four senses are in the drawing, but the anagogic sense is lost when it is transferred. In a drawing by Louis Kahn, you see exactly the opposite. The draftsman prepares the drawing and Kahn puts a piece of yellow tracing paper on top and pulls out the anagogic sense. So three senses—the literal, the moral and the allegorical—are in the *sotto lucido*, while the anagogic comes out only in the *lucido* performed in the drawing in charcoal.

Paper is an amazing device, and if we are going to transfer our understanding of it to the digital world, we not only have to understand how the phenomenon of paper was related to the analogical realm, but how the anagogic condition is located in it. It then becomes very difficult to say whether the architecture is in the stone, in the paper or in the Internet. But the key question is, what is the meaning that we can put behind the line?

Mario Carpo

Palladio published his *Four Books of Architecture* in 1570. Printing, a relatively new information technology in the sixteenth century, allowed him to illustrate his architectural models with scaled drawings and proportional measurements. Vitruvius and Alberti, both dependent on scribal text rather than on reproducible drawings, could only provide measurements by verbally reciting sequences of geometrical constructions. In the sixteenth century, the shift from text to printed images accompanied the transition from classical and medieval geometry to modern number-based calculations. In the 1990s and early 2000s, designers could use numbers (mediated by spline-modelling software) to notate, calculate and fabricate all kinds of geometrical and non-geometrical forms, including free forms.

This text is the transcription of a presentation that was given at the CCA in 2004.

MARIO CARPO

1 Foreign Office Architects. Yokohama International Port Terminal, view of girders designed to support the structure, 2002. AutoCAD file converted to scalable vector graphics format for publication. Original file: girder-template.dwg, 744 KB, last modified 25 July 2002. Foreign Office Architects fonds (AP171), CCA. Gift of Farshid Moussavi and Alejandro Zaera-Polo

BUILDING WITH GEOMETRY, DRAWING WITH NUMBERS

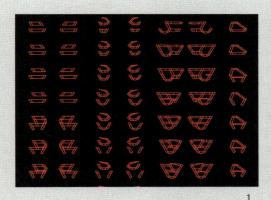

1

According to a commonplace of recent historiography, the Renaissance might have been the only period in architectural history when the rise of a new style was not related to technological change. The Gothic forms of the Middle Ages were abandoned and the old forms of classical antiquity were brought back to life and reinterpreted, but no new machinery, new material or new building technique accompanied this revolutionary change in architectural forms. True as this may be, one might argue that some technological change did nonetheless accompany the rise of Renaissance classicism. These technological changes may have gone unnoticed because they did not pertain directly to building technologies. In the Renaissance, as now, new information technologies, instead of building technologies, were the agents of change.

Mario Carpo

New information technologies brought about some new devices of design that in their turn revolutionized the process of building and changed architectural forms.

The Renaissance design process disrupted the traditional, medieval way of getting things built, but the early-modern way of manufacturing or of reproducing the architectural forms of classical antiquity was also completely different from the method of the ancients. The same forms were obtained using two very different technologies of design. The modern way, invented in the Renaissance, remained a staple of Western architecture for the five centuries that followed; it is only now being replaced. This is, perhaps, one reason why we are more likely to be aware of the historical watershed that took place in the sixteenth century. We tend to recognize the beginning of a historical age only when we have a perception that that age may be coming to an end.

To better illustrate my point, let me show as an example a very simple component of the system of the architectural orders that was a bestseller, so to speak, in classical antiquity, as it was for generations of modern classicists from the fifteenth century to the twentieth century.

The Attic or Doric base of a column, as described by Vitruvius, is composed of six superimposed parts. The rules for establishing the proportions of the path of each part, as explained by Vitruvius and marginally edited for clarity by Leon Battista Alberti fifteen centuries later, read as follows: First, you take the diameter of the column and you divide it into two equal parts. You divide that segment into three equal parts. Take away the lower third, the plinth. Next, take what remains, make a new unit of it and divide it into four equal parts. Take away the upper fourth—that gives the upper torus. Take what is left, make a new unit out of it and divide it into two equal parts. Take the lower half, the lower torus. Divide what is left into seven identical parts and take away the upper seventh and the lower seventh; that gives the two fillets. Take what is left and, fortunately, it is over because there is nothing else to be proportioned. And that's the end of the process.

Alberti, here acting as an editor of Vitruvius, guides the reader through a five-step sequence of successive divisions (fig. 2). Each step, however, is formally identical to any other step in the sequence, and each reads as follows, as I just emphasized: take a segment, divide it into a given number of equal parts, take away one of these parts, take what is left, assume it as a new unit, then go back to step one and rerun the program, as we would say today, this time five times.

This way of determining the proportions, and then the dimensions of an architectural part, has its charms, but it is not the way we would do it. Our way, which is the modern way, came into being by steps in the course of the sixteenth century. First, images of the Attic base were printed thanks to the then-new technology of printing. Neither

2   Mario Carpo. Drawing showing Alberti's divisions of the Doric base

3   Vincenzo Scamozzi. Drawing of a Doric base, in *Tutte l'opere d'architettura et prrospetiva* [sic] *di Sebastiano Serlio...* (Venice: Presso gli heredi di Francesco de' Franceschi, 1600), page opposite p. 140. CCA. NA44.S485 (W3243) | c. 1

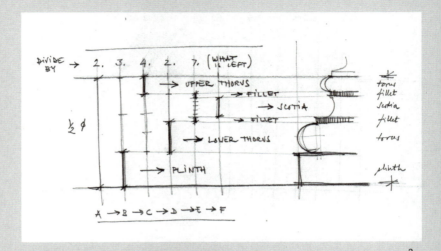

2

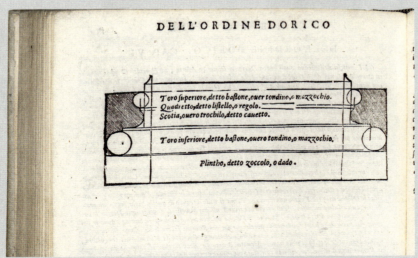

3

Mario Carpo

4   Andrea Palladio. Drawing of a Doric base, in *I quattro libri dell'architettura*… (Venice: Appresso Dominico de Franceschi, 1570), libro primo, p. 25. CCA. NA44.P164 (W161) | c. 2

5   Giacomo Barozzi da Vignola. Drawing of a Doric base, in *Regola delli cinque ordini d'architettura* (Rome: Si Stampa da Gio. Batta de Rossi, 1617), plate XXX. CCA. NA44.V686 (0002785)

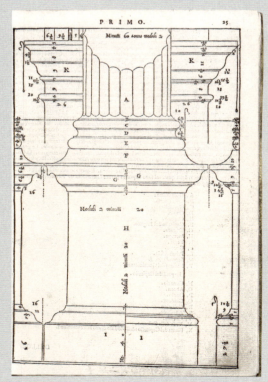

4

5

Vitruvius nor Alberti could have done this. And of course printing depended on the new-found availability of paper in the West. Serlio printed the drawings of the base, proportionally drawn to scale, and he added the names of the parts, which of course can always help (fig. 3). Then a bit later, in the sixteenth century, both Vignola and Palladio printed the same scaled drawing, but they added the proportional or modular measurements of all the parts. Vignola used a module divided into eighteen parts and Palladio used a sexagesimal partition, as we still do with minutes and seconds (figs. 4–5). Vignola and Palladio could not use the decimal point for the simple but determinant reason that it had not yet been invented. However, these differences apart, this is a language both visual and numerical that twentieth-century engineers would still understand and would still be fully conversant with. This would be especially true for engineers trained in the imperial system, which is much closer to Vignola's and Palladio's fractional universe than to the Napoleonic empire of decimals.

In short, what we have seen here are two ways to produce the same object. The first way, the Vitruvius/Alberti way, which is classical but also medieval, is based on text and geometry. The second way, the Palladio/Vignola way, which is modern and basically still the one we use, is based on drawings and measurements. The result may be the same, but the two processes are not. In the first case, each operation in the sequence is an elementary geometrical partition, which can be performed mechanically —perhaps I should say manually—with a straightedge and a pair of compasses, and without the need to perform any number-based operations. A pair of compasses can divide a given segment into a given number of equal parts, without any need to measure the segment or to use numbers to calculate the result.

The second way obliges the user to read the measurements with proportions in the drawing and to multiply these numbers by one or more other numbers in order to determine the final dimensions of the object. This second method, which presupposes—in fact requires—numeracy and the use of Hindu-Arabic numerals to perform the four basic operations of arithmetic, was a relatively new discipline in Europe in the fifteenth and sixteenth centuries, then known as *algorism*, from the Latinized name of its inventor, Al-Khwarizmi, a ninth-century scientist from Baghdad.

The old geometrical method had some advantages. It did not require the use of numbers—a decisive plus at a time when most people did not know how to use numbers, and modern, Hindu-Arabic numbers did not exist. Roman numbers are not good for calculating. A sequence of geometrical instructions is a narration, a recital of sorts. It can be recited aloud, unfolding in real time—the time that is necessary to perform the operations that are described. And then as now, one remembers a story more easily than a list of telephone numbers. Geometry is the daughter of orality, and a good friend of memory. On the contrary, the new number-based instructions of Vignola and Palladio are difficult to memorize, and they are better recorded and transmitted in writing. They are even better recorded and transmitted in print. And mechanical reproduction reduces the risk of mistakes that would inevitably occur when copyists transcribe pages and pages of apparently meaningless numbers. Print made this transmission reliable.

The geometrical way, however, featured another, even more crucial, advantage. A geometrical construction, such as the division of a segment into two equal parts, is an entirely mechanical and analog operation that can be performed regardless of scale or size. With a small pair of compasses, it can be carried out at the scale of a drawing on paper, provided that you do have paper. With a larger pair of compasses, you can perform the very same operation, but at the scale of the building —or at any other scale, for that matter. I tried to bring along a small pair of compasses because I wanted to make an on-site demonstration, but that was foolish of me. I could not carry them on the plane; they were detected by a metal detector. I had to explain to the customs security officer what these things are. I said, "Well, I need them to argue that for centuries this was a weapon of mass construction." In retrospect this was not a wise thing to say —security officers are not keen on learning the history of architecture. But anyway, my point is that geometrical constructions are a tool for building as well as a tool for drawing. In a geometrical environment the making of scaled project drawings may sometimes be unnecessary. Geometry can generate the real thing at real size on the real site without the need to go through the laborious mediation of a preliminary small-scale drawing on paper.

In contrast, small-scale proportional project drawings, with or without the addition of number-based, or digital, measurements, are separated both physically and ideologically from the materiality of building—again, thanks to paper. Project drawings exist and reside on paper. Such paper prefigurations of future buildings must at some later point be translated into real-size, full-scale, three-dimensional objects. This translation of drawings into buildings is an operation of proportional enlargement, also known in French as *homothétie*. Scaled project drawings must be enlarged by a factor of ten, fifty or one hundred, or ninety-six in the imperial system, in order to be converted into stone. But—and this is the snag—this translation or proportional enlargement is not always an easy matter. In some cases, a three-dimensional model might help, but in most cases, the iron law of transference from two-dimensional drawings to three-dimensional objects applies—we can only measure what we can draw, and we can only build what we can measure in a drawing. In short, if you cannot draw it, you cannot measure it, and if you cannot measure it, you cannot build it.

6 Giacomo Barozzi da Vignola. Drawing of an Ionic volute, in *Regola delli cinque ordini d'architettura* (Rome: Si Stampa da Gio. Batta de Rossi, 1617), plate XX. CCA. NA44.V686 (0002785)

It follows that within this logic, the forms that we can build are determined by the power or the potency of the mathematical language at our disposal. If this language is basic *algorism*, or the arithmetic of the four operations, as it was for centuries, we can better measure, and hence build, segments of straight lines that are all parallel or perpendicular to one another or that intersect at fixed angles on the same plane or on parallel planes. Such limits lead to objects that are grid-like, repetitive and discrete, as numbers are. In contrast, geometry can construct lines and surfaces that are continuous and bending, and curves that might be difficult, or even impossible, to measure. This is because geometry does not need to measure lines—lines are simply laid out mechanically. They are made on-site, full-size, using compasses, ropes, nails, chalk, chisels and all kinds of mechanical tricks.

Builders in classical antiquity constructed sophisticated curved surfaces and continuous lines that a twentieth-century engineer would have struggled to describe in numbers, such as the barely perceptible rise toward the centre of the platform, or stylobate, of a Greek temple, the spirals of the Ionic volute (fig. 6) or the entasis of the shaft of the column (fig. 7). The curved, continuous line of the entasis of the column was cut in stone on-site, full-size and without any need to measure it, which was just as well, because if classical builders had needed to measure it, they could not have done it. Using a similar but more advanced geometrical construction, medieval stereotomy built complex curving surfaces that, up to twenty or thirty years ago, would have been almost impossible to draw and measure with numbers.

Geometry is about continuous lines and surfaces. Numbers are discrete entities, and classical geometry neither needed nor used them. Indeed, some classical thinkers and scientists had little affection for numbers, and in the classical age, many practical issues that we now solve with numbers were solved with geometry.

But in the seventeenth century numbers took over. Differential calculus empowered numbers to describe continuity, and through analytic geometry, curves could be written down as algebraic equations. This is in fact what we mostly still do, as for most of us an ellipse is an x-y function, not a concoction to be obtained mechanically with a rope, a stencil and two nails, which is what Serlio could have done. And it is also well known, as Greg Lynn has been reiterating for years, that architects did not start to use calculus as a tool to create forms—as a device of design—until some ten or perhaps fifteen years ago. This was when computers first made differential calculus available to the masses, so to speak—not so much calculus, as the possibility of visualizing continuous functions generated by algebraic equations. And as we all know, this brought formal continuity back to the centre stage of architecture after an exile of almost five centuries.

I am abridging the story and simplifying here a bit; continuity of form did not completely disappear during the five centuries of the dominion of the number. Let us just think of the survival of traditional stereotomy well into the seventeenth century, and occasionally beyond. Or let us think of Antoni Gaudí, Erich Mendelsohn or even the later work of Le Corbusier. But in each of these cases there is some explanation. During the age of architectural numeracy, non-measurable forms could still be built following the traditional geometrical approach, or by using the modern number-based method in disguise—that is, by cheating. We must keep these exceptions in mind. Yet what follows from all the above is a challenging and at times exciting historical paradox.

If all or even only some of the above is true, we must come to the conclusion that one of the main consequences of the digital revolution in architecture is the revival of geometry as a tool for design. As with most revivals, this is not exactly a revival; some more recent developments in geometry are now also involved, and what is being brought back to life is geometry translated first into a new number-based format by seventeenth-century calculus, and second, into a new machine-readable format by twentieth-century electronic

7 Giacomo Barozzi da Vignola. Drawing of the geometrical construction of the entasis of the shaft of a column, in *Regola delli cinque ordini d'architettura* (Rome: Si Stampa da Gio. Batta de Rossi, 1617), plate XXXI. CCA. NA44.V686 (0002785)

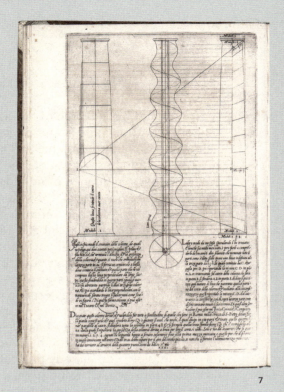

computing. This new geometrical tool for design is managed by machines, and the objects that we can produce using computer-based geometry are machine made rather than handmade. We can now mass-produce what used to be artisanal *pièces uniques*—a marginal point in the economy of this paper, but a major point in the global economy of the present, as this is one reason why we must use the new technologies and make the most of them.

But geometry is still geometry, regardless of the machines that process it—compasses or computers. Not only is geometry about continuity of form, it is also, as it always was, a process that is mostly indifferent to scale. The separation between design and building site, an estrangement that started with the rise of architectural numeracy and the availability of paper in the Renaissance, is now being epistemically challenged by file-to-factory technologies, whereby the same software manages computer-generated images as well as the three-dimensional manufacturing of an object. In time, the gap between design and production, which started in the sixteenth century, will most like-

Mario Carpo

ly be reduced by the logic of the new digital tools. This logic is automatically calculated in a three-dimensional space of x-y-z coordinates. Although endless two-dimensional images of an object can be printed out at will, the source and matrix of all of these variable manifestations make a virtual substitute for the object itself (fig. 1). All parts and each point of this digital archetype can be automatically drawn, measured and built. The iron law of transference from drawing to building—if you cannot measure it, you cannot build it—has ceased to be. In a digital environment, if you have a drawing you already have all of its measurements. Or to be precise, you don't have them; your computer has them.

It is a commonplace of the digital revolution that the new digital environment is in many ways the print environment in reverse. As many have pointed out, the new digital environment is closer to the age of the manuscript as it existed before the age of print than it is to the age of print that is now coming to an end. An assessment of the first ten years of the digital revolution in architecture would appear to reinforce and to corroborate this assumption. Numeracy can exert its influence over architectural design only when numbers and drawings can be printed together. It is the alliance of Arabic numerals and printed images that brought about the rise of architectural numeracy and changed the course of architectural history in the sixteenth century. Now, it seems, the new digital tools are bringing architectural design back to an Edenic state of pure geometry, which is where architecture lived and thrived for centuries before that paradise was lost, as it fell under the dominion of numeracy and of print.

But if this is so, and this is my conclusion, then Thomas Aquinas—a very unlikely name in this environment—and, right on the eve of a revolution of print and numeracy, Leon Battista Alberti could probably understand the present digital environment and the principles of contemporary digital design much better than Walter Benjamin or Mies van der Rohe could or would, to mention only two of the most eminent advocates of art and design in the age of identical mechanical reproduction. Aquinas and Alberti lived, as we do, in a universe of variable media. For them, the fixity of print and measured drawings had yet to come. For us, the fixity of print and measured drawings has already gone. And it is certainly one of the most significant paradoxes that marks the latest stage in the evolution of number-based computing that, thanks to computers, we can now mostly forget about numbers and when necessary manipulate intersecting curves and bending surfaces regardless of scale and measurability, just as our ancestors did in the time of compasses. Computers are just as good, and to be honest, in many ways, I think they could even be better.

<u>In 1837</u>, Charles Babbage developed the concept of the analytical engine, a computer designed to be fully programmable with punch cards and that would have been the first machine with archival memory ever built. The logical, symbolical and memory-based structure of the analytical engine—and of all computers in the contemporary sense—defines the computer as an archive, as a set of gaps punctuated by units of information.

WOLFGANG ERNST

1 Laser-photographic image of a chemically opened section of the microchip surface of a 2114 static random-access memory (SRAM) integrated circuit, showing twelve set–reset (SR) flip-flops. Institut für Physik, Humboldt-Universität zu Berlin

TOWARD A MUSEOLOGY OF ALGORITHMIC ARCHITECTURES FROM WITHIN

1

Wolfgang Ernst

The term *digital architecture* does not only refer to the application of computing in architectural design; in an analytical sense, it also refers to the archive of computing itself. In media archaeology, the archive is a radicalization of Michel Foucault's *Archaeology of Knowledge*, and names the material and logical conditions of possibility for any kind of technical operation. *L'archive*, according to Foucault, means *structure*, and is not to be confused with the place where records are kept, which is the *plurale tantum* term *les archives* in French (a term mostly mistranslated in Foucault literature). Media archaeology implies archivology as well, less in terms of historical contextualizing (with the emphasis on social, cultural and discursive frames), but rather within the techno-archive itself, with a focus on both symbolical (records) and technical (hardware) apparatuses.[1] Let us therefore define *digital architecture* from within the computer itself. This leads to a close examination of the computer's own technological archi-tectonics.

Architecture refers to physical building materialities and to structural conditions, the *arché*. This is also true for computing, which is both symbolical code (software) and physical implementation (hardware). The very term *techno/logy* recalls this split ontology. Technology is not only the science of *techné*; the *logos* (in terms of algorithms) is implemented in the material technique itself (fig. 2).

In its methodological sense, the approach *from within* expresses the media-archaeological—that is, non-human—point of view, departing from the technologies themselves and therefore distant from the cognitive or bodily perception that humans experience through interfaces such as the computer screen. Different from the philological hermeneutics of understanding, the machine- and algorithm-centred epistemology of computational architectures aims to reveal the material and logical, techno-logical principles (*archai*) that drive signal and data processing and build up the architectures (hardware) and archival textures (software) of computing. This essay therefore concentrates on computer architecture itself, which is both structure and process. In order to reveal processual architectures, a sonic approach is proposed.

Such an investigation necessarily departs from familiar historical research. Radical media archaeology is not simply a variant of historiography; it is an alternative way of dealing with temporal evidence. The temporality of the media-archaeological question is not primarily about beginnings and moments in the historic timeline. Rather, the question is, what is the crucial epistemological and structural momentum to be identified and analyzed? Media archaeology, unlike cultural historicism, is always about the archive of the present. Therefore this text concentrates on the moments, both temporal and structural, when symbolic mathematical machines became (and become) physical computing. The oldest-known truly archaeological example of a computing device is the Antikythera mechanism for astronomic calculation, from the first century BCE (fig. 3).[2] What at first glance looks like a rusty, corro-

2   Transistor–transistor logic architecture of the SPACE AGE I demonstration computer, designed by Henry Westphal. Tigris Electronics, Berlin

ded piece of metal is revealed through X-ray images to be a structure of interrelated mechanical wheels. Its operational architecture, though, becomes evident only through the construction of a working replica. In such a re-enactment, historical distance is replaced by a media-archaeological co-presence. Ramon Llull's *Ars magna* proposed a paper machine for symbolical combinatorics of discursive terms in the early fourteenth century (fig. 4), but not until Gottfried Wilhelm Leibniz and later Charles Babbage was a truly digital (decimal, even binary) computing machinery envisaged.
At these moments architecture did not become digital; the digital became architectural, in the sense of three-dimensional material structure. The media-archaeological investigation is epistemologically anchored here. The hardware architecture of the first digital computer, meant to be driven by steam power, was Babbage's difference engine from 1822, a replica of which

Wolfgang Ernst

3   The Antikythera mechanism, the earliest extant portable astronomical calculator, c. 150 BCE. National Archaeological Museum, Athens. X 15087

4   Ramon Llull. *Prima figura* of *Ars generalis ultima*, or *Ars magna*, published in 1305. *Ars magna* outlines a logic system intended to prove Christian doctrine. Each letter in the *prima figura* is assigned an attribute of God that can be combined with other attributes by rotating the concentric circles. The terms are then arranged in a table to outline a set of statements in support of Christian belief.

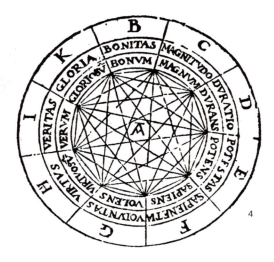

5 Reconstruction of Charles Babbage's difference engine, carried out between 1989 and 1991. Babbage proposed the difference engine to the Royal Astronomical Society in 1822, but it was not built during his lifetime. Science Museum, London

was constructed by the Science Museum in London (figs. 5–6). The analytical engine, which Babbage proposed in 1837 as the successor to the difference engine, was a fully programmable algorithmic computer in the contemporary sense. What are still three-dimensional structures in Babbage's computer engineering have since been flattened to two-and-a-half- or even two-dimensional integrated circuit architectures in present-day computing. Media archaeologically, the structures inside the black box of a microchip can be revealed through an analysis of their chemical anatomy.

But only an abstract circuit diagram, with its gates and transistors, will reveal the internal functional logics of such

Wolfgang Ernst

6 Detail view of the reconstruction of the difference engine. Science Museum, London

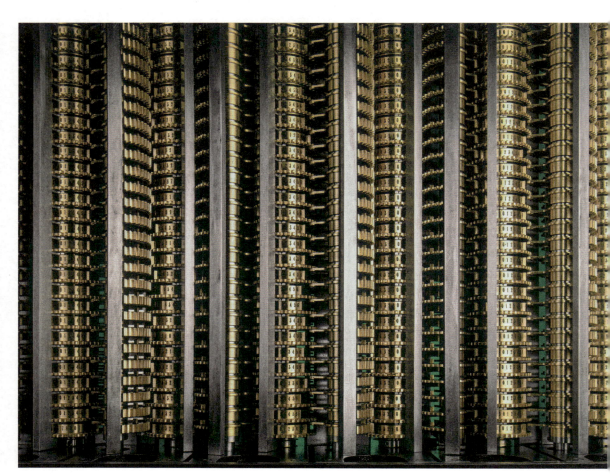

memory architectures. The current transition from computer-aided design (CAD) to computational design has already become an important topic in architecture.[3] The missing links are circuit design itself (hardware) and the flow diagram (software). Media archaeology therefore proposes an understanding of structure as process, and a focus of analysis on computer-architectural functions.

Toward a Museology of the Digital in Computing

The term *digital architecture* most frequently refers to the application of computers in architectural design. But its meaning can be inverted by focusing on the technological condition —thus, the archive—of algorithmic computing itself, which is the von Neumann architecture of storage-programmable symbolical machines. The challenge to archives is how to preserve the hardware and software records of such a computational architecture, whether by paper documentation or by software emulation of obsolete computer hardware. This challenge grows when the notion of architecture, both in its structural and in its processual sense, extends to the functional modelling of the Internet itself: OSI (Open Systems Interconnection) architecture).[4] Therefore digital computing is not just a design medium for architects; in fact, computing has been architectural from the very beginning. In order to become operative, symbolic code must be implemented in physical, material hardware. In other words, algorithmic notation must become architectural in order to happen in the time-defined real world. Nothing is more material than the technological a priori of so-called immaterialities. Any discussion about the role of digital machines in architectural design therefore must be supplemented by a reminder of the archival conditions of architectural digitality.

The physical materiality and the logical design of computer architectures are of primary concern. Computing hardware brings mathematical algorithms from paper into the material world. But the current use of concepts such as virtual worlds —computational phenomena generated by calculation—results in an erasure of the material condition of the computational media themselves. Both physical and virtual access to computer architecture is needed (fig. 1). A truly museological approach to our current computer-based culture insists on what engineers term *computer architecture*: displaying the digital architectures that lie behind all computer-aided design or virtual architecture. Media archaeology proposes a museological scenario in this specific sense of *computer architecture*. The extension of the notion of museum in digital culture does not simply encompass computer-augmented museum space and interactive virtual collections. In a shift away from simple interface metaphors, virtual reality can be applied in a different way; it allows us "to enter the architecture of digital media."[5] Therefore it is the structure of computing, and not its metaphorical representation, that becomes the focus of an architectural display. The fundamental issue is that, at least to most users, the computer dissimulates itself while in operation on the metaphorical interface level. In contrast, open-hardware computer teaching models must be a truly operative media theatre. While the traditional theatre stage allows human performers to make dramatic arguments, the museum space as media theatre presents non-human, techno-logical cultural operators.

Computers in the early years of electronic computing were the size of rooms and were therefore literally accessible. The

7 UNIVAC I (UNIversal Automatic Computer I) Factronic central processing unit, 1956. Deutsches Museum, Munich, Archiv, R2931

UNIVAC I Factronic, exhibited at the Deutsches Museum in Munich, is an example (fig. 7).[6] The challenge is to show how the digital, resulting from the mathematical theory of information, became architectural in its own medium, in terms of hardware and software (with written source code as a new kind of text that deserves to be archived as cultural memory). This takes us toward a museology of algorithmic architectures from within. Architecture shares with digital technologies its twofold existence; it is a conceptual form of diagrammatic reasoning that includes design, theory and epistemology, but it must be grounded in the material world in order to manifest itself. In *The Archaeology of Knowledge*, Foucault rather skeptically insists that it is not possible to describe the *archive* of the present, since it is from within these rules that we speak. But a truly architectural museology media archaeologically reveals such operative computer architectures from within, which is the condition of expression for the digital in architecture.

Media-Architectural Machines: On the Connection Between Architectural Theory and Media Archaeology

There is an affinity between architectural theory and technological media studies when it comes to discussing the notion of the machine. Daniel Libeskind's conceptual knowledge machines, based on the Renaissance idea of book-reading wheels such as Agostino Ramelli's *Le diverse et artificiose machine*, a book published in Paris in 1588, come to mind (fig. 8). Libeskind's *Three Lessons in Architecture* was presented at the Venice Biennale's 3rd International Architecture

8   Agostino Ramelli. Drawing of the book wheel, in *Le diverse et artificiose machine del Capitano Agostino Ramelli*, 1588. Reprinted in *The Various and Ingenious Machines of Agostino Ramelli* (Baltimore: Johns Hopkins University Press, 1979), plate 188. CCA. W10244; ID:88-B10920

9   *Overleaf:*
Asymptote Architecture (Hani Rashid and Lise Anne Couture). New York Stock Exchange Virtual Trading Floor, digital rendering, 1997. Original file: 3D006k.tif, 50.9 MB, last modified 9 March 1999. Asymptote Architecture New York Stock Exchange Virtual Reality Environment and Advanced Trading Floor project records (AP184), CCA. Gift of Asymptote

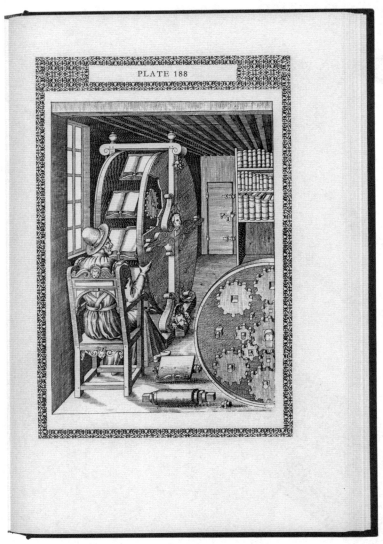

8

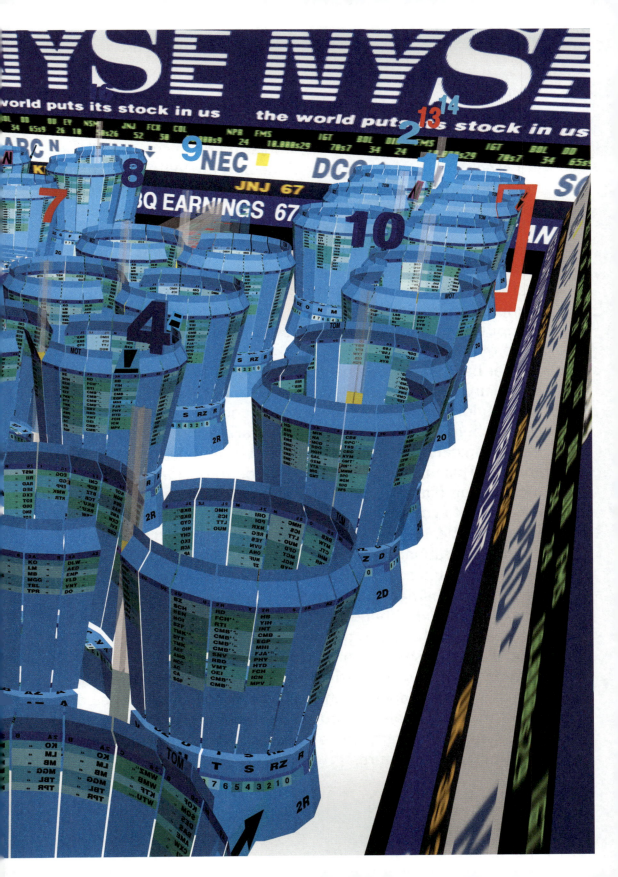

Exhibition in 1985,[7] with a highly architectural material presence that consisted of three modular mechanisms: the Reading Machine, the Memory Machine and the Writing Machine. In Victor Hugo's novel *The Hunchback of Notre-Dame*, the central message is that the printed book has killed the cathedral as a symbolic form of religious authority. Another "paper machine," this one invented by Alan Turing in 1936 as a conceptual diagram to discuss computable numbers in mathematics, similarly transformed culture through material technology. Ironically, today the printed text returns within computing architecture itself, in the form of the alphanumeric code of programming.

Far beyond the mechanical engines driven by steam or electricity, trans-classical machines—machines that process information—have become symbolic and informational devices.[8] Unlike thermodynamic engines, digital computers are primarily logical operations that ask to be materialized as mechanisms. This induced Charles S. Peirce to design the first electrical circuit diagram. Here diagrammatic reasoning occurs in the form of symbolic graphical notation, as designed and discussed in the 1842 "Sketch of the Analytical Engine invented by Charles Babbage" by Luigi Federico Menabrea.[9] In her extensive notes accompanying her translation of Menabrea's text, the mathematician Augusta Ada King, Countess of Lovelace, describes Babbage's difference engine: "The drawings are nearly finished, and the mechanical notation of the whole, recording every motion of which it is susceptible, is completed."[10] Such an "operative script," to use Sybille Krämer's term,[11] is a true paper machine. But symbolical machines on paper must be implemented in the material world as a processual, symbolic time machine in order to become operative computing architecture.

Any media archaeology of digital machines, as both media archaeology *of* the digital and as archaeology of knowledge revealed *by* digital media, does not simply retrace our current media condition in terms of a cultural or social history of technology (as in science and technology studies) but rather reveals its underlying principles and commands in the techno-mathematical sense, framing paper machines as archi-textures.

The temporality of architecture is endurance, and time is architecture's channel of transmission. Architecture endures not only in the material but also in the temporal sense. A building is not an ephemeral presence; it endures in the purest sense of temporality. The archaeology of architectures, whether buildings or technological devices, is not limited to immobile archival structures but pays specific attention to the temporal axis: architecture's *chronopoetics*.

An example is the New York Stock Exchange Virtual Trading Floor and Command Center, designed between 1997 and 1999 by Asymptote Architecture. The purpose of this virtual environment was to visualize real-time numerical and statistical data, detect suspicious trading activity and track the impact of global news events on the market (fig. 9). The crucial challenge in the "virtual architecture" of the project's software was to maintain the connection to real-time data flows, which demand new forms of dynamic archiving.

The Ahistorical in Virtual Reconstructions of Architecture

Dresden's Baroque Frauenkirche is a notorious case of computer-aided architectural reconstruction. The cathedral collapsed as a result of British bombing during the Second World War and for

Wolfgang Ernst

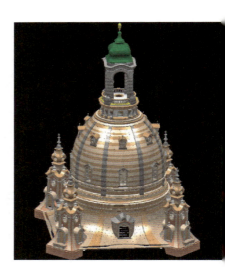

10 Thomas Bauer and Jörg Lauterbach. 3D visualizations and technical drawings used for concrete engineering in the reconstruction of the Frauenkirche, Dresden, 1997–2005. Stiftung Frauenkirche Dresden

11 *Overleaf:*
A magnetic core memory module used in early digital computing as a computer-architectural material diagram. Each of the 128-bit memory units is an electro-numerically addressable point in the matrix of copper wires. Medienarchäologischer Fundus, Humboldt-Universität zu Berlin

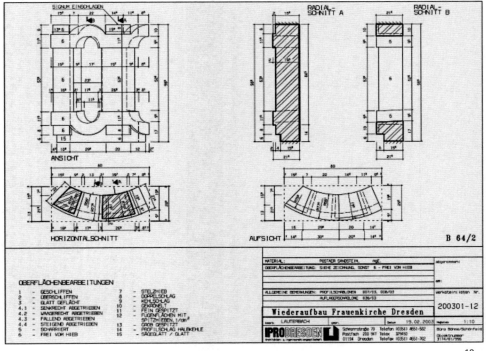

decades remained a ruin, a memorial. What was called "archaeological reconstruction" by the project leaders has since created the impression of reversal against the essential characteristic of historical time, which is material entropy, manifest in this case as architectural ruins. The archaeological reconstruction of the Frauenkirche was in fact a media-archaeological one; supported by algorithmic calculation, the remaining bricks and stones of the cathedral were reconfigured into the core of the reconstruction (fig. 10).

Most archaeological buildings are in ruins, just as an archive implies a set of gaps and absences. Today, computer simulations tend to close up these gaps through intelligent interpolation.[12] But while media phenomenology is mostly concerned with the computer-screen illusions displayed to human senses, there is a parallel, hidden reality at work: the algorithmic infraface, as opposed to the external human–machine interface, to be critically discovered by media archaeology (fig. 11). Virtual architectural reproduction, to quote Friedrich Kittler, "produces a data record that has never existed before." He continues: "The ruin, beyond its imaginary completion," which is realized through computer-aided historical imagination, "is also stored in symbols or algorithms. Each stone, whether preserved or simply presumed, has entered an objective structure"—an archival structure—"that makes it addressable according to its dimensions and characteristiscs. Each stone is both a fetchable data record and a fetchable procedure of its playback.... Computer simulations do not merely form user interfaces, they actually constitute a museum. More precisely: a museum that, as in ancient Alexandria, also functions as a library" of software.[13]

A specific media-archival record is program code that is stored in a masked read-only memory (ROM) chip. Since the chip itself follows a known architecture and its code corresponds with open assembly language, the only reverse engineering required concerns the recovery of the actual instructions stored in it. For example, Aperture Labs managed to visualize the data records kept on ROM microchips within computer architecture by creating code, a disassembler, to extract the bits (fig. 12).[14] Between chips and codes, there is both hardware and software hacking, which is the more militant practice of media archaeology. Such media-philological criticism understands the actual logic of a proprietary chip by reverse engineering its construction. But here, a second-order observation paradox arises. Computer software cannot watch and archive itself; a second institution is needed to maintain and archive software. Memory agencies of computer architecture would have to store flow charts, hardware architectures and software solutions "so precisely as to preserve at least the validity of mathematical algorithms."[15] But this has to be done through executable programs instead of passive reading, which makes all the difference for the "Gutenberg galaxy" of handwritten or printed texts, beyond the stasis of traditional textual archives and libraries.[16] Because media archaeology is concerned with software as well as hardware, archiving needs to address the operations described in Turing's machines as well as the paper they are written on, the virtual space of Asymptote's trading floor as well as the ROM chip.

Archivology of the Digital: Archival Tectonics

Traditional archives of architecture are predominantly paper based. There have even been proto-digital forms of transmitting architectural memory to posterity.[17] But in a kind of recursive argument, the archive returns even *within* computer architecture; that is why a core element in the central processing unit is aptly called the *register*, a term taken directly from archival science.

Beyond the straightforward (though not simple) task of preserving records of pivotal works of virtual architectural design, another specific epistemological imperative of the digital media archive arises. Computer-archaeological strata, once conceived as essentially processual by nature, are operative diagrams, close to Peirce's diagrammatic reasoning.[18] Future archivistic activities will have to deal with this kind of dynamic object. The archive here is not only the data set but also its organizational agency, "defined by *constraining* laws or by an *algorithm*," according to communication theorist Abraham Moles.[19] This definition is more in accordance with Foucault's logical notion of *l'archive* than with the traditional notion of archives as record depositories.

The increasing temporalization of the archive, which had previously been considered to be static, leads to the theorem of the dynamic and algorithmic archive. But this does not imply a liberation from traditional boundaries. Still present is *l'archive* in Foucault's sense, which must be addressed in its rigid, non-discursive and non-debatable structure. Any administrative or techno-logical structure is the archival essence per se, even if the endurance of such structures increasingly shrinks to short temporal intervals.

Against an overall virtualization, let us insist on architecture in its material sense, which today encompasses a new class of architectural objects: the micro-architectures of computing machinery, as expressed in the von Neumann architecture, beyond modish visual metaphors that compare close-up photographs of microchip circuits with bird's-eye views of a city.

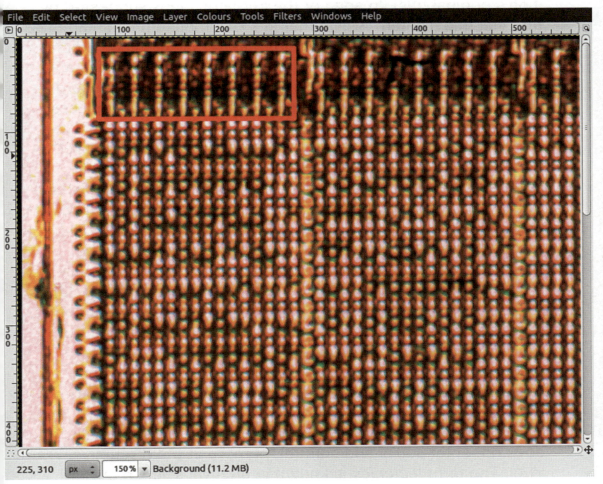

12 Pattern recognition on a ROM microchip to identify program code. Aperture Labs

The future museology of computer and computing architectures will be a true escalation of the legendary exhibition *Les Immatériaux,* curated by Jean-François Lyotard and Thierry Chaput at the Centre Pompidou in 1985.[20] Lyotard took as a point of departure the Indo-European linguistic root *mât*, which means both "measurement" and "construction," to unfold the different layers of the material (hardware) as well as the matrix (code) of new materials and creation (which was the exhibition's original title). In spite of the immaterialities suggested by the final title, Lyotard insists that in a real museum exhibition nothing is more materially grounded than the seemingly immaterial objects on display.[21] Architectural macro-dimensions are invertedly mirrored by the architecture of microchips. According to Paul Virilio: "The access protocol of telematics replaces that of the doorway. The revolving door is succeeded by 'data banks,' by new rites of passage of a technical culture masked by the immateriality of its components."[22] The more radical update of *Les Immatériaux* will be an equally co-original display of computer architectures from within. Once the time-critical element becomes essential for the very possibility of virtual architectural spaces to emerge, the term *computer* is to be replaced by *computing*, with an emphasis on the processual—a challenge to the traditional notion of the static archive (fig. 13).

The new kind of archival tectonics is the revelation of computer and source-code architectures. We therefore move from the computer-based representations of architecture to the architecture of digital computing. There is a veritable information architecture behind the current forms of digital communication and Internet use, consisting of several layers. It is such information that needs to be archivized since it usually does not enter social and cultural memory at the discursive level. The term *tectonics* is known in archival science but will

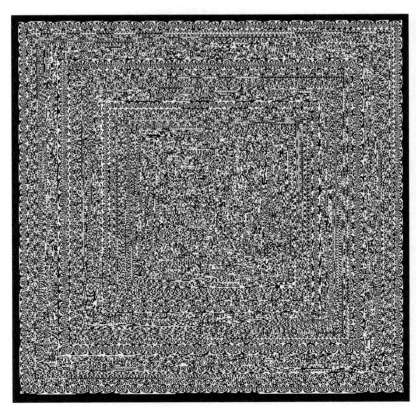

13 Ulam spiral, a visualization of the calculations by the digital computer PASCAL for producing prime number series, c. 1960

Wolfgang Ernst

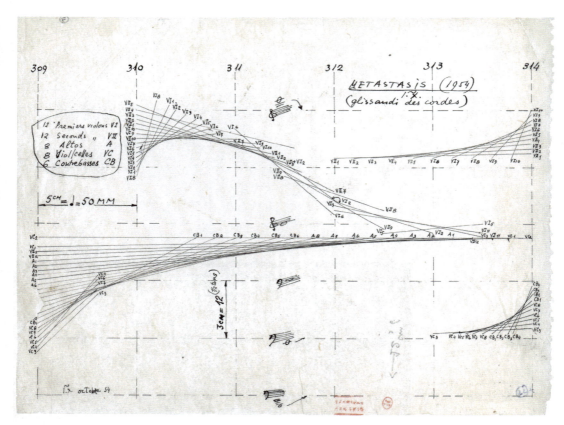

14 Iannis Xenakis. Study for Metastaseis (A), 1954. Collection Famille Xenakis

be given a new meaning. According to the online glossary of the Swiss Federal Archives, *archive tectonics* "describes the hierarchical structure of an archive's holdings."[23] This is the symbolical order as architecture of the archive. Tectonics applies to the archival structure and not to its contents; therefore a future archive of digital architecture will be an archive of an archive, involving two layers of information architecture.

Architectural Sonicity: Listening to Computer Architecture with Media-Archaeological Ears

Displaying the architecture of computational systems addresses hardware elements as well as processual forms of implementing data and instructions, and cannot be reduced to the visual display of images and artifacts. The appropriate channel for experiencing the *chronopoetics* of algorithmic media architectures is auditory perception. Special attention must therefore be given to the inherent sonicity of computational architectures.[24] Examples are the first programmable digital computers built by the engineer Konrad Zuse in Berlin beginning in 1936. These constructions were based on mechanical elements and electro-magnetic relays for each bit; therefore each step of computation was audible and created a sonic rhythm of what had been algorithmically programmed before. Such techno-sound, coming from within the machine, resonates with computational processuality itself.[25]

Actual sound from the media-archaeological archive allows for an exploration of computer-architectural space. When an early Datassette is loaded from external tape memory into the random-access memory (RAM) of a Commodore 64 home computer, the user is listening to data music—not popular musical sound but rather the sound of computer memory itself, a software program that is an alphanumeric script. We are listening to the data archive, which is not sonic memory but sonicity. Today, there are numerous artistic and scientific experiments that involve the sonification of data. We can imagine the virtual trading floor of the New York Stock Exchange addressing the ears as well as the eyes, just as earthquake analysis is best done through acoustic alerts, since the human ear is most attentive to micro-temporal changes.

Let us turn the traditional metaphor of architecture as frozen music upside down. Far beyond simply audifying or sonifying spatial architectural structures by transforming them into time signals,[26] there is an implicit sonicity in computational architecture itself. Computational space can be made viable not only by metaphorically wandering through the inside of technical computer architecture. We should pay special attention to the sound-related epistmology, the sonicity, of architectures, which are not physical spaces but rather closer to Marshall McLuhan's structural notion of acoustic space.

If we apply sonic analysis to the flat and condensed architecture of digital computing, the sound we experience is of a different kind. Since the essence of digital computing is the literal temporalization of mathematics by media-operative algorithms, we must change the sensational mode from the visual to the auditory, the time organ of human senses. Usually high-performance computing is not associated with music, aside from Iannis Xenakis's stochastic music, which originated from his concern with architecture (fig. 14). But there is implicit music within the computer—the rhythm of algorithms. In order to become operative in the real world and to acquire temporal agency, mathematical algorithms (which symbolically exist as lines of source code, a form of alphanumerical text) must be implemented in real physics, usually with electronic elements.[27] Since architecture is becoming more processual as it becomes more digital, its true archive, which consists of its driving algorithms, must be displayed to our time-critical auditory sense.

Antoine Picon

The tabulating machine was patented in 1884, having been invented in response to the need to process United States census data more efficiently. The machine, which used punch cards, was a product of a new society of information dependent on vast quantities of data for the purposes of commerce, administration and city planning.

This text is the transcription of a presentation that was given at the CCA in 2013.

ANTOINE PICON

1 Still from *Metropolis*,
directed by Fritz Lang, 1927.
Friedrich-Wilhelm-Murnau-
Stiftung

HISTORIES OF THE DIGITAL: INFORMATION, COMPUTER AND COMMUNICATION

1

I'd like to talk about the histories of the digital and the way digital technology has impacted architecture. More than a single narrative, what we see emerging is a multiplicity of narratives regarding the digital in architecture, and hence I propose *histories* of the digital. The plural might have to do with the complexity of the digital itself, and so I would like to ask: What is the digital? What are we confronted with? I will try to outline how complex and layered it is. I will also invoke where we are in terms of historiography, what has been covered and what still remains to be documented.

Histories of the digital in architecture constitute a rapidly expanding field; it's actually easy these days to find PhD students dealing with the history of the digital, whereas scholars of the eighteenth century are becoming a kind of

Antoine Picon

endangered species. Nevertheless, much remains to be done. The digital raises fundamental questions regarding the architectural discipline itself, which I'll address. I'll also briefly evoke the urban dimension and I will conclude on the need to rethink, perhaps, the agenda of the history of architecture as a result of the digital. I'm aware that this is a relatively complex itinerary, but the subject is complicated. My goal is not to deliver my latest thoughts on the digital but rather to contribute to the clarification of some of the issues that are at stake.

The term *digital* may be misleading if we confuse it with the use of computers. The digital is indeed a pervasive condition in technology and culture, and I'm not sure that we can limit the study of the digital in architecture to computing because architecture is related to an array of dimensions linked to the pervasive digital world in which we live.

I'd like to show how our digital present is the result of a complex set of historic strata. I believe that we have to go quite far back, at least to the late nineteenth century and the emergence of the society dependent on massive quantities of information. This is now a well-documented subject among historians. What is often called the Second Industrial Revolution is just as much an information revolution in which society began to manipulate larger and larger quantities of data for administration, business and other purposes. This is the first phase in a history of the digital. Here are the Prudential Insurance Company offices at the turn of the twentieth century (fig. 2). The offices produced kilometres of data.

It's not the computer that gave birth to the society of information, but rather it is the emergence of the society of information—let's say sometime between 1880 and 1920—that made the invention of a machine like the computer necessary. The best proof is that the institutional—not the technological—ancestor of the computer is the tabulating machine, invented in the 1880s. The tabulating machine is what IBM produced until the Korean War. Most of the big businesses that eventually went into computer manufacturing were tabulating machine companies. Again, it was the society of information that made something like the computer necessary, and this is a good antidote to the temptation of technological determinism.

The second phase coincides with the invention of the computer proper and the beginning of the modern computing world. This happened between the early 1940s and the 1960s, and we could say that the invention of everything that goes with the computer continued through the 1970s and 1980s.

We are now in the middle of the third phase, which is more difficult to characterize but is marked by a series of key evolutions. The first, beginning in the early 1970s, is the Advanced Research Projects Agency Network (ARPANET), later the Internet. This indicates the rising importance of communication between machines as well

2   Interior view of the Prudential (Guaranty) Building in Newark, New Jersey, c. 1916, showing the accounting, audits and claims offices of the Prudential Insurance Company of America

as between man and machine. The Internet is only part of this evolution. The second evolution is the increasingly ubiquitous presence of computing. This is something that was foreseen by Mark Weiser, who was the director of the Computer Science Lab at Xerox Palo Alto Research Center (PARC), in his 1991 article "The Computer of the 21st Century." Today cell phones are part of this ubiquitous computing. For example, there are connections from our phones to dishwashers and to many other appliances. The third phenomenon that characterizes what has happened is the individual turn. Social networks and Web 2.0 are evidence of this, but it's something that goes beyond digital culture. The sociologist Ulrich Beck insisted on this dimension very early on in books like *Risk Society* of 1986. The link between what was happening in the field of the digital and the individual dimension was underlined by Nicholas Negroponte in *Being Digital*, which is very much about the difference between the mass information age and the individually customized information age; Negroponte characterizes this as a digital condition. That said, and to complicate the picture, I've tried to show in my work that the rise of the individual in relation to information is actually a much older story. This is one of the reasons I became interested in the cyborg as a kind of recurring mythological figure of the information age.

So, there are at least three layers in this history. One could be tempted to go to the technology to get clearer ideas, but the technology possesses the same layered structure. I'm arguing therefore that the digital has always been deeply historical. We have the legacy of machines from the past, for example. If the tabulating machines are gone for good, the ghost of the typewriter is still with us, to say nothing of the telephone. The diversity of the various pieces of equipment that surround us is even more spectacular. The digital age, as we all know, is as much the age of the smart phone as it is the age of the computer. Actually, one of the questions today would be what an architecture of the age of the smart phone is, as much as an architecture of the age of the computer. A related question is whether, more than the machines themselves, what really matters are their connections to each other. Because of the dependence of machines on networks, some scholars have given them a quasi-object status. It's true that a machine that is connected to the Internet is no longer a traditional machine; it's a terminal. The Internet has transformed the architectural profession. Think of all the transcontinental offices; without the Internet they would not be possible.

If we try to limit ourselves to looking at the computer, we discover that even the computer is a multi-layered reality. When the computer appeared, it was meant to be a computing machine. But very quickly it was understood—this dates almost to von Neumann—that the computer was a machine that could, in a certain sense, think. And that was the big theme at the time of cybernetics. Around the same time, the idea emerged that the computer was a machine that enabled you to see. In the Semi-Automatic Ground Environment (SAGE) anti-missile system, the computer network is meant to enhance your vision of missiles and bombs, to let you see the world in a certain light.

And then we have the idea that the computer is a machine to fabricate, which dates from the early computer numerical control (CNC) machines like the Milwaukee-Matic-II through to the present (fig. 3). So, the computer has become a machine that is leading to a profound evolution of our senses and their relations, what is often referred to as the sensorial. This is probably the deepest character of the digital age. The computer has reformed our vision; for anyone less than ten years old, a non-clickable image is almost a scandal. Zooming out and in has become a natural visual condition. The computer has also reformed our sense of touch. The first time I saw someone flexing thumb and index finger was at the time the iPhone was released, and now everyone is used to this gesture. The computer is also reforming modes of music, of course, and even the perfume industry is becoming more and more dependent on computers.

3   Milwaukee-Matic-II computer numerical control (CNC) machine, 1959

Antoine Picon

4 Dennis Crompton. Computer City, axonometric, 1964. Archigram Archives. 063-001-TC02

5 Lionel March. Boolean description of the Seagram Building, 1972

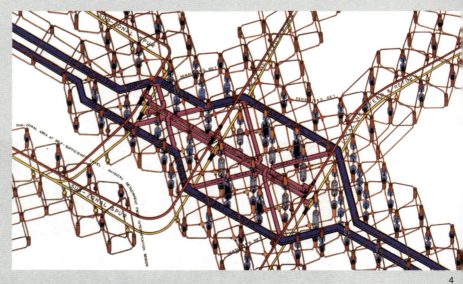

4

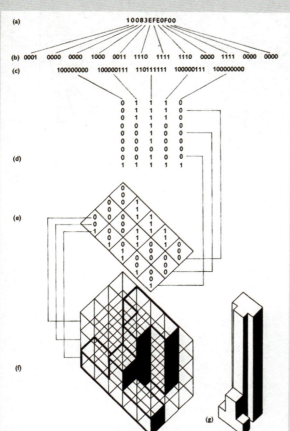

5

Fabrication is back, with the utopia of universal printing. We are no longer facing traditional machines or even quasi-objects, but a seamless technological environment—something like an ecology with deep historical structures. This situation suggests that instead of having something that is purely technological, we have something that is, at the deepest level, social and cultural. This is something historians have dealt with extensively; the computer is as much a perspective on the social world as it is a machine. This is what the historian of science Paul Edwards has tried to argue.

I'm especially concerned with the question of the subject, of the individual. From the information age to the digital age, one of the constant questions has been that of the subject, and this is one of the threads that link the four books that I have devoted to the rise of digital culture and its impact on architecture in the city, from *La ville territoire des cyborgs* to the most recent ones on ornament and smart cities. This is the recurring question: what is the subject of the city, of the new digital city and the new digital architecture?

I'll now say a few words about where we are in terms of the history of the digital in architecture. Throughout the twentieth and early twenty-first centuries there have been multiple interactions between architecture and phenomena like the rise of information, the development of the computer and, of course, the advent of the digital age. These connections have been documented by historians, but unevenly. The problem is not that we don't have histories of the digital—we actually have many of them—but that they are very unevenly distributed in terms of time.

For instance, there have been relatively few studies of the influence of the rise of the information-based society on architecture. This influence does exist —just think of all the spaces devoted to information in early-twentieth-century architecture, especially control rooms in which you see information. This is a theme in *Metropolis*; what you see in the office of the director is information, and not the suffering of people (fig. 1).

Most of the histories of the digital that have been written so far are concentrated on the period roughly from the 1940s and 1950s to the advent of postmodernism, although we're far from knowing everything about this period. For instance, in *The Organizational Complex* Reinhold Martin has documented the rise of the notion of pattern at the intersection of deep information structures and spatial information. Pattern in the 1950s is where information becomes synonymous with spatial as well as social regularities. He has shown convincingly how the social pattern combined with cybernetics influenced Saarinen and corporate architecture.

We are beginning to better understand the relationship between the corporate strategies of IBM, for example, and architects like Eero Saarinen, Charles and Ray Eames and Eliot Noyes. John Harwood's book *The Interface: IBM and*

6 Warren Chalk and Ron Herron. Control and Choice, detail section, 1967. Archigram Archives. 104-013-NM01

the Transformation of Corporate Design is full of precious insights, such as the fact that the computer was a spatialized machine at the beginning. Eliot Noyes designed the computer as an environment.

We are by now well aware of the relation between the megastructural movement and computing perspectives, something that is epitomized, for example, by Yona Friedman's Flatwriter, in which a computer would allocate space in the spatial cities Friedman envisaged. We also know that Archigram and others were influenced by the perspective of computing, as we see in Computer City (fig. 4). Of course it's important to study Cedric Price, and I think that the audacity of the Generator project has not yet been reached again in the field of digital architecture.

There are studies of crucial places of teaching and research, like Cambridge University in the 1960s and 1970s, where people as diverse as Leslie Martin, Lionel March, Christopher Alexander, Bill Mitchell, Peter Eisenman and Tony Vidler were present. This is one of Lionel March's studies on the application of Boolean logic to architecture (fig. 5). By the same token, we're beginning to know better what happened at the Massachusetts Institute of Technology (MIT) and at the Hochschule für Gestaltung Ulm. On the latter we have the work of Ingeborg Rocker and more recently Andrew Witt. I could go on and on. Almost every year there is a new kid on the block who wants to study this subject. All this work reveals an extreme diversity of places and people. It's not only North America, but also the United Kingdom, Germany, the Netherlands, France, Italy and Croatia—Ivan Rupnik has unearthed how important work from Croatia was at some point in the story. So it's a wide-ranging story, to say nothing of Japan and other places.

Many of the questions we're currently dealing with as if they were brand new had already been raised at the time. For example, the question of code-writing and its relation to design was central in the 1960s and early 1970s. There is also the definition of the computer as something that has to do with ambience and environments, what Hani Rashid calls the atmospheric. During this period, many designers addressed this definition, including Buckminster Fuller and Archigram, whose Control and Choice project is especially relevant (fig. 6). On the subject of the environmental, the sensory and the immersive, one should note the intensity of architecture's relationship with the emerging electronic and later video arts, a connection that has not been fully restored yet.

The most pervasive feature of the period is that people really did believe that the computer would not only draw but participate in the design process. Computer-aided design at the time was truly conceived of in the sense of design, and we are barely beginning to recover this ambition today, after about twenty years of computer-aided drawing.

The next period, the 1980s and early 1990s, has been less thoroughly

Antoine Picon

explored and it often appears as an interlude between yesterday and the present, although it has been well documented as a crucial period in engineering. We know the genealogy from deconstruction to folding in architecture and to the paperless studios. Mario Carpo wrote an excellent paper in the revised edition of "Folding in Architecture" on that matter. We know the part played by Eisenman in the early formulation of this particular agenda. What is less known—in my opinion this is a big subject still to be explored—is the link between postmodernism and the computing perspective. Postmodernism was obsessed by a question of language, and the computer appeared as the perfect semiotic machine. In the last chapter of *Architecture and Utopia*, Manfredo Tafuri evokes the new age when capitalism will no longer manipulate money, but rather symbols through the computer.

At the end of the 1990s and in the early 2000s we see the rise of real computing in architecture, the digital projects, the blob and so on. Most of the key projects are documented by architects, and there is a lot of theoretical writing by architects, beginning with Greg Lynn's *Animate Form* and going up to, for example, *The Sympathy of Things* by Lars Spuybroek. There have been relatively few historians trying to make sense of these very recent histories: Mario Carpo, Georges Teyssot, me and probably a few others. This is because the period is close to the present, and things move very quickly.

In the early 2000s, form was still an important topic; it was the time of the blob and *Animate Form*. Today fabrication is the most popular subject, and parametricism is in decline. The most pressing challenge may have to do with the fact that this is a domain that raised theoretical questions.

I'd like to address a few of the theoretical questions that are on the table. It's important to avoid techno-determinism. The machine is not the ultimate cause but rather something that reveals and accelerates. Above all, the technology mediates between architecture and the shifting social and cultural background. In other words—this might be where I'm very much a historian—I think what is primarily happening is a huge cultural change. The aim is not to pass from techno-determinism to social determinism. Architecture is not a mere reflection of what's happening. Rather, what I would suggest is the idea of a co-evolution. Society and culture are changing, and architecture is changing. It's a bit like Sheila Jasanoff's notion of co-production as a way to describe the relationship between technology and society. There might be a co-production of architectural change and social change.

We're seeing a destabilization of key notions in architecture, such as representation. This may have to do with the radical questioning of architectural form, which we used to take for granted. One of the questions today is whether designing form is a relevant concern for architecture. Karl Chu suggests that it is more important to design a sort

7   Eadweard Muybridge. *Animal Locomotion. An Electro-Photographic Investigation...of Animal Movements. Commenced 1872, Completed 1885. Volume VII, Men and Woman (Draped), Miscellaneous Subjects.* (Philadelphia: University of Pennsylvania, 1887), plate 49. Photogravure. Metropolitan Museum of Art. Rogers Fund, transferred from the Library. 1991.1135.7

8   Étienne-Jules Marey and Charles Fremont, chronophotograph, 1894. Gelatin silver print from glass negative, 20.2 x 16.3 cm. Metropolitan Museum of Art. Purchase, The Horace W. Goldsmith Foundation Gift, through Joyce and Robert Menschel and Rogers Fund. 1987.1054

7

8

of DNA that can give birth to different forms. This has been a question since Gilles Deleuze and since Bernard Cache's Objectile: should we design form or mechanisms that trigger form?

Another reason for the destabilization of form is that in a dynamic and fluid world like the one the computer proposes, form is no longer the crowning achievement of the design process but rather something that appears as an instant, as an occurrence. To use an approach from Eisenman in his Derridean period, one could say that form is no longer synonymous with stable presence. Form could be different. It's a frozen moment—this explains the enduring fascination of the pictures of Muybridge and Marey (figs. 7–8) —as if architecture were the section of a certain moment in a time of theoretically limitless geometry and technological flow.

According to Pierre Lévy, information is not a thing. A bit is not a thing, but an occurrence. It's an elementary event. In this respect, one could say that form in the digital world is not in the ontological mode of presence. Form happens and becomes commensurable with a form of action. For me this is the root of the performative turn in architecture. Architecture becomes more thinkable as an action, as a thing. The reluctance to use the term *representation* may have to do with this. Is performance replacing representation as the perspective from which design must be approached? Scale is also becoming problematic with some designers, because of course digital information has no scale. This François Roche object looks like a sponge, but it's meant to be a city (fig. 9).

The crisis of tectonics is also striking. This is a crisis of a certain kind of attachment to structural legibility; structure is no longer a clear guideline. That may account for the obsession with stacking, as a kind of rejection of traditional tectonic modes. Preston Scott Cohen's Tel Aviv Museum of Art is based on this principle. At the same time we have a return of ornament, and more profoundly a kind of blurring between structure and ornament that is very different from what we used to know. For example, in the Beijing National Stadium, the structure is partly ornamental.

The relationship between memory and history is also at stake today. Why do we have so many spaceship forms in architecture? Perhaps the reason is that spaceships do not have history. This is an architecture of the everlasting present that has difficulty connecting to a clear past and to a very different future. This may have something to do with the crisis of tectonics because it creates projects without parts; George Legendre made this remark a few years ago. Parts are replaced with relation. Parts were what used to be revealed in the ruins, so we have projects that are difficult to imagine as ruins. This was one of the classical exercises of architecture: to imagine architecture as a ruin, as a way to inscribe it in time.

As all these big questions are being asked, fundamentals are returning. Rem Koolhaas is now talking about the

9   R&Sie(n). I've heard about, digital rendering, 2005. Original file: motion3.tif, 8.8 MB, last modified 28 July 2005. R&Sie(n) project records (AP193), CCA. Gift of New-Territories/R&Sie(n) by François Roche and Stéphanie Lavaux

Antoine Picon

10 Jacques Bertillon. Map of Paris showing average revenue from taxes levied on various goods, according to revenue office. *Album statistique de la ville de Paris*, 1884–1888. Bibliothèque nationale de France. FRBNF40734119

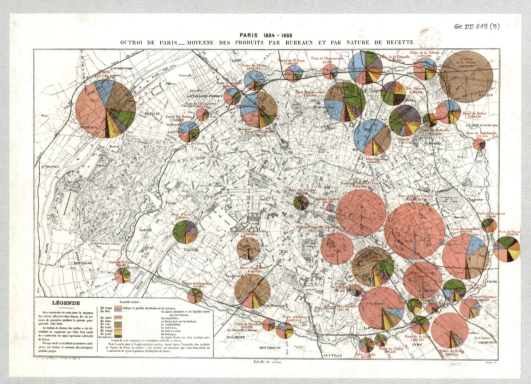

elements of architecture, and Bernard Tschumi is talking about the founding concept of architecture. There seems to be the need to rethink the foundations of the discipline, of course with a few guidelines. We know that a more acute sense of materiality linked to a new tactile condition may have something to do with the way we create that foundation.

I argue in my book on ornament that it is necessary to reinvent the question of symbolism and meaning. This is not architectural meaning as something frozen, but as something that unfolds dynamically. In the old analogy, the column is never a body but the suggestion of becoming the body. The current dismissive attitude toward meaning that we have today because of postmodernism does not acknowledge that in earlier periods architectural meaning was certainly not frozen, but was something dynamic.

I believe that we are living in a period of evolution of the discipline that is comparable to the Renaissance, a kind of radical rethinking of the foundation of architecture. The Renaissance rethought building, invented the perspective as a new mode of what was called representation at the time, and was contemporary to the invention of a new subject, the humanist subject. I don't believe in the cyborg anymore, but what is the new subject with the emerging condition of architecture in society?

I'll now briefly discuss the urban. Many architects working with digital tools do not seem to see the gaps between the two stories, but it's absolutely evident that the rise of the society of information is linked to urban questions. This is one of the things that gave birth to urbanism as a modern discipline. Urbanism emerged in the period between the 1880s and the early 1900s, and it is linked to an understanding of the city as a series of information flows and as something that is not reducible to urban design.

This map is from the statistical album of the city of Paris in the 1880s, done by Jacques Bertillon, brother of Alphonse Bertillon of the anthropological measurements (fig. 10). Jacques Bertillon was at the head of the statistical bureau of the City of Paris. I would say that in all the periods that I've discussed, information and the digital are linked to urbanism. In the 1950s and 1960s, we see a direct attempt to apply cybernetics and system theory to urbanism. This is partly documented in Jennifer Light's *The Nature of Cities*.

This is Melville Branch's project for a kind of control room to plan Los Angeles in the 1960s (fig. 11). Branch was trained as a planner, worked for a big corporation dealing with missiles, designed a control room for this company and then designed a control room for the City of Los Angeles. This is the dream of the cybernetic city. It's a fundamental story because if you don't understand this period, you don't understand why planning separated from architecture. Cybernetics and system theory were a failure in the 1960s and early 1970s, but they contributed to the divorce of the plan-

Antoine Picon

11 Melville C. Branch. Continuous master city planning: central mechanism of analysis, display and decision. In *City Planning and Aerial Information* (Cambridge, MA: Harvard University Press, 1971), p. 21. CCA. W7363 | c. 1

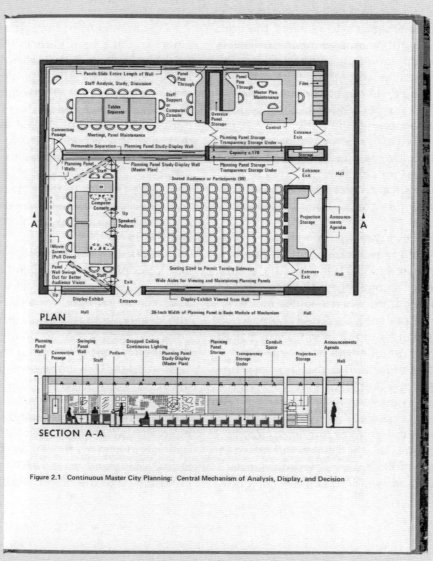

Figure 2.1 Continuous Master City Planning: Central Mechanism of Analysis, Display, and Decision

ning profession from architecture in the United States. Planners were making models of traffic, which were non-architectural. Urban design developed in response and that led to the development of computing.

The smart city is partly marred by a return of the cybernetic dream. When IBM or Cisco want to design control rooms for cities, we see the return of the same temptation. There are very few relationships these days between research on smart cities and what's happening in architecture. That's a huge problem. And work like Zaha Hadid's parametric project for Singapore doesn't connect the two, nor do all the augmented reality screens on building facades. That doesn't mean that there are no possibilities to connect. One possibility is the sensory dimension; both the smart city and digital architecture have very strong tactile dimensions in common. But the problem is that, unlike the technology of the automobile and many other technologies, digital technology does not have a clear impact on the urban form. The automobile inevitably changes the urban form— architects like Le Corbusier heralded these changes—but digital technology does not. In *City of Bits*, Bill Mitchell evokes a kind of green condition of the city, but so far this hasn't happened. The urban experience is fundamentally changed—the city is reinterpreted and mapped in a different way, and urban cartography is developing rapidly—but so far the urban form has not changed significantly. So we need to reconnect, and history might be a good way to explore a number of questions.

I first studied material from the seventeenth, eighteenth and early nineteenth centuries and then became interested in the digital because I am interested in periods in which rapid technological and cultural change intersects with architectural and urban issues. For the first part of my career I studied what happened between 1750 and 1850 in relation to industrialization. I often have the impression that something just as massive is happening today.

All these histories of the digital raise a series of classical historical problems. For example, we have problems of periodization. I think the first period, the rise of the society of information, and the second period, the emergence of the computer, are very clear. When the digital really takes over is a more complex question. It may begin in the 1970s or it may begin in the 1990s. For a historian, twenty years is a very long period of time and it changes one's perspective completely.

Another classical question concerns the role of the avant-garde in relation to more widespread evolutions. To be clear, the paperless studios were not the only avant-garde. We shouldn't forget that they would not have existed without a larger network. So, should we write a history centred on the avant-garde, or should we write a different history?

There is a need to connect to an archaeology, which has been at the forefront of historical inquiries in the history of science, with Peter Galison's inter-

Antoine Picon

est in concrete processes and machines, apparatuses and experiments. This is something we haven't done enough in architecture. We have worked so little on the material condition, and we must ask about the kind of paper and pencils that were used. For example, I'm one of the last representatives of the Rotring generation. We had the problem of the ink dripping, and of the 06 that became an 08. FedEx changed a number of processes in architecture, to say nothing of the Internet's role. And this history must be connected to many other histories. For instance, you cannot understand what was happening in the 1950s and 1960s in architecture if you don't consider electronic art, if you don't think of places where art and architecture intersect. Media history, media theory and social history are just as important, and above all we need to connect to the urban dimension.

I think the greatest challenge is that if we write this history, it's impossible not to deal with very concrete questions that have to do with the definition of a profession. If you write these days on Giulio Romano and the problem of Mannerism, you are not completely obliged to deal with what's going on in the profession. But if you deal with what happened in the 1950s, with even relatively distant moments in the history of the digital, you have to address the professional questions of today. The problem is how to write a history that is linked to social history, political history and so on, and that at the same time is intimately linked to the discipline. In terms of history, the problem is how to be both external and internal. There is the classical opposition in history between external, which is something that relates the discipline to social issues, and internal, which is a history of the discipline. I think today we have to do both at the same time.

Because of that, we must find a new answer to the relatively old question, what is the role of history in design? Without returning to the postmodern or the Tendenza—we're no longer in the time of Rossi—we may have to reconnect history to the question of design. Of course, historians should be first and foremost historians and not designers, without any pretensions to tell designers what they have to do. This is not our role. But we should find a new regime, a new economy of a relation between history and design education. As a historian, what I ultimately find interesting in the digital is that it obliges us to rethink the content and the status of history vis-à-vis the profession and professional education.

Peter Galison

<u>In 1895</u>, C. T. R. Wilson invented the cloud chamber, a device that can detect radiation and produce pictures of the movement of subatomic particles. Wilson drew from the theory of matter and from experiments carried out for the study of thunderstorms, forming a new segment of scientific culture that encompassed both theory and technology. The most productive moments in the history of the digital are moments like this one, when the approaches of experimentalists, technologists and theoreticians overlap to create a shared understanding.

This text is the transcription of a presentation that was given at the CCA in 2004.

PETER GALISON

1 The volcanologist Frank Perret during the Royal Scoiety Montserrat Expedition in 1936. He holds a thermograph, a device used to record temperature. The Archibald Gordon MacGregor Archve, British Geological Survey. EA16/161

EPISTEMIC MACHINES: IMAGE AND LOGIC

1

What interests me in the history of physics and the history of science in general is to follow history not through theory, but through the instruments and techniques that divide history into three parts. One part represents the point of view of the experimentalists, a second part represents the perspective of the instrument makers and a third represents the perspective of the theoreticians —these three parts divide the periods, the continuities and the discontinuities in the history of physics. For the theoreticians there is a big change—a rupture—in the history of physics with the introduction of quantum mechanics in 1926, but for the instrument makers and the experimentalists there is no break at that time. And where there are discontinuities for the instrument makers, there are very often theoretical continuities. I would like to address how we

Peter Galison

can see the history of modern physics, and especially abstract particle physics, following this history across instruments, across material culture. In particular I will trace how two traditions developed in the twentieth century: one tradition that represents the logic of non-visual statistics and another that is visual, which I will call the image tradition. Image and logic: that is the topic, and it is possible to make analogies to the histories of other subjects through material culture.

These two traditions organize the material history of modern physics. They divide up the history of physics very differently from the way you would understand the history of physics if you followed it only from a theoretical perspective. From the point of view of theory, which is how we usually organize the history of science, you would see the great breaks occurring at the introduction of special relativity in 1905, general relativity in 1915, quantum mechanics in 1926, quantum field theory in the 1940s, quark theory in the 1970s and so on.

But there is a very different way to approach the history of modern physics. If one looks at history through the material culture of the discipline, one gets a very different perspective on how history might be parsed. In particular, there's a traditional way—that goes back to the time of the logical positivists—of thinking about science as being grounded in observation. Observations (for the positivists) were cumulative, continuous; they mounted one after the other into a great aggregation of observations, advancing at each step in ways that encompassed the past. Theories came and went. You had a theory, then a break and then another theory. But theory was there only to organize the observations; observations were the true arbiter and strength of what science was about. I'll call this "the positivist periodization" for short.

Then in the 1960s and afterward, there was a new way of looking at the development of science that was made very popular by Thomas Kuhn, Mary Hesse, Paul Feyerabend, Gerald Holton and many others, who said that essentially that's not right—there is no thread of observation that carries through all of science. In fact, so they argued, science is divided into blocks that are discontinuously related one to the other. Theory and observation went together in the old account, for instance, of Newtonian and classical physics, and that was replaced by a new way of looking at theory and observation under Einstein. Between them was a revolutionary rupture, a paradigmatic break, a change in program, a radical disjuncture so enormously deep that it became impossible to speak about science as a unitary phenomenon that carried on over time, instead of only in discontinuous blocks. What I want to propose in this discussion, and what I have been pursuing in my work for quite some time now, is to restructure periodization in a way that is neither positivist nor anti-positivist. The anti-positivists, like Kuhn, for instance, were on to something very

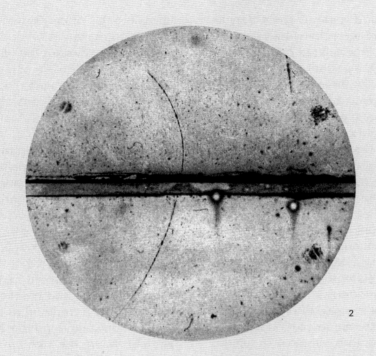

2 Cloud-chamber photograph, showing the first positron ever observed. The photograph was taken by Carl David Anderson in 1932 and was published in his 1933 article "The Positive Electron."

important when they said that observation was not continuous, that certain things came into view as possible observations and other things became impossible as theory changed—that's true. But from the point of view of the different subcultures of physics, from the subculture of the experimentalists, the theorists and the instrument makers, there are different periodizations—these other histories don't march in lockstep. Instrument makers may find a break with the invention of the cloud chamber, for example—that's not a break for the theorists. The theorists may see a break in the development of general relativity—that's not a break for the experimentalists, and so on. In fact, the intercalated nature of this periodization, the way that the subcultures fit together like an old stone wall, produces the strength that we recognize in science. What's interesting to scientists is, in fact, that they are able to move across different theories. But I want to suggest that this is not because theory is continuous or indeed any part of science by itself is continuous. Rather, this new view is that the strength of the discipline derives from the circumstance that the breaks occur differently since they are intercalated rather than lined up.

But this intercalated periodization immediately raises another question. If there are really three or more subcultures of physics, how do they talk to one another? The experimentalists find different ways of proving or demonstrating things than the theorists do. If they have different epistemic approaches to the discipline, then how do they have contact?

It is useful to think about the different cultures of physics, or of science, more generally, as being rather strongly analogous to languages. When anthropological linguists address the way languages relate, they don't look only at radical disjunctions of language, which is the model for, say, the Kuhnian picture of great epistemic revolutionary breaks. Rather, the anthropological linguists have increasingly been interested in the way partial exchange languages or inter-languages function. They distinguish between jargons, very limited terms that are shared by different languages, and pidgins, which are more developed sets of ways of speaking that allow, for instance, a wheat-growing culture to exchange goods with a fish-based culture. But these are more developed in order to allow these very important exchanges to take place, to negotiate agreements and to form cultural commonalities between speakers. And then there are creoles, which are full-fledged inter-languages that are developed to the point where you can grow up in them, and in a certain sense, all of our modern languages are themselves creoles of earlier combinations. There's no reason to think, from everything we know about the history of language, that English, French or German are primordial languages—they are themselves compositions of earlier languages. And in fact, that's the rule, not the exception.

Take, for example, chemistry and biology. An inter-language forms that eventually becomes biochemistry, but it begins with very limited terms, develops into a more elaborate form of exchange and eventually blossoms into a discipline that one can indeed grow up in. That also happens, in ways that I'll point to, between the instrument makers, the experimentalists and the theorists. What do I mean by a tradition of material culture? I have in mind three layers of handing-down, the literal meaning of *tradition* in this sense.

First, there is a tradition (literally and analogically, a handing-down) of technology. So, for example, one goes from the cloud chamber (fig. 2), which is a device that precipitates little droplets of water around the track of a charged particle as it moves through the chamber; to bubble chambers (fig. 3), which are devices that produce tiny bubbles if a charged particle goes through them; to film, which can be used to allow a particle to skim along the surface and then developed to see the small silver composites that make it possible for the observer to follow the tracks under a microscope. So at one level, I'm talking about a technological tradition, a handing-down on the one side on the

3 Bubble-chamber image showing particle tracks, from the Big European Bubble Chamber (BEBC), CERN, 1990

4 The oil-drop apparatus used by Robert Millikan in his 1909 experiment to determine the charge of the electron

5 A Geiger counter made by Hans Geiger in 1932

105

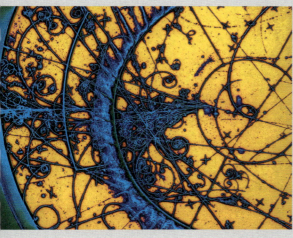

3

5

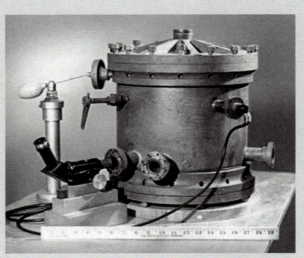

4

6 Multi-wire proportional chamber, invented by Georges Charpak, 1967–1968. Musée des arts et métiers-Cnam, Paris

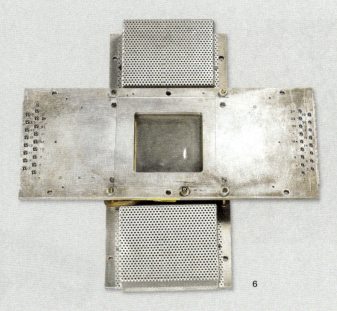

image tradition of optics, photography and the measurement of the path of particles, and on the other side the more electronic, logical and statistical tradition. On the logic side I have in mind the use of high-voltage machines, electronics, scalers—which are devices that count—and the logic circuits that record, say, when A, B and C do happen and D does not.

In addition to the technical, machine traditions, there is a tradition of pedagogy. When one looks at the history of experimental science, one sees that there are certain forms of devices that are handed down, just as the cloud chamber, the bubble chamber and the film share certain techniques. This tradition involves a conveyance of expertise and orientation from one generation of teachers to their students. Think, for example, of a physicist like Robert Millikan, who won the Nobel Prize for showing that you can make little droplets form around individual electrons (fig. 4) and by so doing determine their charge. Millikan's student Carl David Anderson, who built more sophisticated cloud chambers, was not only able to make fog out of which a droplet could be isolated, but precision cloud chambers that could track particle trajectories in stunning and quantitative detail. Anderson's student, in turn, was Donald Glaser, who began building cloud chambers but then went on to construct the first bubble chamber. People tend to remain, generation after generation, scientific generation after generation, within these pedagogical traditions that carry on, for instance, from the cloud chamber to the bubble chamber, or from the emulsion to the bubble chamber, or from the cloud chamber to nuclear emulsions, rather than crossing from one tradition to the other.

Finally, there's a tradition of demonstration—an epistemic tradition. There are certain ways of arguing that are characteristic of each of these traditions. For example, within the image tradition, for physicists from many scientific generations and across all of these different instruments—bubble chambers, cloud chambers, nuclear emulsions, films—there are golden events, individual images that are so clear, so compelling to the physics community that each image forms a kind of demonstration. Whereas, on the other side, clicks and counts of objects from a device like a Geiger counter are combined and any one click means nothing. Only the statistical aggregation of clicks amounts to something. So we have these three dimensions of tradition at the instrumental level: technological, pedagogical and epistemic handing-down.

Making use of these considerations, I want to look back at the history of particle physics over the course of the long twentieth century. Let's set aside the theory-centric periodization and instead acknowledge that instruments, experiments and theory each have their own dynamics. As we have seen within instrumentation, on the one side, there is a tradition of image, in which the cloud-chamber physicists hand down techniques, pedagogy and forms of argumentation to the nuclear-emulsion and bubble-chamber physicists. On the other side, the logic tradition begins with the ordinary Geiger counter (fig. 5) that you've probably seen many times, which clicks when it gets near a radioactive source, but then the image and logic traditions can be combined in much more sophisticated ways. For example, three Geiger counters in a row are all struck by a charged particle and begin to click, and then they could form not just tubular Geiger counters but flat sheets of conductors that can be used to make spark chambers and wire chambers (fig. 6), which consist of thousands of wires that are used to measure the passage of a charged particle—all of these share specific pedagogical, technological and epistemic forms of argumentation.

In the 1970s these traditions began to join, as instrument makers and experimentalists began to use electronics to produce images and even to argue from individual images in the way the image tradition had done for many decades. And yet, just by virtue of the electronic grounding of these machines, they were able (as was characteristic of the logic tradition) to control the situation, to have a kind of statistical approach and an

Peter Galison

7 Postcard showing a view of Ben Nevis. Produced by Valentine and Sons, Dundee, Scotland, c. 1920

8 Ernest Rutherford in his laboratory at McGill University, 1905

108

7

8

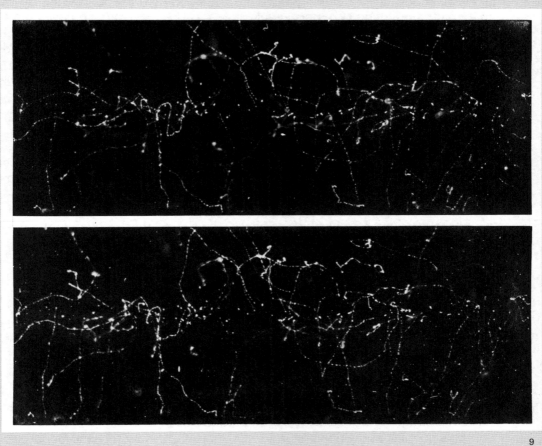

9 Cloud-chamber photograph by C. T. R. Wilson, c. 1913. C. T. R. Wilson Collection, University of Glasgow Library. GB 248 DC 448/2/4/55

ability to manipulate the device and the phenomena the way one had with Geiger counters.

I would argue that this coming-together is indicative of and connected to a much more general pattern. Look, for example, at how optical astronomy and radio astronomy have joined in image-making electronics. Consider how, in medicine, a non-visual and a visual tradition have joined in nuclear magnetic resonance and computers and other devices that produce pictures based on the combination of thousands of channels of electronic data.

Just to elaborate on this a bit, it's what physicists mean when they say, for instance, that counter A gives off a signal and counter B gives off a signal, but either counter C or counter D does not. It's this combination of "either/or," "not" and "and" that composes the way these electronic devices function. And that's true for spark chambers, which are an extension of those ideas. Spark chambers are unrolled Geiger counters, if you will. It's also true for wire chambers, which allow you to make extremely precise determinations of where the particle went and reconstruct its path.

Let's go back and explore some of these ideas in a bit more detail. The cloud chamber sits at the beginning of the development of the image tradition and it leads to looking at tracks on film, nuclear emulsion and the bubble chamber, where the tracks leave not a wispy line of droplets as they do in the cloud chamber, but a wispy line of bubbles boiling along a highly compressed and superheated liquid. That image tradition begins out of natural history, not out of anything to do with atomic physics or chemistry.

C. T. R. Wilson, who invented the cloud chamber, began by being interested in clouds. He was fascinated with beetles, and with natural history and all of its aspects in the Scottish Highlands, where he grew up, but especially with clouds and weather formations. He spent time, for instance, as an apprentice to the meteorologist on top of Ben Nevis (fig. 7), and there he saw devices, including what is called a dust chamber. A dust chamber was used by meteorologists to take samples of the air and then to change the pressure around it and allow water droplets to condense around the dust particles, which then fell on a glass slide, so you could count them. Victorian Britain was obsessed with dust—they thought it was the source of disease but also the mark of progress—and these devices became very popular and part of the standard account of how rain worked. Rain was, the Victorians thought, the condensation of water around dust particles.

Wilson saw this and began to wonder whether it might be possible to change the device. John Aitken, who invented the dust chamber, would take a sample from the local atmosphere, pump it into a reservoir, and then it would go into the chamber where the pump would change the pressure and cause the droplets to go around the dust particles, which would fall on a glass slide. Wilson took essentially the same device, but he filtered the air before it went to the reservoir. Now on the face of things, that should have made this device completely useless; it was designed to measure dust. But Wilson had the hope that he might be able to show that water droplets could condense around ions, atoms that were somehow more or less charged than their normal neutral state would indicate. He changed this, because he had been exposed to the new physical theories and approaches of the Cavendish Laboratory at Cambridge. Wilson asked how we could use this device that's meant to measure dust—just ordinary dust that you can sometimes even see with the naked eye, or certainly with a microscope—to explore a possible source of rain on the one side or a way of tracking these ions on the other, by looking at water droplets condensing around purified air that has no dust in it.

Wilson soon began to see something quite astonishing. People had begun to predict that atoms, when they collided with one another, were like little pellets hitting one another. Not that matter was more like a pudding, but rather it was divided, as Ernest Rutherford argued (fig. 8), into very hard nuclei surrounded by electrons at a distance. So people began to speculate about how those collisions would look. When Wilson could actually show photographs of charged particles moving through his cloud chamber (fig. 9)—it's called a cloud chamber because it issued from his interest in clouds, but was able to see the paths of individual particles—they looked so much like what the physicists had expected that it caused a true sensation. Almost immediately, physicists around the world—this is starting in about 1913—began to say that this would be a way of actually seeing atoms, of making the invisible world of physics visible.

On the other side—that is to say, on the logic side—people were beginning to combine Geiger counters using complicated electronics, and even began exploring ways to use Geiger counters, under certain circumstances, to launch a cloud chamber. They were trying to take the enormously helpful ability of the counters to pick out a certain kind of event and to count only those events that are interesting, and to combine that ability to be selective with the beautiful visualization capabilities of the cloud chamber. Some physicists in the early 1930s were trying to use counters to launch the cloud chamber only when something interesting happened—only when, say, counters A, B and C fired, and D, E and F did not. By using counters in this selective or logical way, they could get more control over the cloud chamber.

The cloud chamber, meanwhile, blossomed into a very influential instrument. In some ways, the first half of the twentieth century had the cloud chamber in the way earlier centuries had the microscope or the telescope. Scientific atlases of cloud-chamber pictures began to be produced. And young physicists would study these atlases the way young doctors would study atlases of physiology, abnormal physiology or pathological physiology—in order to recognize things that were new. In this case, the physicists, rather than finding departures from the norm to be pathological as the doctors did, would say that once you learned what the standard pictures were, if you saw something different it would be a discovery.

So this new form of device became the basis for a new kind of epistemology, a new way of looking at the world, and new kinds of arguments began to develop out of it. In a sense, you could see the history of the cloud chamber this way. You could imagine, in 1895, Wilson joining two completely disparate fields. On the one side, there is Cambridge-style matter theory—what is matter made of? Is it made of little ions? How big are these ions? How do they compose the ordinary objects that we know? And then there is this other tradition, practised, for instance, high up on Ben Nevis, trying to understand what made thunderstorms, how they work, how lightning happens and how large-scale meteorology functions. Wilson did something that was a contribution to both, and indeed was inseparable from both. He was looking at how water condensed on ions that showed the ion physicists where the ions were, because you could see these droplets, watch the paths that they made and even move the droplets around, as Millikan did, to determine how much charge there was on an electron. It was also a way of showing how rain formed, and Wilson believed very strongly, contrary to what we later came to think about rain, that this was the true source of the rain that made up thunderstorms.

Between 1895 and 1911, roughly speaking, there was one subject, a new subject composed as a hybrid of matter theory and thunderstorm theory, if you will, or thunderstorm observations, which you might call condensation physics; it was the condensation of vapour around a charged particle that was at one and the same time part of understanding matter and part of understanding drops. In about 1911 that began to splinter into all these other areas, but for this period of sixteen years there's a feeling of coexistence. They form what you could call a trading zone, an inter-language that is materialized in these new devices, a form of acting in the laboratory that is connected both to morphological meteorology and to Cambridge-style analytic matter theory.

And that's the phenomenon that interests me, where you see different scientific cultures or even scientific and non-scientific cultures joining together, sometimes for long periods, sometimes for short periods, borrowing pieces of each and combining them into a conjoined effort. Wilson's students go on to become the leading cloud-chamber physicists. They are also the people who begin to develop nuclear emulsions. One of his students, C. F. Powell, was interested in steam, in the way turbines work. He did detailed studies of how something as practical as steam functioned in these massive turbines. He also became interested in how steam worked in explosive volcanic eruptions. In fact, Powell was sent to Montserrat by the Royal Society in 1936 to study these very dangerous explosions in which superheated steam goes down under the lava and makes it possible for the lava to travel, not at a stately pace, but racing down the slopes too fast for anyone to get out of the way (fig. 1). These are extremely dangerous forms of volcanic eruptions, and Powell went to the island to understand the way this condensation physics works.

He set up what he called "untrained observers," who made seismographic and other forms of observation all over the island. That became extremely important for him when he heard about the new discoveries being made in physics, and, in particular, about the discovery of nuclear fission in the 1930s. So he came back and tried to use the cloud chamber to study this new phenomenon. He soon discovered that it's not a very good instrument for that, but he took this visual orientation and asked, "How else could I make these charged particles visible?" And he thought, "Maybe I could do it with film." He took a piece of film—probably no bigger than a couple of postage stamps—and divided it into little sectors, and sent them out to what he called "untrained observers" (fig. 10). He modelled what he was doing in the laboratory on the way these observations of volcanic activity had been organized on Montserrat. And he sent them out to group A, group B and group C. Each one of them received a tiny slice of the film and then had to study it, making enormously delicate measurements through the microscope. That instrument was then adapted using film in this way to study how nuclear fission works in bomb physics.

In fact, for a long time it was a great mystery to me why in the middle of and just after the Second World War this study of these nuclear emulsions—just ordinary film, to try to see how and where particles go—was so lavishly funded, while in Britain, everyone, in the sciences in particular, was desperate for money. They had no money for any of this. It turns out—we know this from declassified documents—that the emulsion had actually been very useful in understanding how neutrons move around in atomic bombs, and this was work that was conducted in part in Chalk River in Canada, in England and in the United States. And so, little by little, the scientists needed to get better and better film. One of their problems was that they had film on which it was very difficult to see the track and measure it against the background of other random silver particles. So the physicists struck what I think of as a Cassandra deal with Ilford and Kodak. The physicists asked the film companies, "Will you make us an emulsion that will show the tracks of all particles very beautifully?" and the companies said, "Sure, we'll make you a film like that, but we'll have to do it in such a way that we will never tell you, ever, how this film works. We will design

Peter Galison

10 Emulsion photograph
of a cosmic ray pion
by C. F. Powell, 1947

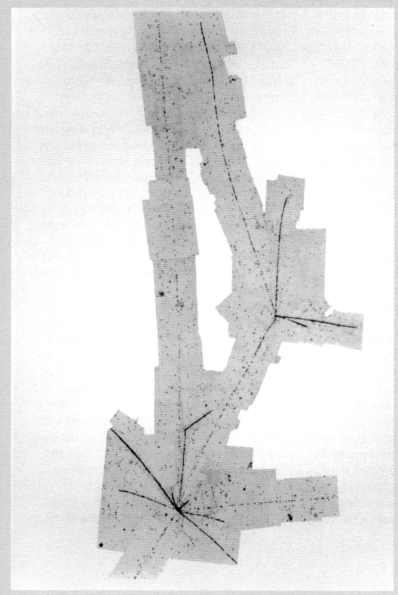

this in such a way that you will never really have the confidence to understand your own instrument. We will make you a film where you can see everything, but you may not be able to believe it."

The physicists accepted the deal. They had little choice. It was such complicated chemistry that there was only one physicist in the world who was actually able to make these emulsions: a Canadian physicist named Pierre Demers. He said that there are two aspects: the *aspect processus* and the *aspect détection*, and he essentially divided the world into physicists who are looking at the way cosmic rays work, the way the basic elements of matter function—they're on the top and all the applications that these films are used for are up there. And then there are the people, in some ways like him, who are interested in how film works and what this tells us, much in the way Wilson was interested in how the droplets condensed over the ions. You could either think of that as telling you about droplets or telling you about ions.

So Demers said you could either look at this from the detection aspect or from the process aspect, and he formed a kind of trading zone between the two with his allies and co-workers. And they began to form a way of thinking in which the physicists could communicate with the film people, but which required a lot of adjusting because the people who made film knew nothing about nuclear fission or other processes of physics, and the physicists knew nothing about how emulsions worked or how suspended colloidal particles worked; this was really a mystery. In fact, when you wanted to make these films, you had to use the hooves of pigs that had grazed in a certain form of clover—the kind of things that physicists never wanted to know. But they could form a trading zone where they could learn enough of each other's language to communicate, and pictures then became crucial, again providing golden events that were able to show individual phenomena well enough to persuade people on the basis of a single image.

After the war, the Americans took a path into physics that was predicated largely on these very large-scale approaches to the discipline, but which, in fact, they had developed during the war, either with the two-billion-dollar radar project or through the development of the atomic bomb, which was another two-billion-dollar project. The Europeans obviously had nothing like these resources in the postwar scene. Many of their laboratories had been destroyed, and many of their students had been killed or had emigrated. So the Europeans turned hopefully to the idea that you could make small-scale physics work by taking your cloud chamber or nuclear emulsions up to the top of a mountain. But these were tiny experiments that cost nothing, whereas the Americans had drawn up plans for their laboratories during the war, based on the large military and industrial-scale efforts.

By looking at the material culture of science, you can begin to see these

Peter Galison

11 Donald Glaser and the bubble chamber at the University of California, Berkeley

12 Luis Alvarez (*at left*) and the bubble chamber at the University of California, Berkeley

11

12

13 Oscilloscope trace of the first proton beam guided through the Main Ring, which houses the main synchrotron of the Fermilab National Accelerator Laboratory, 1971

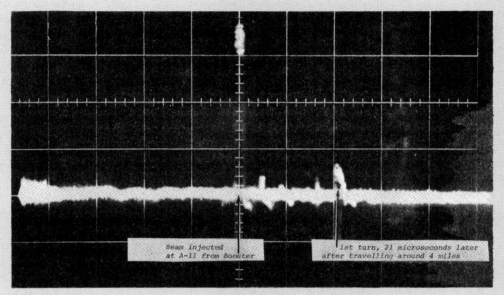

much broader features that reveal what scientists want from their discipline, what kind of culture they want to live in and what counts as being a physicist. It wasn't all Europeans versus Americans in this sense. As I mentioned before, Millikan was used to working by himself or with one collaborator. He won the Nobel Prize for work that was done essentially by himself. His student Anderson won the Nobel Prize for work that he did with the cloud chamber—a two-person collaboration. Glaser, Anderson's student, was too young to participate in the Second World War projects, and he began to wonder whether he could make a device that would be able to show a much more accurate development of an image, say, in a liquid—causing bubbles to form in a liquid rather than droplets in a vapour. And in these tiny bubble chambers, tracks can be photographed. Glaser took pictures with a Polaroid camera taped into his notebook, and used his parents' old 16-mm movie camera and the speaker magnet from his stereo. This is very small-scale physics built deliberately, so he wouldn't have to work in laboratories of the scale and scope that had come out of the war.

But as soon as this device was shown, the big-physics types, like Luis Alvarez at Berkeley, said, "I want one of those, only I don't want it as big as my thumb; I want it as big as a factory," and within a few weeks Glaser was working with the people who came from the atomic bomb tests in the Pacific to build versions of this behind a blast wall. The scale of these things is immense. But even then, as physics was growing in size, there were others who wanted to keep it small. In fact, at Harvard, joined with the Massachusetts Institute of Technology (MIT), there was a bubble-chamber laboratory just down the street from my office, where they insisted on not following Atomic Energy Commission rules; they didn't have safety officers, military-style discipline, security systems, code words and so on. Instead, they allowed people to build bigger and bigger chambers on their own. Unfortunately, they were working with liquid hydrogen, and one day in the early 1960s the much-feared event happened: one of these chambers blew up. It not only killed one technician and wounded several other people—young physicists—but it also put an end, definitively, to big physics conducted in the style and manner of an earlier age of physics. After this event—and even some of the physicists admitted that it could have happened in one of the more militarized laboratories—nowhere in the world were people allowed to work with bubble chambers outside of this much more industrial scale and form of work.

The bubble chamber at Berkeley represented, in a sense, the pinnacle of the pure visual tradition (figs. 11–12). But by the early 1970s, the increasingly sophisticated electronic tradition and the increasingly sophisticated image tradition began to realize that in some way they needed each other. Instead of trying to do experiments in which particles came and went through a series of detectors, physicists wanted to make experiments in which a proton and an anti-proton or an electron and an anti-electron would collide head on and annihilate each other, producing much more energy than would be possible from these so-called fixed targets. The target is another particle heading in the opposite direction, and the amount of energy released is enormous. These sorts of experiments created devices at a scale that was going to produce, in some ways, electronic images, and these devices were built out of teams that were composed half from the image tradition and half from the logic tradition. The image folks began to produce images from an oscilloscope (fig. 13), and the logic tradition people started counting and doing statistics on the images. The image people tried to treat electronically produced images, even very rough ones, like old-fashioned precision bubble-chamber pictures. It shows you how powerful the epistemic aspect was—the trusted, characteristic form of argumentation that accompanied each of these traditions.

Soon—by the early 1980s—you had collaborations that, instead of being two or ten or fifty members came to have 150 or more. The great experiments of the early twenty-first century at CERN—billion-dollar devices (ATLAS and CMS)—were carried out to find the Higgs boson, each with teams of between two and three thousand physicists and an equal number of engineers. These are more than big experiments; they are world-spanning communities that create a new sociology of work and knowledge.

So in the architecture of hardware, the architecture of software and the architecture of the machine, one begins to see the sociology of the material culture itself that affects the kinds of arguments that are made. But eventually, by the 1980s, one begins to see images that are electronically composed across a huge range of science, from the tiniest bits of matter and energy through the human body and out to astronomical scales. If we look out at the big history of science not from claims of unified theory but from instrumentation, we would say that the long twentieth century is a history of image and logic—and their confluence.

The last thing I want to mention is that these trading zones, these zones of exchange between these different cultures, can sometimes be seen in the physical architecture of the laboratory itself. In the first nucleus of the radar laboratory at MIT, each of the components of the radar had a different room. Within each room—within the antenna group or within the transmitter group—you would find engineers, experimentalists and theorists, all talking to one another, all desperate to figure out how to understand devices like this that required some theoretical work as well as more engineering. In fact, you can see that structure in the creation of these exchange zones. During the Second World War, the physicists and the engineers at Chicago were at such loggerheads that the physicists told the president of the United States they would fail in the war effort against the Germans if they were not allowed to dominate the project. And the engineers wrote back and said, "It'll fail if you trust the physicists." Finally, one of the heads of the atomic bomb project specified exactly how the lines of communication were going to work. The forced contact brought engineering, experiment and theory together and gave rise to a new way of understanding physics. So I leave you then with this thought: if we look at the development of physics or of science, or of science and technology, by focusing on practices and techniques, we find ourselves very quickly raising questions that are on the one side as grubby as machines, as sociological as who talks to whom, as linguistic as the kinds of terms that are used and as abstract as the forms in which scientific knowledge is composed.

Orit Halpern

The article "A Logical Calculus of Ideas Immanent in Nervous Activity," by the mathematicians Warren McCulloch and Walter Pitts, appeared in 1943. It outlines the neural net model for cognitive and computer science, which defines neurons as semiotic units that can be represented as yes/no or true/false signs operating in a communication structure—a net. The neural net model was one of the foundations for the work of the Architecture Machine Group (AMG) on responsive machine-learning projects. The group developed environments that could monitor and redesign themselves in response to change. The smart city, both pre-emptive and responsive and obsessed with demonstration, has inherited these environments.

ORIT HALPERN

1 The Architecture Machine Group laboratory with SEEK under construction, 1970. MIT Museum

ARCHITECTURE AS MACHINE: THE SMART CITY DECONSTRUCTED

1

Orit Halpern

Today, "smart" grids and operating centres surround us. Littering the world with interfaces, luminous data visualization rooms exist in cities across the globe. Interfaces show data on the environment, traffic and other measures of urban space being gathered through closed-circuit televisions and other systems. Take, for example, an IBM operating centre in Songdo, South Korea (fig. 2). But South Korea, for all its fabled technology, is hardly alone. London, Rio de Janeiro and New York have similar systems installed in different emergency and management agencies. What is most curious about this architecture is that it serves no clear purpose for human beings. Large panels show snippets of information culled from various sensor systems, but the actual flow of information is too great for human cognitive processing capacity. Most of this data is autonomously analyzed by IBM algorithms that alert the operators only in case of emergency, sometimes after already having initiated emergency protocols. These architectures are performances, demonstrations of big data enacted for individuals who can neither see nor directly analyze the images. Managers in Songdo's control rooms speak of an extremely rapid turnover of operators due to excesses of boredom and fatigue, for which operators are offered therapy, exercise and shopping coupons. Forced to sit for hours with no event structure before largely algorithmically analyzed data, individuals are losing their minds, it seems.

But losing minds, or perhaps reason, appears to be what smartness is all about. These gleaming rooms are merely the flagship displays for vast infrastructures of computing, performances of control and surveillance on ever-larger and increasingly global networks. They are the visible and sensible manifestations of a much greater set of concerns with climate change, energy scarcity, security and economic collapse that has turned the focus of urban planners, investors and governments toward smart infrastructures as sites of value production and potential salvation from a world consistently defined by catastrophes and crises. Such smartness and resilience directly refer to computationally and digitally managed systems—from electrical grids to building management systems—that can learn, and in theory adapt, by analyzing data about themselves. Whether threatened by terrorism, sub-prime mortgages, energy shortages or hurricanes, the responses are remarkably similar, and we therefore turn to interactivity and the management of attention as ways to negotiate our environmental and social condition.

The original concept of such a responsive or smart environment, one that is so gleamingly enacted by these sleek, screen-filled rooms, is often dated to the 1970s, and attributed to Nicholas Negroponte's work with the Architecture Machine Group (AMG), later to become the Media Lab at the Massachusetts Institute of Technology (MIT), where Negroponte

2 Control room, Songdo International Business District, 2013

3 *Overleaf:*
The Aspen Movie Map experienced in the media room at MIT, c. 1979

supposedly coined the term *responsive environment*.[1] Negroponte, who was trained as an architect and led AMG, proposed that designers would be able to make architecture better serve populations and address the context of urban degradation and racial segregation in the United States and in the decolonizing nations by integrating computation into built environments. Relying on technology, AMG envisioned buildings and urban designs that could monitor fluctuations in their environments, alter their forms in response to possible changes and, if necessary, redesign themselves.

Emerging at the same time as a global energy crisis, rising ecological consciousness and an increase in both urban violence and terrorism, the concept of the responsive environment has long been married to catastrophe. Negroponte's famous adage "demo or die" captures the high-technology start-up mentality of the 1990s, as well as the mode of futurity and preemption that underpins so many of our smart systems. In order to elucidate this double logic of smartness and "demoing" that is reshaping how we understand architecture, territory and urbanism, I will move between the inside of the nervous system and the scale of populations, showing how AMG assimilated and recombined numerous principles from cybernetics, computing and histories of architecture to produce the epistemology of the demo and the practice of the responsive (now smart) environment, which continues to shape our imagination of the future of human life.

Simulation and the Urban System

I began this essay with an image of a data-inundated urban operations centre because, in many ways, such a centre is the scaled replica of one of the more infamous early experiments in "virtual" reality—AMG's Aspen Movie Map of 1978 (fig. 3).[2] One of the first fully interactive digital environments, the map was both a way to navigate space and the outcome of a new epistemology that correlated emerging notions of computation and cognitive science with design. The Aspen Movie Map was commissioned from MIT by the Cybernetics Division of the Defense Advanced Research Projects Agency (DARPA), part of the United States military. Inspired by stories of the Israeli army's use of a mock built environment in training for the mission to rescue Israeli hostages in Entebbe, Uganda, in 1976, DARPA sought to build an entirely simulated training space. The function of the Aspen Movie Map from a military perspective was to implant geographic knowledge and cognitive maps into soldiers before they arrived at the real site in combat. But for members of AMG, including project director Andrew Lippman, the main purpose of the project was not related to human memory, training or geographic specifics. Rather, it was to develop more interactive environments for engaging with computers, and to test the emerging technologies of video discs and high-resolution storage and replay systems.[3] The map was built through a careful survey using gyro-stabilized cameras that captured an image at every foot they covered on the streets of Aspen, a high-end ski resort town in Colorado. The system worked through a computer, laser discs and a joystick or touch screen. The map could be navigated at the user's speed. Today, this model is often touted as the predecessor of first person–shooter video games, military simulation for both battlefield training and post-traumatic stress disorder treatment, and Google Earth.[4]

Importantly, the Aspen Movie Map was not a classified military project. Counter-terrorism and urban warfare due to decolonization became pressing issues by the 1960s, particularly after the conflicts in Algeria and Vietnam, but there was another war going on. The urban riots of the late 1960s in the United States sparked by Martin Luther King Jr.'s assassination, and the increasing tensions as white Americans fled urban areas, refusing to desegregate and erasing tax bases as a result, prompted a new discourse of "war" and "crisis" in America's cities. Historian Jennifer Light has shown that this discourse of crisis was heightened by an influx of defence intellectuals leaving the analysis of nuclear strategy to apply their operations research and cybernetic methods to the burgeoning and increasingly profitable sector of urban security and development.[5] The history of the Architecture Machine Group expands on this condition.

As Aubrey Anable has argued, by the 1970s, the discourse of urban "crisis" had dissipated or dissolved. It was replaced by the Nixon administration's investment in privatized solutions and a turn away from the programs of Lyndon B. Johnson's Great Society. This privatization and fatigue, according to Anable, are refracted in the movie map's hyper-individualized mode of traversing urban space.[6] Certainly, the movie map sat within a longer tradition at MIT of more than three decades of investment in behavioural and computational sciences in schools of planning and architecture. Planners at MIT had not answered even the original "crisis" with a turn to sociology or structural discourses. Rather, they continued to make use of the tools of environmental psychology, communication theories, cognitive science and computer science. Kevin Lynch, who developed environmental psychology, and computer engineer Jay Forrester, who implemented cybernetic and computer programming methods and simulations in response to environmental problems and urban design issues, had been working since the 1950s to apply cybernetic approaches to human habitation.[7]

Forrester's work was particularly influential for AMG, and important in introducing new ideas of technical obsolescence into urban planning practices. In *Urban Dynamics*, a study that introduced models of computation to urban simulation, Forrester concludes that cities must be treated as systems of industries, housing and people. For cities, as for all technical systems, "processes of aging cause stagnation."[8] More widely, he argues that the social sciences, and the study of society as the foundation for urban planning, must be displaced. The report opens with a statement to the effect that the entire research project had no grounding in the literature of urban studies or planning. Instead, Forrester espouses the direct application of approaches from business and computer science that had been previously used to model the growth of corporations.[9] The research was conducted under the rubric of the Urban Systems Group, a Ford Foundation–funded initiative to apply management and computing to urban problems. The group existed at MIT in the late 1960s and was critical in linking its schools of urban planning and engineering, as well as in forming cross-disciplinary projects at the University of Michigan, Harvard and elsewhere. *Urban Dynamics* details efforts to use time-shared computers to run generic models of common urban revitalization programs and of urban growth, testing how different policies produce different outcomes. Forrester systematically sorts urban processes into categories: *inputs*, which today might be labelled *stakeholders*; *valves*, which were actions that would impact demographic and economic activities, such as increasing education and investing in housing; and *outputs*, or desired results (fig. 4). The Urban Systems Group then spent enormous energy and capital to build computer simulations that would project different arrangements of inputs and valves, impacting the entire city's productivity, measured through economic output and demographic indicators such as class, profession and birth rate.[10] It is important to note that these were *sui generis* models grounded in policy and planning at MIT, not in studies of existing cities. The MIT approach to urban design and planning through computing was distinguished by its focus on process rather than on end point, and by its reformulation of urban problems through the direct application of organizational management represented through the flow charts and feedback loops of programming.

Forrester's discourse of "obsolescence" and management marks a critical turn in reimagining urban territories and the practices of urban planning and design. According to historian Daniel Abramson, such discourses of obsolescence are historically specific, differing radically from modern discussions of urbanism as a rapid and industrial, albeit often dehumanizing, process. Cities in the 1950s and afterward were increasingly imagined as obsolete technical systems, a conception that demanded new approaches emerging from organizational management and computer-aided manufacturing.[11] Forrester thus anticipates a logic of refreshable newness invoked by "demo or die" in envisioning aging and non-growth—or stagnation—as the central causes of urban problems, race conflict and environmental issues. The implication is that cities, like corporations, must invent, or age and die.

Conceiving of cities as corporate-computational systems distanced the imaginary of planning from ideal or utopian forms and reframed urbanization as an ongoing process of calibrating cities for constant change. Throughout the nineteenth and early twentieth centuries, modern designers and

135

4   Jay Forrester. Feedback loops and circuits: "the major levels (rectangles) and rates (valve symbols) for the model of the urban area." In *Urban Dynamics,* Jay Forrester (Cambridge, MA: MIT Press, 1969)

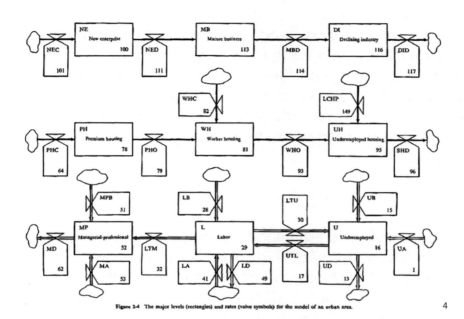

Figure 2-4 The major levels (rectangles) and rates (valve symbols) for the model of an urban area.

4

urban planners, including Ebenezer Howard, Le Corbusier and the Bauhaus, produced utopic and replicable forms of the city.[12] The planners working from histories of communication and computer science replaced ideal forms with pragmatic methods: the demo and the flow chart. The historian Shannon Mattern defines this obsession with data-driven analytics and computation as "methodolatry," and it now largely shapes contemporary urban planning practices.[13]

Scale and Complexity

AMG reflected and advanced the history of systemic thinking already in existence at MIT by emphasizing a concept of design as a matter of systems and not of discrete buildings, and of an architectural practice dedicated to scale. If one thinks of the replacement of the term *architecture* with *media* when the group became the Media Lab in 1985, perhaps this new concept of design implied the disappearance of discrete space and architectural expertise altogether.

In keeping with a systems approach, scale and complexity were central concerns for AMG. Negroponte's book *The Architecture Machine: Toward a More Human Environment*, written in the late 1960s and published in 1970, would become a bible for computer-aided design. This is a text that, according to architectural historian Molly Wright Steenson, precipitated the spread of computers within the field of architecture, and that was critical in producing an emergent do-it-yourself ethos in the design fields that started in the late 1960s and early 1970s and continues into the present, an ethic not of expertise but of constant experimenting, versioning and what we might now label "hacking."[14] As Negroponte argues in the book's introduction, the functions of inserting machine intelligence into design are twofold. The first is "evolution": "I shall consider the physical environment as an evolving organism... [and] I shall consider an evolution aided by a specific class of machines," he writes.[15] The second function is to promote "an environmental humanism," which, according to Negroponte, "might only be attainable in cooperation with machines that have been thought to be inhuman that can respond intelligently to the tiny, individual, constantly changing bits of information that reflect the identity of each urbanite as well as the coherence of the city."[16] This environmental humanism that could only be created in symbiosis with machines was, for Negroponte (but also for Forrester, among others), understood to be a necessary corrective to the human inability to deal with "large-scale problems." AMG thus insisted on both a constant demand for change and technical solutions to infrastructural and social issues in design. Humans, Negroponte implied, simply were not good pattern seekers; they could not see systemic problems resulting from changes over time or changing contexts. Human beings were either specific or abstract, but they could not negotiate the space between the local and the global. Arguably, machines could assist in this function.[17] Computing can thus be understood to have served two related ends for AMG: the automation of change and the production of new practices that could scale between the individual and the urban environment or even the planet.

As if to emphasize the grandeur and vast scope of AMG's ambitions in liberating humanity from history or stagnation, major concepts in *The Architecture Machine* are introduced through a wide range of examples, such as informal planning in Latin America and community developments in Boston (fig. 5). Central to these examples are images of cities in

Orit Halpern

5 Nicholas Negroponte. An example of urban planning (Brasília) and two examples of informal development (Mojácar, Almería, Spain, and Positano, Italy). In *The Architecture Machine: Toward a More Human Environment* (Cambridge, MA: MIT Press, 1970), p. 4–5. CCA. 0005334; ID:87-B19491

The diagram is a metaphor. The many little forces are not summed or averaged, rather they are constantly and individually affecting a single body. It is this multitude of forces, causes, and effects that the machine can so readily handle as individual events in a particular context.

Handling design problems solely at the building scale can provide a monumentalism by ignoring all the local forces. Of course, Brasilia works, but only as a symbolic statement of power and not as a place to live and work. It is the result of global and general (and perhaps unethical) goals housed at the wrong scale.

Mojacar in the province of Almeria, Spain. This is an example of local forces shaping the environment. The unity, which results from more global causes, comes from the limitation of materials, resources, weather, and so on. (The photograph first appeared in *Architecture without Architects* [Rudofsky, 1964]. Photograph courtesy of José Ortiz Echagüe)

Italian hill towns. "The very thought that modern man could live in anachronistic communities like these [Positano, Italy] would seem absurd were it not that they are increasingly becoming refuges for city dwellers" (Rudofsky, 1964). The unmentioned amenities are in fact attainable in high-density urban life, now that the serial, repititious, and generalized aspects of the industrial revolution can be superseded. (Photograph courtesy of Gabinetto Fotografico Nazionale, Rome, Italy)

personal needs in antihuman structures. The result is an urban monumentalism that, through default, we have had foisted upon us by opulent, self-important institutions (that can at least control large chunks of the beach); our period is a period of neo-Hancockism and post-Prudentialism. The cause is the distinct maneuverability gap that exists between the scale of the mass and the scale of the individual, the scale of the city and the scale of the room.

Because of this, an environmental humanism might only be attainable in cooperation with machines that have been thought to be inhuman devices but in fact are devices that can respond intelligently to the tiny, individual, constantly changing bits of information that reflect the identity of each urbanite as well as the coherence of the city. These devices need the adaptability of humans and the specificity of present-day machines. They must recognize general shifts in context as well as particular changes in need and desire.

The following chapters have a "pebble-prejudice." Most computer-oriented tasks today are the opposite: the efficient transportation system, the public open space, the flow of goods and money. Our bias toward localized information implies two directions for the proposed relationship between designer and machine. The first is a "do-it-yourselfism," where, as in the Marshall McLuhan (1965) automation circuit, consumer becomes producer and dweller becomes designer. Machines located in homes could permit each resident to project and overlay his architectural needs upon the changing framework of the city. The same machine might report the number of shopping days

Orit Halpern

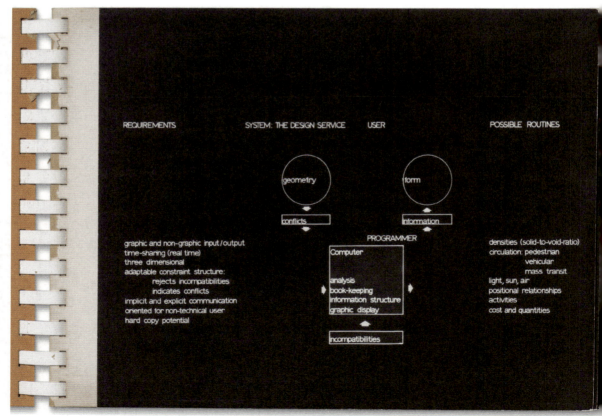

6 AMG. Page from the URBAN 2 presentation booklet illustrating a computerized urban design system, 1968. URBAN 2 involved an exchange between the user and the computer, based on a set of twelve thousand solids and voids. Using a light pen, a user could select design operations on the screen.

7 AMG. Page from the URBAN 2 presentation booklet, 1968

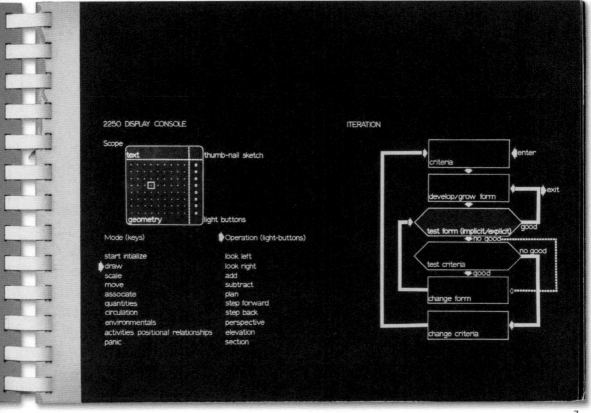

former colonies. These cities are juxtaposed with vernacular construction produced after or against colonial authority, as in the case in which colonial Spanish planning in La Paz, Bolivia, is contrasted with the informal development that emerged as the city grew after the withdrawal of direct Spanish control.

These allusions to an emancipatory design that would relieve humanity from both colonialism and modernism implicitly offer evidence of the context within which this text was written and its research conducted, a context of rapidly changing political-economic geographies and new modalities of race, class and sex conflict. Within this context, the Aspen Movie Map must be understood as both a technology and an imaginary to answer to American race riots and to decolonization, of which the Entebbe incident was part. The movie map was an individualized but networked way to negotiate space, a new form of habitation and perhaps even life that might respond to what seemed to be the ruins of modern urbanity, colonialism and nation.

Demo or Die: Race in the Machine

Even before 1970, AMG had been involved in efforts to demonstrate the application of computing to urban redevelopment and racial struggles. AMG's initial efforts in the late 1960s to integrate machines into the urban design process conceived of human–machine interaction in terms of symbolic logic and language, perhaps representation, and inductive reasoning influenced by the work of computer scientists such as Marvin Minsky, Simon Papert and Terry Winograd.[18] These initiatives to integrate machines into the design process began with a series of programs emerging from urban design studios that were

8 Nicholas Negroponte. The URBAN 5 system, a more advanced version of URBAN 2 meant to create a unique dialogue between the user and the computer. In *The Architecture Machine: Toward a More Human Environment* (Cambridge, MA: MIT Press, 1970), p. 80–81. CCA. 0005334; ID:87-B19491

In this photograph the shutter of the camera was left open during the complete operation of "questioning" an element. The user detects the QUESTION light button, the verb, and then points to the cube, the noun. The list that appears at the top of the screen is a partial inventory of qualities ascribed to the form by the machine.

Handling Qualities
URBAN5 handles qualities either explicitly or implicitly.

Beyond the traits of solid and void, each ten-foot cube (whether solid or void) has pre-allocated receptacles for ten characteristics that refer to aspects of sunlight, outdoor access, visual privacy, acoustical privacy, usability, direct access, climate control, natural light, flexibility, structural feasibility. All these qualities are implicitly ascribed to elements. In other words, without the user's permission, intervention, or even awareness, URBAN5 automatically assigns the absence or presence of these features using a predefined geometry for each quality. (This geometry can be changed by the user at a later date when he is more familiar with the workings of the system.) This means that when a ten-foot cube is added (making a solid) or removed (making a void), URBAN5 tacitly rearranges the local and, if necessary, global characteristics. For example, the addition of an element not only casts shadows on other solids and voids but might obstruct another element's natural light or visual privacy.

Implicit qualities are occasionally reported to the designer (depending on their importance), but in most cases the designer must explicitly interrogate the cube to find its qualitative status. URBAN5 is more prone to divulge implicitly ascribed qualities when the neighboring influences are significant. Certain characteristics are strongly communicative, and their presence is directly transposable to neighboring elements or members of the same space (natural light, acoustical privacy). Other qualifications are less communicative (visual privacy,

81

Orit Halpern

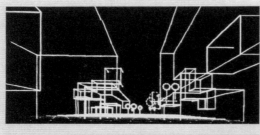
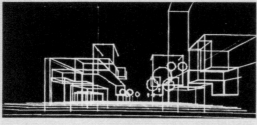
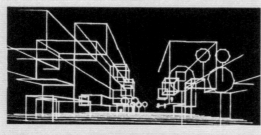

The adjacent illustrations, as well as many on the following pages, are prints taken from the 16mm movie, URBAN5. They are a sequence of frames that depict travel through an environment constructed jointly by the architect (Ted Turano) and the machine. You will note that the illustrations are quite crude, hidden lines are evident, circles are polygons, and straight lines are usually short segments butted together. In no way do these crudities represent the state of the art in computer-generated perspective drawing, not even for the time in which they were done. However, since computer graphics is not computer-aided design, this roughness is not important. What is important is that it took only a few days to implement this mode of viewing.

9   Nicholas Negroponte. Images from the URBAN 5 system, in *The Architecture Machine: Toward a More Human Environment* (Cambridge, MA: MIT Press, 1970), p. 76–77. CCA. 0005334; ID:87-B19491

45

text of ELEMents for the path of the sun and for growth patterns.

The next row of buttons, the therapeutic ones, are instructional modes that are "intended to make the designer-machine interface as conversational and personal as possible, permitting the user to articulate himself in the privacy of himself" (Negroponte and Groisser, 1967a). The PANIC button, for example, summons instructions on the usage of other modes, directions on how to proceed, and an accounting mechanism that can be interrogated for computer time spent in dollars (often affording cause for greater panic). The therapeutic modes were often inconsistently designed. In truth, PANIC should never be depressed for reasons of total distress. In a true dialogue the machine should sense the designer panicking long before the button is pushed. PANIC, in fact, was erroneously designed as an alarm monologue rather than a teaching dialogue.

The remaining modes are primarily procedural ones that act in a janitorial fashion. STORE mode, as an example, permits design studies to reside in either short-term or long-term storage devices, to be given arbitrary names, and to be recalled in a few hundredths of a second (recalled by either name or time of creation).

Within these modes there is no predetermined sequence of usage; there is no presupposed chain of events. URBAN5 has one central "attention" mechanism that either listens to or hears from the designer, always giving him the opportunity to change his mind or restate a situation at any time. However, the reader

should notice that the context, which is so important to intelligent behavior, is explicitly stated by the human designer and not, in URBAN5, implicitly discerned by the machine.

9

demoed under the labels URBAN 2 and URBAN 5 (figs. 6–9). The programs were micro-worlds, simplified abstract models of the real world that were made of blocks that designers could move around using commands in English. The computer was supposed to "learn" about the design process by studying the relationship between the English command and the action, and then be able to replicate or anticipate future design decisions. It didn't work. In Negroponte's words, the system was not very full of "play."[19] Given the inability to make machines learn from language, AMG turned away from creating discrete intelligence in the machine to figuring out how to make computing and life more seamlessly compatible. In doing so, the place of computing in architecture began to shift away from emulating human behaviour and thought and toward forming a non-linear conversation between humans and machines. This was not a conversation framed in terms of language or translation, however. Machine intelligence was redefined outside of human intelligence; Negroponte writes that "we are talking about a symbiosis that is a cohabitation of two intelligent species."[20]

In creating this "symbiotic" relationship, race played an important role as a site to justify computer-aided urban planning. Among the first public demonstrations of computer-aided design run by AMG in the interest of urban planning was a series of Turing-style tests carried out with tenants in Boston's under-privileged South End neighbourhood, where battles over eminent domain and the clearance and resettlement of residents for commercial development and transport infrastructure were pervasive.[21] These political battles were happening within a context of rapid transformations of the urban economy and geography, related to the rise of the finance, insurance, real estate and high-technology industries.[22]

In the interest of addressing the apparent decay of Boston's urban core and rising racial tension, AMG ran a study known as the Hessdorfer Experiment. Three African American men were recruited from the city's public housing projects and were asked what their main concerns were regarding urban planning and neighbourhood improvement, specifically what they wished urban planners and designers would take into account (fig. 10). Interestingly, this demo involved no actual computers. At the time, computers could not handle such sophisticated questions. The test was run by a human being. The participants, however, were kept ignorant of this fact, believing that they were speaking to a machine. One can read, therefore, the whole test as an interface and a demo of what a computationally aided interaction in service of a responsive government might be.

The implication of this demo was that if social structures of race could not be changed, then hyper-individuated, technologically managed responsive environments might be necessary interventions. In the work of AMG, race conflict in the United States was transformed into an evidentiary example for the necessity of computing through the strategy of the demo. This is a future contingent on excavating the disjuncture between the desire for how a technology should work and the physical realities of system performance. Despite the lack of "real" infrastructure or machine intelligence, the demo convinced many designers of the necessity of integrating computation into human decision making at the scale of the city.

Cybernetic Cognition

Responding to structural transformations in the urban fabric through immersion in interactive environments was neither

Orit Halpern

10 Nicholas Negroponte. The Hessdorfer Experiment, in *The Architecture Machine: Toward a More Human Envrionment* (Cambridge, MA: MIT Press, 1970), p. 56–57. CCA. 0005334; ID:87-B19491

The three protagonists of e Hessdorfer experiment, aurice Jones (top right), rry Adams (top left), and bert Quarles (bottom). It is interesting to note e button Robert Quarles ppened to be wearing at day: "Tenant Power."

Picturephone. Copyright 69 Bell Telephone, Inc., rray Hill, New Jersey. Reinted by permission of the itor, Bell Laboratory RECRD.

mediately entered a discourse about slum landlords, highways, schools, and the like. Second, the three user-inhabitants said things to this machine they would probably not have said to another human, particularly a white planner or politician: to them the machine was not black, was not white, and surely had no prejudices. (The reader should know, as the three users did not, that this experiment was conducted over telephone lines with teletypes, with a human at the other end, not a machine. The same experiment will be rerun shortly, this time with a machine at the other end of the telephone line.)

With these domestic (domesticated) machines, the design task becomes one of blending the preferences of the individual with those of the group. Machines would monitor the propensity for change of the body politic. Large central processors, parent machines of some sort, could interpolate and extrapolate the local commonalities by overviewing a large population of "consumer machines."

What will remove these machines from a "Brave New World" is that they will be able to (and must) search for the exception (in desire or need), the one in a million. In other words, when the generalization matches the local desire, our omnipresent machines will not be excited. It is when the particular varies from the group preferences that our machine will react, not to thwart it but to service it.

obvious nor predetermined. It is therefore worth examining the genealogy of logic and computation that underpinned AMG's attitudes to temporality, demoing and intelligence. Cybernetics and machine learning, not urbanism and sociology, were central to AMG's imaginaries of responsive environments and conceptions of computer-aided design.

In his introduction to *The Architecture Machine*, Negroponte opens with a statement to the effect that computer-aided design demands a new form of intelligence, one that is no longer beholden to the human. He writes that "computer-aided design cannot occur without machine intelligence, in fact it would be dangerous without it…[and that intelligence] must have a sophisticated set of sensors, effectors, and processors to view the real world directly and indirectly. Intelligence is a behavior."[23] This form of intelligence is behavioural, sensory and decentralized; it is a smartness that is out in the world. In his definition of architecture machines, Negroponte draws explicitly from cybernetician Warren McCulloch's concept of "ethical robots." Ethics here is not about morality. Rather, it is about the ability to anticipate the future and learn from the past, to evolve and adapt to changing conditions. Ethics is machine learning. Cybernetics has long had a complicated relationship to temporality, storage and performativity that speaks to the demo as an experimental practice and as an epistemology. I call attention to this genealogy because the reformulation of "intelligence" and experiment is central to the epistemology of the demo. Negroponte's invocation of cybernetic forms of networked machine learning and intelligence signals a discursive shift from practices grounded in deduction to those anchored in induction and performance. There is also a temporal aspect to these nervous networks. In computer-aided design, the necessity of predicting or representing future states was replaced by an incremental demand to version. Rather than designating a clear final form or attempting to predict the outcome of a project, AMG made constant and regular adjustments to suggested designs. For AMG, as for contemporary designers working with parametric algorithms and techniques, any design or plan could always be further optimized, enhanced and modulated without end. Time itself, within the structure of cybernetic ideas of mind, is neither historical nor predictive.[24]

Finally, in changing the constitution of both evidence and temporality, AMG refracted a broader transformation occurring at the time in the human, social and computer sciences in redefining human agency and consciousness in terms amenable to machine modelling and learning. Focusing on practices and actions—behaviours—rather than on memories, desires, motivations or intentions, the social and human sciences created a new idea of the agent that is always pre-emptive but never psychological, and that could be assessed by the same criterion as machine systems, as an agent that could be a seamless part of networks. These points may seem insignificant in isolation, but when reattached to the historical context within which AMG operated, they become essential in understanding the group's interest in transforming both design and politics in urban spaces.

As is now well documented, the sciences of communication and control first emerged within the context of anti-aircraft defence and radar research in the Second World War.[25] The MIT mathematician Norbert Wiener, working with neurophysiologists and doctors and influenced by Vannevar Bush's work on early computational machines such as the differential analyzer (fig. 11), argued that human behaviour could be mathematically modelled and predicted, particularly under stress,

Orit Halpern

11 Vannevar Bush examining the interconnection gearing of a differential analyzer at the Aberdeen Proving Ground in Maryland, c. 1930. The differential analyzer features integrating mechanisms (*left*) and input/output tables (*right*). MIT Museum

thereby articulating a new belief that machines and humans could speak the same language of mathematics.[26]

In 1943, inspired by a pre-cybernetic paper by Wiener and his colleagues, and influenced by the idea that machines and minds might be considered together through the language of logic and mathematics, McCulloch and the logician Walter Pitts, working at the University of Illinois at Urbana-Champaign, decided to take the conception of the machine-like nature of human beings quite literally.[27] Their article "A Logical Calculus of Ideas Immanent in Nervous Activity," published in the *Bulletin of Mathematical Biophysics*, has become one of the most commonly referenced pieces in cognitive science, philosophy and computer science.[28] The model of the neural net put forth by McCulloch and Pitts has two characteristics that are fundamental to our contemporary idea of smartness. The first claim is that every neuron has a "semiotic character"; it may be mathematically rendered as a proposition. To support this claim, McCulloch and Pitts imagined each neuron operating on an "all or nothing" principle when firing electrical impulses over synaptic separations. The pair interpreted the fact that neurons possess action potentials and delays as equivalent to the ability to make a discrete decision. This effect affirms or denies a fact or an activation. Neurons can be thought of as signs (true/false), and nets as semiotic situations, or communication structures (fig. 12). This discrete decision (true or false, activate or do not activate) made neurons equivalent to logical propositions (yes/no or true/false decisions) and Turing machines.[29]

The second element of the neural-net model that is relevant is the adoption of a strictly probabilistic and predictive temporality. Neural nets are determinate in terms of the future (they are predictive), but indeterminate in terms of the past. In the model, given a net in a particular time state (T), one can

Orit Halpern

12 Warren McCulloch and Walter Pitts. Diagram of nervous nets, in "A Logical Calculus of Ideas Immanent in Nervous Activity," reprinted in *Embodiments of Mind*, ed. Warren McCulloch (Cambridge, MA: MIT Press, 1965), 19–39

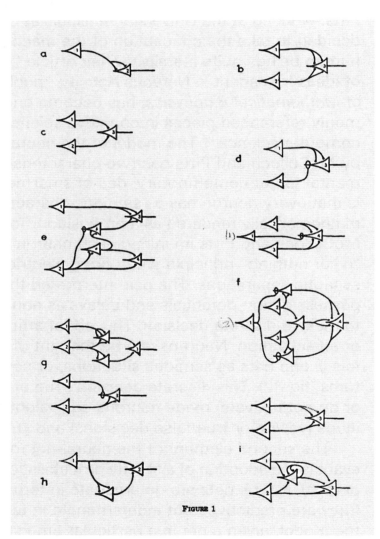

Figure 1

13 Frank Rosenblatt. Perceptron diagram. Originally published in "The Perceptron: A Probabilistic Model for Information Storage and Organization in the Brain," *Psychological Review* 65 (November 1958): 386–408

14 Oliver Selfridge. Pandemonium diagram. Originally published in "Pandemonium: A Paradigm for Learning," in *Mechanisation of Thought Processes; Proceedings of a Symposium Held at the National Physical Laboratory on the 24th, 25th, 26th and 27th November 1958* (London: Her Majesty's Stationery Office, 1959), 513–531

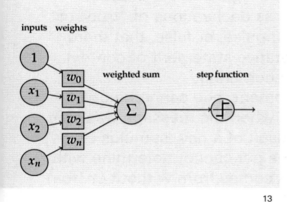

13

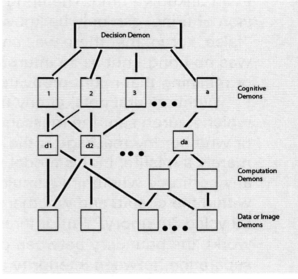

14

predict the future action of the net (T+1), but not the past action. McCulloch offered as an example the model of a circular-memory neuron activating itself with its own electrical impulses. At every moment, what results as a conscious experience of memory is not the recollection of the activation of the neuron, but merely an awareness that it was activated, at an unknown time. The firing of a signal, or the suppression of firing, can only be known as declarations of "true" or "false"—true, that there was an impulse, or false, that there was no firing—not as an interpretative statement of context or meaning that might motivate such firing.

Within neural nets, at any moment, one cannot know which neuron sent the message, when the message was sent or whether the message is the result of a new stimulus or merely a misfire. In this model the net cannot determine with any certitude whether a stimulus comes from without or from within the circuit, and whether it is a fresh input or simply a recycled "memory." Put differently, from within a net (or network), the boundary between perception and cognition, the separation between interiority and exteriority and the organization of causal time cannot be differentiated. But McCulloch and Pitts saw this as an advantage. These cybernetic notions of "processing" and amnesic yet pre-emptive "thought" found fruition in the context of machine learning, character recognition and research on computer vision.

In 1958, the psychologist and artificial intelligence pioneer Frank Rosenblatt, working at the Cornell Aeronautical Laboratory, published the article "The Perceptron: A Probabilistic Model for Information Storage and Organization in the Brain." Grounded in the McCulloch-Pitts theory of the neural net, the paper argues that information processing does not take place exclusively in a centralized location like a brain (fig. 13). Citing

British empiricism as a model, Rosenblatt hypothesized that "the images of stimuli may never really be recorded at all, and the central nervous system simply acts as an intricate switching network, where retention takes the form of new connections, or pathways."[30] In fact, it is possible that there is no way to know if an input is new or simply recycled, no way to separate the "interior" from the "exterior" of the organism. Rosenblatt argues that rather than being concerned with the "truth" of interpreting stimuli, or with older ideas of consciousness and representation in the sensory-perception-cognition system, computer scientists should focus on the route that the signal takes to arrive. It is the structure of the communication channel or the electrical or nervous circuit that creates particular responses and actions.

Assuming a non-deterministic temporality and a data-rich environment, storage in this model is not indexical, and not every stimulus is stored. What is stored are "connections or associations" and a "preference of a particular response."[31] The perceptron operates, in Rosenblatt's formulation, much like the mathematical theory of communication, as a "probability theory rather than a symbolic logic."[32] The theory does not lay out a linear and Boolean representation of the process with singular and well-defined outcomes, but rather sets up a network with certain potentials for future behaviour of the machine. This model was intended to be a way to ask how intelligent computer systems might store sensory information, and then how that information might impact future behaviour, to develop systems that could learn and respond to their environments without having implanted images of those worlds already within memory.

The perceptron model was not the only effort to produce a machine learning that did not rely on symbolic representation or past knowledge of a situation. In 1958, the MIT engineer Oliver Selfridge, in communication with McCulloch and Rosenblatt, presented the pandemonium model (fig. 14), an architecture for pattern recognition at a conference on the mechanization of thought processes held at the National Physical Laboratory in London that included many of the top figures in the nascent fields of neuroscience, computer science and cognitive science.[33] The pandemonium model of decentralized intelligence without symbolic processing would come to influence AMG's conception of interactivity. Negroponte admits that much of AMG's work was indebted to Selfridge, who later went on to consult for the National Security Administration on pattern-recognition softwares and methods.[34]

Pandemonium was—and still is—the bedrock of many machine-vision and pattern-recognition programs. It is based on the principle that instead of describing the "gestalt" or "essence" of a form, and giving the system an explicit definition of an object to be identified ahead of time, the system could, through smaller incremental decisions, eventually find a pattern match. It is, to use a colloquial framing, a bottom-up instead of top-down approach to software architecture. The system is comprised of "demons," programs that run quasi-autonomously in a decentralized manner as background processes, rather than falling under the direct control of the user. Each demon, comprised of a neural-net cluster, or a series of logic gates, has a tightly constrained task, and there are parallel demons at different layers of the operation. For example, the first task is to recognize an input—a line, for the sake of argument. Demons go out into the environment to find this input. They shriek when they find lines of particular shapes. The demon's shriek is equivalent to a neural fire/do not fire response to a yes/no or true/false statement. For instance, one demon deals with horizontal strokes and emits a shriek whose intensity is proportionate to how closely the data fits its search and decision-making criteria: louder for the letters A or T, which contain straight lines, and quieter for O or S. At the next level up, a cognitive demon listens to the shrieks of the demon population below it and assigns a value based on the relative intensities of the shrieks—in other words, based on how many nets were fired. Other demons simultaneously perform different tasks at this level, subjecting the letter to grids of various kinds, and the data they gather is continuously funnelled up the demon hierarchy until, finally, a judgment is made by the decision-making demon in response to the part of the network that shrieked loudest. For example, if the part of the network seeking out curves sends out the most signals, and another part seeking straight lines shrieks less, then the next level of decision-making demons weights the signal sent toward an O or an S rather than an A or a Z. Cumulatively, more signals coming from a certain region of the network linked to particular shapes indicate closer similarity to the letter in question. Within such an architecture, reading can occur without centralized thinking, and intuitive actions arise as computers make decisions in a way that appears human.

  The pandemonium model for character recognition marks a historical shift in both the forms of reason and logic being applied to, and enacted by, computational and engineering problems. As Selfridge argues, "*Pandemonium* is a model which we hope can learn to recognize patterns which have not been specified." He goes on to say that "the basic motif behind our model is the notion of parallel processing," which he asserts is both seemingly "natural" and "easier to modify" than other linear or representation-grounded pattern-matching approaches. What is critical in these statements, made at the start of the era of machine learning, is a move toward inductive reasoning, what McCulloch would label "epistemological experiment," rather than defining or representing problems beforehand. The principle is to allow machines to learn without having to stipulate an end point, or to fully represent a problem—to allow machines to deal with what today we might label "fuzzy" or "wicked" problems. This is both a pragmatic engineering approach and a new epistemology for defining intelligence and learning in machines and perhaps other organisms as well. This somewhat jarring use of the term *organism* to refer to machines is a deliberate strategy on Selfridge's part. He insists that "we are not going to apologize for a frequent use of anthropomorphic or biomorphic terminology. They seem to be useful words to describe our notions."[35] Smoothing away the question of machine or human or animal intelligence, in a double displacement of both nature and ontology, Selfridge implies that working inductively without a predefined pattern will also be closer to the natural processes of cognition that occur in living beings. Computers and animals are both rendered into information-processing machines. The pandemonium model is, as media theorist and architect Branden Hookway argues, "predatory," colonizing any object and rendering it into a networked process.[36]

Both the neural net and pandemonium models of sense perception and character recognition suggest a new cognitive-sensory paradigm grounded in making process a thing in the world, a material and technical entity amenable to algorithmic manipulation and production. Sense perception and cognition are compressed into a single channel and envisioned as both material and scalable; what applies to individual organisms can also scale to environments. These models posit a decentralized and networked understanding of mind and analytics.

Scalability is grounded in the fundamental confusion between boundaries and the pre-emptive logic that is literally wired into nervous networks.

In Negroponte's epistemology, the observer is reconfigured as an agent and the environment is rendered computationally active through an idea of intelligence as agent based, amnesic, pre-emptive and environmental, lacking clear distinctions between interior and exterior. Negroponte argues that the goal of computing is "making the built environment responsive to me and to you, individually, a right I consider as important as the right to a good education."[37] Equating the mandate for public education, long a staple of democracy, with individualized and "meaningful" environmental responsiveness, AMG embraced both a new idea of a networked observer and the self-organizing, responsive territory as the central concern of design. Cyberneticians and architects thus imagined a world of neural processing, what we might label now a "smart" or "cognating" planet where our very nerves could be directly linked to networks.

Demo or Die: In the Museum

According to Negroponte, "Computing isn't about computing anymore. It's about living." This life world, he argued, was to be a "machine… [conceived as both] a 'cybernetic world model' and a 'behaviorist laboratory for observation and experimentation.'"[38] Now defined as "omnipresent," "behaviorist" and "cybernetic," the place of computing in design was envisioned as consuming life itself. Increasingly, the "life" would occur in a new architecture that would be full of sensors and would include the extension of computerized intelligence into the

Orit Halpern

162

15 SEEK installed at the Jewish Museum, 1970

environment. Soon after attempting to demonstrate the need for computing in urban policy decision making, AMG turned to an effort to build a computerized city.

In an installation done for the important—and infamous—*Software* exhibition at the Jewish Museum in 1970, the group demoed another micro-world, titled SEEK (figs. 1, 15). This demo, however, no longer had screens or linguistic commands; it was a world within which inhabitants (albeit non-human) were entirely surrounded by an environment managed by machines. SEEK consisted of a small group of Mongolian gerbils, chosen according to Negroponte for their curiosity and inquisitive nature, placed in an environment of Plexiglas-mirrored blocks that was constantly rearranged by a robotic arm. The basic concept was that the mechanism would observe the interaction of the gerbils with their habitat—the blocks—and would gradually "learn" their "living preferences" by observing their behaviour and how they moved the blocks. The gerbils were meant to introduce chance and unpredictable, non-mechanical behaviour into the environment. The machine was originally set up as a city, a state it would try to homeostatically maintain. The gerbils would start to undo this model and the machine would have to learn about how they changed the environment, and attempt to return the system to equilibrium.

This experiment in rethinking the conventional definition of intelligence, or even of life, went awry, though perhaps productively. The machine ceased working because of problems with both the software and the hardware, and the museum almost went bankrupt. In what might be seen as an omen, the gerbils, in their computer-managed environment, confused the computer, wrought havoc on the blocks and became sick and aggressive, often attacking each other. The art critic Thomas

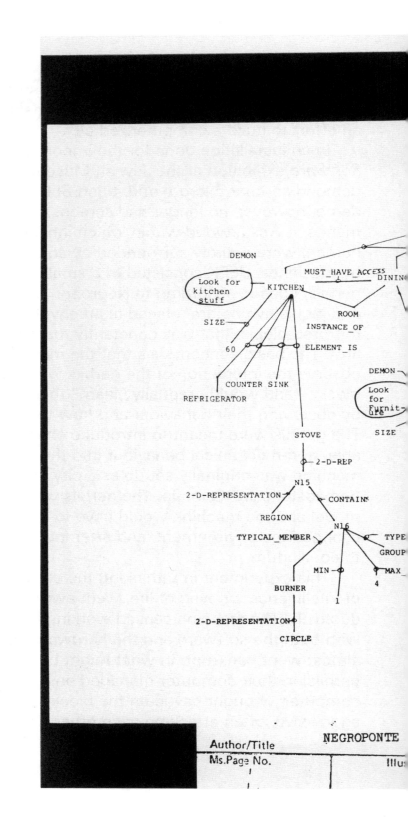

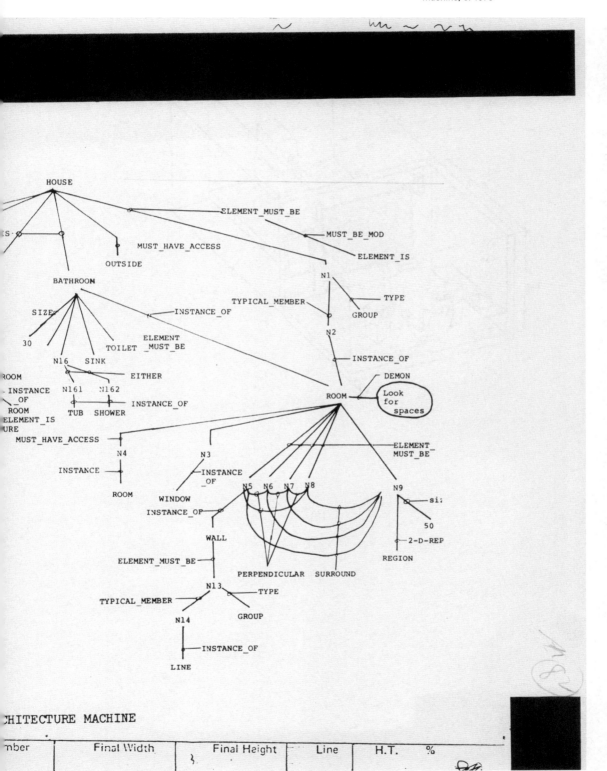

16 Nicholas Negroponte. Diagram outlining the soft architecture machine, c. 1975

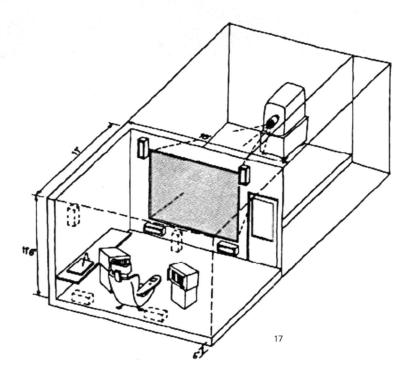

17 William Donelson. Media room, axonometric, c. 1977

Hess wryly responded to this in an *Art News* editorial. He described the gerbils as covered in excrement and shadowed by the broken arms of the robot and concluded, "Artists who become seriously engaged in technological processes might remember what happened to four charming gerbils."[39] No one thought to ask, or could ask, whether gerbils wish to live in a micro-world built with blocks.[40] No one could ask, because conversations in this case were interactions and behaviours, without translation. This demo, now a world, was subtly mutating from a conversation between machines and animals to a network between agents. Architecture as a machine was about design as a process to network humans (and animals) and machines into new assemblages, to assimilate differences through this a-temporality and homeostasis of the demo that is always "new" and yet methodologically consistent. This is a world rendered as a demonstration or a prototype, one where death is not a failure but the very rationale for increasing the penetration of computing into life.

Demo or Die: Immersion

In 1975, Negroponte published the book *Soft Architecture Machines*. In this new "soft" world, the computer disappears from sight and the user is immersed in the environment. Negroponte speaks of "omnipresent machines" that will make environments full of "responsiveness" (fig. 16).[41] Computing, which began as a conversation and then became an experiment, had now become environment, while the question of intelligence was now measured through the metrics of usability and engagement.

This new approach was centred on a structure completed in 1977: the media room. This room had quadrophonic sound, seamless floor-to-ceiling displays and probably several million dollars worth of hardware (fig. 17).[42] It was an immersive environment, fully networking human sense and computation, suggesting an end to architecture and its absorption into media. The name of the Architecture Machine Group was changed to the Media Lab in 1985, with the explicitly articulated goal of integrating the industries of broadcasting, motion pictures and publishing through computing. The new lab was meant to be a machine for assimilating differences—between people, media and economies.

One of the media room's first projects, and one of the first three-dimensional digitally mediated responsive environments ever built, was the Aspen Movie Map. In this project, there are no computers to be seen; it was not envisioned as a model. It is *Aspen*. According to Michael Naimark, an artist who worked on the project, "Aspen [is a] *verb*…. Aspen is known for two processes, or 'verbs' relating to heritage and virtuality. One is to 'moviemap'…the other is to 'Aspenize,' the process by which a fragile cultural system is disrupted by tourism and growth."[43] Naimark's point implies that the movie map is not a representation; it is an operation, a way to live, a way to be in the world. It is also a self-directed, trauma-inducing event; it "Aspenizes" or disrupts ecologies. Whether disruptive or emergent, the project was imagined by its architects, designers and engineers not as a room, or simply an interface, but as a cultural system and an ecology.

As we watch the film of the original demo, the questions of race, urbanization, war and society fade into the calm embrace of interaction. What had started therefore as game theories around military concerns, and then the simulations of artificial

18 Cameras being attached to the roof of a truck for filming in Aspen, c. 1978

intelligence, becomes about total life. Today it is about ubiquitous computing, or smartness. The video that the MIT team produced to record the project shows an individual slowly navigating the space of Aspen. Surveying the tranquil, affluent neighbourhoods, the interface bears no resemblance to the military purpose for which it had been built. The developers took care to ensure that footage of Aspen would be recorded at the same times each day in order to maintain a kind of timeless sunny consistency in the environment (figs. 18–19).[44] The film was shot both forward and backward so the user could navigate in reverse, place new objects into the space and move them and stop at sites to learn about their histories. The intent according to Negroponte was to have so much recorded that the experience was "seamless."[45]

The design of the movie map's interface implicitly uses a double strategy of deferral and *méconnaisance* to prompt the user to interact with the system. The interface resembles the familiar world, using conventions of documentary cinema and first-person perspective, while the mapping system at the top of the screen recalls the usual abstract maps for navigation. As architectural historian Felicity Scott notes, the system was built to include animations and additional data in order to obscure any cuts or lags in the flow of images, and to produce experiences that repressed and rendered invisible any editorial or cinematic cuts into the space, thus inducing a standardized temporal movement.[46] But while history, as a form of homogeneous time in the way Walter Benjamin describes the "shocks" of modernity, is available by clicking on objects and extracting data, historicity as a discontinuous or heterogeneous flow of time and data is banished as an experience in the interest of producing an ideal of movement without interruption through the environment. (This is not to say that the actual

19 Cameras mounted on the truck, c. 1978

19

20 Still from the Aspen Movie Map

system did not suffer lags and stoppages as a result of limitations in memory and communication between devices.) This is a temporality emanating only as a matter of user choice and self-reference, not as a feature of engaging with the environment or with others—whether human, machine or animal (fig. 20).

What makes this interface seductive is that the coordinates of "real" and "virtual" cease to exist and that this floating "map" is not stable in time and space, but is rather generated from within the system. Users are prompted to engage with seemingly familiar things—such as houses, cars and streets—that represent urban and suburban spaces, while their visual plane is deflected from observing a space that represents a specific locale. They interact with the interface, modulating their body and their responses to the timings and sounds of the networked space. One is at once in the local and in the global; the user is in a particular place experientially while being able to see on an abstract map the relationship of that space to a broader territory. As the map slowly unfolds and the video immerses the user in media with historical distance, the self-organizing system is networked into an attentive system. The individual here is given a sense of control over the space while simultaneously being subsumed within the network. The structural politics of militarism, race, war and security are rechannelled into interactivity in a logic that integrates users as part of a circuit, in keeping with cybernetic ideals of agent-based machine learning and sensing.

The Aspen Movie Map's particular relationship to both temporality and territory recalls the "demo or die" adage. Negroponte clearly distinguished between the idea and practices of simulation and these new "responsive" architectures by designating the demo as distinct from a simulation.[47] The demo is not a simulation, since it has no reality, not even a fictionalized reality or a future to which it corresponds. Rather, the demo is a technical practice analogous to a test bed in engineering, or to a prototype. It is neither a representation of the real world nor a finalized reality in itself. The demonstration of the technology hangs in anticipation for the next technical development. The demo is a particular technology for negotiating uncertain futures and for producing realities and potentials for action; it emerges from a history of machine learning and neural nets that are always in a pre-emptive but amnesic state. The construction of demonstrations was part of a process whereby the environment and the user would be adjusted to one another, and eventually the demo itself would be dispensed with. The culminating success of this approach was the movie map: a system that could integrate hearing, sight and touch to create an immersive environment that is also a place and that could train users to live in this new technically generated world.

Today this model of constant repetitive futurity, technical failure and demoing has enormous implications for how we design buildings, cities and technology. It dominates our imaginaries and affects our responses to everything from global warming to terrorism. We live life in demonstration; media is not simulating or separating us from a "real" world, but is rather creating worlds and futures.

This form of time, and its attendant form of violence, recalls the sad gerbils in their excessively responsive environment. In this case the logistics of computation had folded in upon itself to produce something other than what was intended—a result that was also radically nihilistic. The essential question is how to encounter this demo, or test bed, that has now become our world. While this essay hardly offers a solution,

75 it suggests the importance of thinking about a history of our responsive environments in terms of difference rather than homogeneity, and of recognizing that there is still critical work to do—in architecture and in scholarship—to envision alternative images of the future and different forms of time and experience that do not operate at the scale and tempo of our eternally pre-emptive, affective, nervous networks; to demo without death.

Mark Wigley

<u>In 1963</u>, the Sketchpad program was invented, allowing designers to draw directly on the computer screen. The black screen replaced the white page as the blank surface, a move that had an effect even on architects like Cedric Price and David Greene, who did not use computers.

This text is the transcription of a presentation that was given at the CCA in 2004.

MARK WIGLEY

1 David Greene. CSB 63.4, A
   Mechanised Pod House, 1964.
   Archigram Archives.
   057-003-NM01

BLACK SCREENS: THE ARCHITECT'S VISION IN A DIGITAL AGE

1

Drawing, of course, happens classically on paper, and the classical understanding is that the drawing is the shadow of a shadow. It's not even the shadow of something clear, like the ideas in the mind of an artist. The artist is from the beginning a mind, a thinker. But this is a special kind of thinking, usually with the artist sitting in the light beside the window, receiving the glories of the cosmos from over their shoulder. And these leave their shadow on the page: a dark shadow on a light surface. In fact, shadows can only be seen against a light surface. The shadow is then treated as a residue, a delicate trace, a ghost of a ghost.

It's as if the white paper is a screen for catching the trace of an immaterial thought, the surface that allows us to think the relationship between the two. So the whole point of the paper is to be

Mark Wigley

there, but also to be absent—to be there as the support, but invisible and unseen, so that the marks upon it can be seen. We have been trained over the last five hundred years to act as if the paper is not there, in the same way that when we read a book we tend not to reflect upon the nature of the white surface on which the words appear. We have been trained to see through paper, noticing only the dark marks made upon it.

This invisible white paper explicitly institutionalized by figures like Vasari is tied to the definition of art—Vasari being, of course, a privileged figure in the innovation of the concept of the education of the artist, of the criticism of art, of the collection of drawings and of history itself. This very long history has left us with an understanding of drawing, to quote the definition of the Museum of Modern Art, as "an original work on paper." That is how they decide what should be collected, and most institutions that collect drawings use some variation of the Museum of Modern Art definition.

This is a bit of a problem for us today because drawings in the hands of architects—and I don't know if we can say in the "hands" of architects, but let's say what used to be the hands of architects—are obviously not original works on paper. They are not originals, for a start. They are mainly prints, or even *printouts*. So then the question is, printouts of what? What is the interior out of which a print appears? Famously, they are paperless, but this doesn't mean that there is no paper; it just means that paper is no longer the surface on which the original mark by an artist is traced. In fact, there are mountains of paper being used precisely because we are in a paperless mode; paperless studios print everything out endlessly. The paper, though, is understood to be just a provisional printout, and in that sense, I suppose, we have a kind of unexamined theory that the drawing is in the machine. The interior from which the printout comes out is a machine, and even there in the machine it's not an original, a stable figure, but rather some kind of fluid organization of information. So we are describing the interior of the computer in a similar way to the interior of the mind of the artist. But from a technical point of view, the state of architectural drawing today is that it cannot be exhibited as drawing. From an institutional point of view, the Museum of Modern Art actually cannot exhibit architectural drawings as drawings according to its own definition.

In digital drawings, white paper with black marks on it has given way to white lines on a black field. Architectural presentations, lectures and publications are now entirely filled with glowing forms suspended in black space. People are now drawing with light rather than with shadow, and black has become the default setting. Black is, of course, the actual default setting of the software. If you want to define black in the hexadecimal system, it's zero, zero, zero, zero, zero, zero. If you're in the RGB system, it's zero, zero, zero. The logic in the world of digital drawing is that you start

2   Ivan Sutherland using Sketchpad, 1963

3   DAC-1, developed by General Motors and IBM, 1968. General Motors Media Archive

2

3

with black. Black is also the colour of your monitor when the monitor is off. The entire world around you is bristling with electronics and when they are not doing anything, they are black.

How does this shift occur? Computer graphics, of course, began as a military research program at a laboratory at the Massachusetts Institute of Technology (MIT) set up by the United States Air Force in the mid-1950s. For the first time, information could be entered into the computer with a light pen, an electronic pencil with light rather than graphite at its tip. Ivan Sutherland, who was a young graduate student working at the MIT laboratories, was very low ranking and therefore only allowed to use the machine in the middle of the night. During that time, he developed Sketchpad (fig. 2), which is the first program that allowed drawing directly upon the screen. The architectural ambition of the project was revealed for the first time to engineers in 1963, and later that same year, the first commercial systems evolved. Among these was the DAC (design aided by computer) system (fig. 3). At the time, DAC was a rival label to CAD. Sketchpad allowed for very sophisticated modelling of objects in perspective, but the big challenge at that time was how to hide the lines that you would not see—in other words, how to make a non-solid look like a solid.

Numerous conferences, school courses, organizations, essays, special issues of magazines and books promoted "computer graphics," as it was then defined by one of the people working for the IBM General Motors team. And along with this came an entirely new iconography of the architect, no longer leaning over a horizontal table, not looking down at the drawing and letting the shadow fall on the paper, but lined up with the screen. The drawing is being constructed in front of the person rather than behind the person. And there is no longer a window for the light to pass from behind, because any kind of light that's not coming from the screen is an interruption.

It's important to remember that initially the computer was not in the hands of architects. It was in the hands of the military, then of the aerospace industry, then of the automation industry, then of city infrastructure administrators, then of large engineering firms, then of corporate architectural firms of global scale and then slowly it moved to wider society. Not by chance, this dissemination coincided with machines getting smaller. In 1982 the first official minicomputers were released, and medium-size architecture offices could afford them. That's also the year in which AutoCAD was released—what would become the generic software package for design. And importantly, of course, AutoCAD starts with a default black background.

What I deeply admire about the work of the so-called digital architects is that they're carrying out an essentially intellectual labour on the history of certain technologies in relation to thinking about space. It's subversive not because it's breaking new ground, but because it's

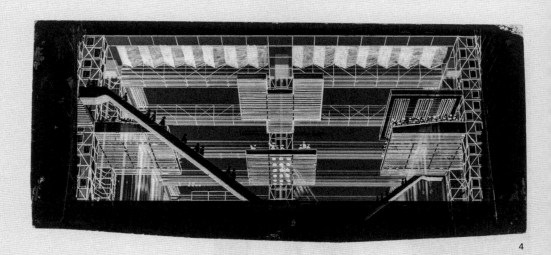

4　Cedric Price. Fun Palace, worm's-eye interior perspective, c. 1964. Black and white ink over photostat, 19.1 x 8.7 cm. Cedric Price fonds (AP144), CCA. DR1995:0188:519

reassessing, reimagining and reconsidering an entire generation of research. This has always been the role of the architect: to provide some kind of coherent way of thinking about heterogeneous forces. As early as the 1960s, the visionary architects—and this is the title of a number of exhibitions from back then—challenged the Museum of Modern Art about how to handle this kind of drawing, even if architects were the last to use the computer. Exactly in the year 1964, architectural discourse was awash with these new dark images—architects started drawing white on black. Architects who didn't have computers, like David Greene (fig. 1) and Cedric Price (fig. 4), immediately started drawing this kind of image. They were all thinking about what the computer means for architecture and all starting to simulate the drawing style that became possible as a result of the computer. But in fact, there had been a genre of white-on-black drawings that had already emerged in the 1950s and early 1960s done by architects who had no interest in computers, and even by architects whose work was entirely opposed to them.

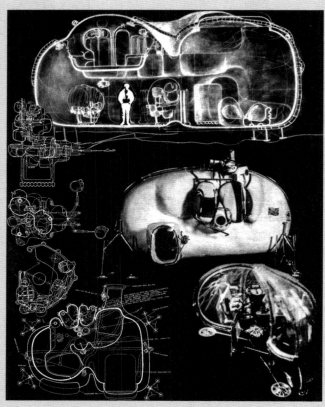

5 David Greene. Living Pod, collage including sketch section, section and plan of food dispenser, plan of teaching machine, elevation of model, plan of upper level and model of teaching machine, 1966. Archigram Archives. 086-021-PM02

6   Yona Friedman. *La ville spatiale*, drawing, 1958
7   Yona Friedman. *La ville spatiale*, drawing, as published in *Form*, 1964

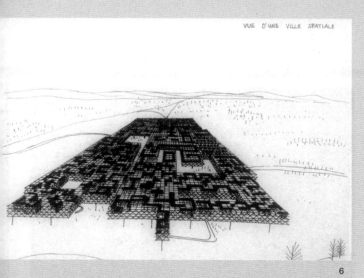

6

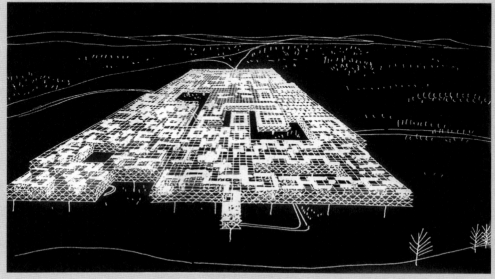

7

Mark Wigley

8 Ivan Leonidov. Tsentrosoyuz Building, Moscow, photograph of a plan for the competition, 1929–1930. Gelatin silver print, 18 x 13.1 cm. CCA. PH1989:0012:045

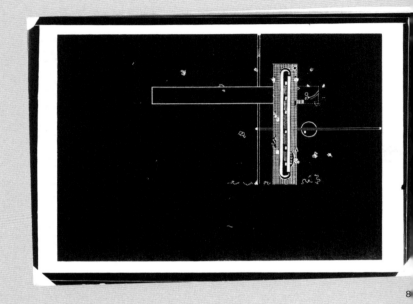

And some drawings are drawn to be flipped. In 1966, David Greene drew his Living Pod in black and white only to have the image reversed photographically in publications (fig. 5). And he was the one doing the publishing, so we know this is the intention. Other drawings were published one way and then flipped another way. This is the case with Yona Friedman's *Ville spatiale*, drawn in 1958 (fig. 6) and republished in reverse in *Form* magazine in 1964 (fig. 7). Some architects are retrospectively flipped. There are a number of famous Mies images that people treat with great affection, not knowing that they are photographic reversals of images that were never drawn that way.

In the late 1950s and early 1960s, images start to flip backward and forward on the same page—this, of course, has the effect of making the background visible as a background for the first time, and then making it invisible again, so there's a kind of a flicker of the background. The background becomes a sort of mark, even if it becomes a trace of the photographic medium in which architectural drawings primarily circulate. Obviously, if one image is a photographic negative of the other and you are asked to flip backward and forward, you are experiencing photography. I associate this with the postwar rise of the technologies of light lines against dark backgrounds. We can go through the whole history of radar and how it related to the development of computer graphics. But what I am interested in as a historian are the precedents, and what is quite shocking is how few examples there are of such behaviour as we move back in time. The great exception is Ivan Leonidov (fig. 8). His images are almost always seen as white on black. But it's not a photographic flip here; Leonidov actually drew with white ink on black paper or cardboard, or even on the table. He worked with prephotographic media in a photographic way. In this magnificent exception to the rule, somewhere between 1926 and 1930, Leonidov produced a kind of intellectual commentary on the relationship between architecture and photography. His sources were the Suprematists, primarily El Lissitzky and Malevich. Of course, Malevich was the high priest of black and white. But the black background is actually quite rare in the work of the Suprematists. There is a sort of evolution of the concept of black as a building site, as a site for building production. The rarity of the kind of images Leonidov made is absolutely astonishing given how easy it is to flip a drawing from a negative in the publication process and the fact that almost all experimental architects wanted to do dramatic visual things. All of them collaborated intimately with the most experimental graphic designers of the day.

Of course the issue is photography itself. By the early 1960s we could argue that the reader of an architectural magazine might not even notice an image that's white on black even if the majority of the images are still black on white. As a result of this, computer images could be later absorbed by the discourse extremely easily. Computer drawing

Mark Wigley

was seamlessly naturalized with a photographic legacy, and this is entirely consistent with McLuhan's argument that the only effect of a medium is the effect of seeing the previous medium. In other words, just as this kind of drawing reveals the photograph, the computer reveals these drawings. From that point of view, then, this huge revolution in architectural drawing from white to black is maybe not such a rupture in the history of architectural drawing, but instead something like an extension of the long-standing although usually recessive photographic sensibility in architecture. But perhaps the negative photographic flip had itself only become visible in the 1950s because this period saw the demise of an even earlier form of white line on a dark background: the blueprint.

The blueprint is an image applied to linen or paper. It was invented in 1842 and mass-produced in the 1860s for architects and engineers, and by the end of the century, tracing done by hand, which was the single biggest activity of any architect or engineer's office, had become redundant. In other words, the office was transformed. The blueprint took over from the hand and mechanized the discipline, and you could make an argument that it is the blueprint that made modern architecture possible because you can't have a modern architecture if you don't have a modern office.

A blueprint is the result of a photographic process. In fact, it began at the very beginning of photography. More than that, it was invented by William Herschel, who played a key role in the early history of photography, a medium invented by his friend William Henry Fox Talbot. Herschel even coined the word *photography*—drawing with light—and later coined the photographic use of the words *negative* and *positive*. It's important to note that Herschel and Talbot explicitly invented photography as an improved form of drawing and upgraded their own landscape drawings with a camera. Talbot's book on his invention of photography is called *The Pencil of Nature*. The camera is not understood as the technological substitute for the pencil. It is understood as an improved pencil, and photography as an upgraded form of drawing. But blueprints in the world of architecture were always treated as secondary negative copies rather than as drawings per se—construction documents rather than as artworks. They were almost never published, despite being the one form of drawing that the architect was symbolically identified with in the consciousness of the client. In that sense, blueprints were the hidden ghost image of architecture, only seen in engineering magazines and advertisements for architects. Popular magazines like *House Beautiful* and *House and Garden* in the 1930s developed a genre of a kind of simulated blueprint (fig. 9); they just basically published plans and sections in reverse. The only exception to this repressed tradition of the blueprint was Frederick Kiesler, who was the first to exhibit and publish blueprints as final projects. But it's precisely only in the mid-1950s, when the blueprint as a

9 The Wellington, one of the Liberty Homes of the Lewis Manufacturing Company, 1935. This advertisement features an example of the pseudo-blueprint style of plan.

The WELLINGTON - *A Prize Winner* - *Attractive* - *Economical* - *Well Planned*

The neat English exterior of this favorite design, with the brown stained sidewall shingles, encloses an interior plan that will please the tastes of many modern families. Modern home makers require more in a home than an attractive exterior, as they become more and more economical in the saving of time and steps. Convenience is one of the first requisites of a good design. In both plans of the Wellington we find the happy combination of an attractive exterior and a most convenient plan combined with good taste and real economy.

Plan A is designed for the family requiring only two bedrooms with a large attic space that can easily be made accessible by having an attic stairway leading up out of the kitchen over the present cellar stairs. The small additional cost for attic stairs, extra door, etc., will be quoted on request.

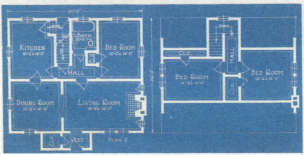

In Plan B the large attic space has been utilized to provide for two bedrooms in addition to the splendid large bedroom on the first floor.

Ornamental window shutters and flower boxes are furnished for front windows as shown in illustration.

Height of ceilings first floor 8'6", second floor 8'0".

— 10 —

Mark Wigley

190

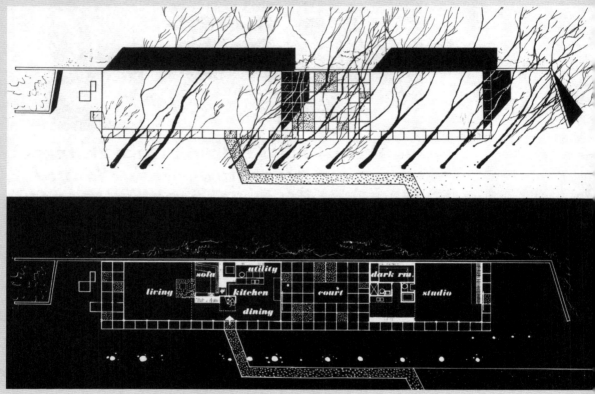

10 Charles and Ray Eames. Case Study House no. 8 (Eames House), Los Angeles, floor and site plans, as published in *Arts and Architecture*, December 1949

transfer technology was made redundant by the success of the so-called whiteprint or diazo machine, that the ghost image was brought to the surface in the form of the photographic negative. In other words, what happened, in my view, is that the blueprint was actually the backbone of architecture, but was buried as the antithesis of the classic image of the shadow drawing. Blueprints are all about technical production and not about reflection and thinking. The blueprint suddenly came to the surface in the 1950s precisely because at that moment it became redundant. Architectural magazines were very slow to pick up on it. *Arts and Architecture*, which is not a professional magazine—I think that's the key—absorbed the white-on-black pseudo-blueprint style of popular magazines (fig. 10).

The medium, the black background itself, rose to the surface only at the moment of the death of the blueprint, as if to hand over the tradition of the ghost images to a different form of photographic negative before it would then be turned over to the computer screen. So digital drawing is deeply embedded in the history of architectural drawing, the history of drawing with light, a history of the ghost image that extends back to Vasari. After all, the traditional black-on-white drawing is itself already a negative if you think about it. The shadow is what will become the substance.

We have to remember paper itself, that thing which was turned into the privileged site for original production by an artist and made possible the very idea of the architect as an artist. Drawing on paper in the sixteenth century was just a technology for imitation, a kind of early form of Xeroxing that was gradually turned into the centre of the emerging art world. Paper was at that time first and foremost an expensive technology of transfer. Pieces of paper were glued together and were pricked in order to transfer an image from one surface to another. The purpose of the paper being white was only to facilitate their transfer. The artistic original actually emerged right out of the heart of systems of copying, but architectural drawings never quite survived this logic of mechanical transfer.

But we might argue that the same thing will happen with digital architectural drawings. Just as with paper and then with photography, this will require institutional shifts and redefinitions. What are we going to collect? Are we going to collect the files or the prints in architectural design departments? Where will we keep these things? In drawing collections, photography collections or print collections? Should we keep the file, or do we need to keep the software, or do we also need to keep the computer, but especially the printer, since obviously the printer affects the quality of the image? I don't accept the idea that there's a fundamental difference between the calculation and the printout. There is, in my mind, never a possibility to completely separate the algorithm from the printout. In fact, it's in the particular form of the printout that one can sense what is being defined as an algorithm by the architect. Therefore, we cannot simply say that we should just keep the formulas and that we don't need the examples.

Secondly, I think there will be a question of preservation. And I think emulation is probably the key area in this regard. There is a growing expertise in the area of emulation and we could consider the ways in which drawings in one media can be emulated by another. We could make the argument that we should be systematic; we just collect every tenth drawing no matter what it is, no matter who does it. That would be a reasonable argument for detecting movements. We could also do it randomly; we just send a machine to randomly collect anything, any program, any machine, any software. That would actually be a very thorough way of collecting digital material. We could curate by obsessively collecting those things that we think are the right things to keep, but that is the old form of collection. If you know it's the right thing to keep, you've already got it in your head. How to collect those things whose meaning you don't yet know requires other kinds of strategies.

Anyway, for all the talk about computers, I don't think we really ever got to talk about the things that we claim that we want to collect, and I would say that's where we have to start. And maybe we could, just for a moment, hesitate and look into that kind of black screen.

Molly Wright Steenson

Christopher Alexander's *Notes on the Synthesis of Form* was published in 1964. Alexander used diagrams to frame design problems and spatialize data; information provided the structure for an approach to architecture practice. The legacy of Alexander's concern with formatting information can be seen in work that uses digital tools to organize data-rich environments.

This text is the transcription of a presentation that was given at the CCA in 2013.

MOLLY WRIGHT STEENSON

1   Cedric Price. Generator, view of working electronic model, c. 1976. Chromogenic colour print mounted on cardboard, 17.3 x 12.6 cm. Cedric Price fonds (AP144), CCA. DR1995:0280:108

INFORMATION ARCHAEOLOGIES

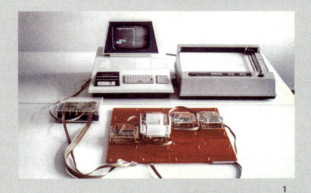

1

Occasionally, jumps happen, as Bernard Tschumi says, in the continuity between a design intention and the available technology. With this in mind I will address other archaeologies of other digitals, focusing specifically on information not as representation but as the structural mode and the technology for architecture.

In 1970, C. Peter McColough, president of Xerox, said, "What we seek is to think of information itself as a natural and undeveloped environment which can be enclosed and made more habitable for the people who live and work within it." This was when he announced the founding of Xerox Palo Alto Research Center (PARC). What does it mean for information to be inhabitable? This is an explicitly architectural problem.

It is helpful to consider Friedrich Kittler's statement, quoting Nietzsche, that "our writing tools are also working on our thoughts," as well as Cornelia Vismann's idea of the *in-format-ion*—

formatting information. Issues of formatting are fundamental to an understanding of the ways information and architecture cross over. Visualizing, generating, mediating and spatializing data are all different formats and modes of other archaeologies of the digital in architecture.

I will discuss selected projects by three architects: Christopher Alexander, Cedric Price and Nicholas Negroponte. These examples show how architecture formats information or how information is used to format architecture, the ways in which visualization structures possibilities, how unexpected solutions are generated beyond the control of the architect or the user, how architecture produced a definition of media and finally how the spatialization of data surrounds the user.

Christopher Alexander is, of course, best known for *Notes on the Synthesis of Form*, published in 1964, and *A Pattern Language: Towns, Buildings, Construction*, published in 1977. He studied mathematics at Cambridge and then went to Harvard for his PhD. His dissertation committee consisted of a broad group of people: Jerome Bruner, a cognitive psychology luminary; Serge Chermayeff, an architect and industrial designer; and Arthur Maass, a political scientist.

Alexander was interested in representing form through information and structure. He developed different modes of representation: a tree, a semi-lattice and eventually a network. He was completely circumscribed by what is possible with those visualizations. The idea in *Notes on the Synthesis of Form* is that form is a matter of finding misfits. You list what is wrong and then you group these things together to find the relative density. You structure this as a tree, and you use a computer to calculate the densities (fig. 2). Alexander presents a program consisting of the sets and diagrams that define a set of requirements: production, safety, use, capital and maintenance. These are all the things that go together into making a tea kettle, for example (fig. 3). Alexander thought that once you could structure a design problem in that way, you could make it stable. He called this ultra-stability, a notion he took from W. Ross Ashby, the cyberneticist. Ashby modelled this with a Homeostat, a computer that uses water, electricity and magnets and that knocks itself into a stable state (fig. 4). Alexander was also inspired by D'Arcy Wentworth Thompson's diagram of forces (fig. 5).

Before his dissertation was published, Alexander worked on a set of civil engineering projects for highways, which gave him the opportunity to use the IBM 7090 computer in the Massachusetts Institute of Technology (MIT) Computing Center. Working with Marvin Manheim, he structured his first problems as civil engineering problems (fig. 6). The problems are produced through descriptions of conditions for designing changes to a highway. Alexander and his colleagues determined where the services were, clustered accordingly and then made drawings to represent the clusters. Alex-

2 Christopher Alexander. Trees, in *Notes on the Synthesis of Form* (Cambridge, MA: Harvard University Press, 1964), p. 94. CCA. 2894; ID:85-B1051

3 Christopher Alexander. A tree that could be used to determine how to design a tea kettle, in *Notes on the Synthesis of Form* (Cambridge, MA: Harvard University Press, 1964), p. 62. CCA. 2894; ID:85-B1051

4 A Homeostat built in 1948 by W. Ross Ashby

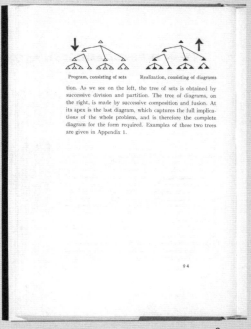

2

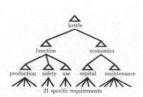

3

4

5   D'Arcy Wentworth Thompson. Shear mappings used to demonstrate the transformation of species of fish, in *On Growth and Form* (Cambridge: Cambridge University Press, 1917), p. 1062–1063. CCA. PO8255

1062   THE THEORY OF TRANSFORMATIONS   [CH.

which fossils are subject (as we have seen on p. 811) as the result of shearing-stresses in the solid rock.

Fig. 519 is an outline diagram of a typical Scaroid fish. Let us deform its rectilinear coordinates into a system of (approximately) coaxial circles, as in Fig. 520, and then filling into the new system,

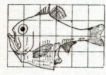
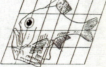

Fig. 517. *Argyropelecus Olfersi.*   Fig. 518. *Sternoptyx diaphana.*

space by space and point by point, our former diagram of *Scarus*, we obtain a very good outline of an allied fish, belonging to a neighbouring family, of the genus *Pomacanthus*. This case is all the more interesting, because upon the body of our *Pomacanthus* there are striking colour bands, which correspond in direction very closely

Fig. 519. *Scarus sp.*   Fig. 520. *Pomacanthus.*

to the lines of our new curved ordinates. In like manner, the still more bizarre outlines of other fishes of the same family of Chaetodonts will be found to correspond to very slight modifications of similar coordinates; in other words, to small variations in the values of the constants of the coaxial curves.

In Figs. 521–524 I have represented another series of Acanthopterygian fishes, not very distantly related to the foregoing. If we

XVII]   THE COMPARISON OF RELATED FORMS   1063

start this series with the figure of *Polyprion*, in Fig. 521, we see that the outlines of *Pseudopriacanthus* (Fig. 522) and of *Sebastes* or *Scorpaena* (Fig. 523) are easily derived by substituting a system

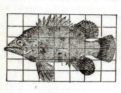

Fig. 521. *Polyprion.*   Fig. 522. *Pseudopriacanthus altus.*

of triangular, or radial, coordinates for the rectangular ones in which we had inscribed *Polyprion*. The very curious fish *Antigonia capros*, an oceanic relative of our own boar-fish, conforms closely to the peculiar deformation represented in Fig. 524.

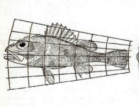

Fig. 523. *Scorpaena sp.*   Fig. 524. *Antigonia capros.*

Fig. 525 is a common, typical *Diodon* or porcupine-fish, and in Fig. 526 I have deformed its vertical coordinates into a system of concentric circles, and its horizontal coordinates into a system of curves which, approximately and provisionally, are made to resemble

6 Christopher Alexander. A traffic flow diagram, in *Notes on the Synthesis of Form* (Cambridge, MA: Harvard University Press, 1964), p. 88. CCA. 2894; ID:85-B1051

7 Christopher Alexander. A diagram of an Indian village, in *Notes on the Synthesis of Form* (Cambridge, MA: Harvard University Press, 1964), p. 153. CCA. 2894; ID:85-B1051

6

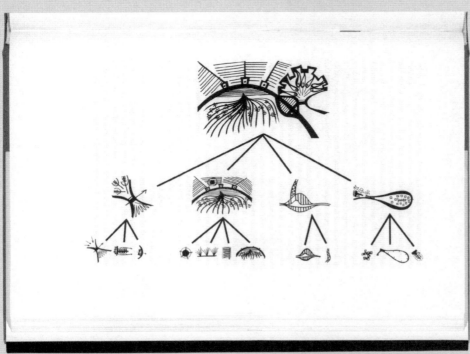

7

8 Paul Baran. Network diagram, 1962

9 Lyons Electronic Office (LEO) II/1 computer units, c. 1953. Science Museum, London

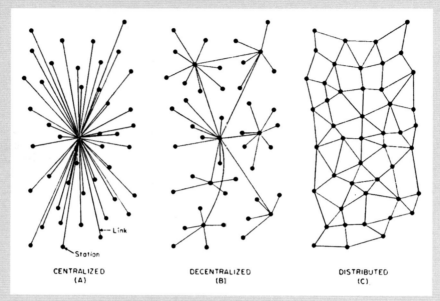

8

9

ander would put these drawings in trees, and these trees would evoke the conditions. This is what we see reflected in the diagram of the Indian village in *Notes on the Synthesis of Form* (fig. 7).

Alexander applied this to the Bay Area Rapid Transit (BART) system in San Francisco in 1964. He and his collaborators Van Maren King and Sara Ishikawa came up with over three hundred different requirements for the design of a mass-transit system. But this did not fit with the engineering culture at BART or with the San Francisco city government, and so the project didn't continue. There was too much top-down administration and too much computation where it wasn't required.

Alexander eventually started to calculate multiple relationships in set theory and graph theory, and a semi-lattice became possible. His rhetoric is a bit ridiculous. In "A City Is Not a Tree," he writes, "The city is not, cannot and must not be a tree," now that he has the more complex semi-lattice method. "The city is a receptacle for life. If the receptacle severs the overlap of the strands of life within it—because it is a tree—it will be like a bowl full of razor blades on edge, ready to cut up whatever is entrusted to it. In such a receptacle, life will be cut to pieces. If we make cities which are trees, they will cut our life within to pieces," he writes.

This shows the strength of the visual structures that organize and format the information. In "A City Is Not a Tree" he looks at existing cities and determines that Kenzo Tange's Plan for

Molly Wright Steenson

Tokyo 1960 is a tree, that Chandigarh is a tree and that perhaps the model of an open society is a semi-lattice. But he writes that "you are no doubt wondering, by now, what a city looks like which is a semi-lattice, but not a tree. I must confess I cannot yet show you plans or sketches." He goes on to explain that although the ideal is not there, eventually thinking will catch up.

From about 1968 until 1977, Alexander worked on *A Pattern Language* and developed a format for defining a design problem as a network and a set of formats that link together. This is Paul Baran's network diagram from 1962, showing centralized, decentralized and distributed networks (fig. 8). Distributed networks are redundant and have multiple nodes of connection. In *The Timeless Way of Building*, published in 1979, Alexander defines the relation of all of these different patterns, these ways of solving design problems, as a network, and these networks between patterns create the language that he has in mind. As he moved away from physical modes of representation, from the tree to the semi-lattice network, his method became open ended; he didn't use a computer, and he didn't need to force things backward into a linear model.

Alexander writes in *A Pattern Language* that each design problem has an image problem statement, a diagram that solves the statement and a pattern that addresses the problem solved and its relationship to the rest of the network of patterns. Users get a mental image of something they want to build, create a pattern, make a form and then reiterate back through the network. This is a formatting language for architecture that looks quite a bit different from the kind of procedures that Peter Eisenman used. But it is very computational; it has the logics of information and formatting within it and it is defined by visual information structures.

I am also interested in how Cedric Price represented information, and how he used architecture as a way to grapple with information networks and communication possibilities. The Oxford Corner House project that he started in 1966 was a feasibility study for Lyons Corner House, a restaurant chain that was once thriving but had fallen on hard times. J. Lyons Ltd., the company that started the restaurants, also created the first business computer in Britain—the LEO—in 1953 (fig. 9). They used it to manage payroll and inventory. It wouldn't be too great of a jump to say that the Oxford Corner House might be reframed as an information hub, and that's what Price envisioned.

In the Cedric Price archive at the CCA there are a number of network diagrams that deal with information utility. There's a user, a keyboard terminal and a conversational machine, and, for example, a square in a diagram announces: "Immense national batch processor serving all regions." A large amount of networked space has been conflated in one diagram. Price worked through how different learning and social activities could be distributed throughout this

10 Cedric Price. Oxford Corner House, network analysis, 1965–1966. Ink and traces of graphite on paper, 70.6 x 38 cm. Cedric Price fonds (AP144), CCA. DR1995:0224:114

11 William R. Martin. A site development network, in *Network Planning for Building Construction* (London: Heinemann, 1969), p. 21. CCA. W3664; ID:87-B16832

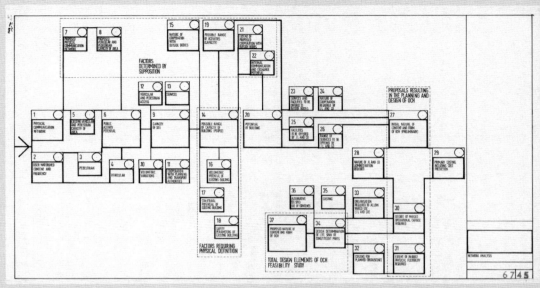

10

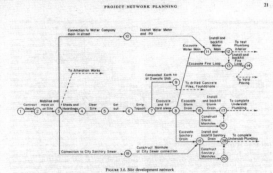

11

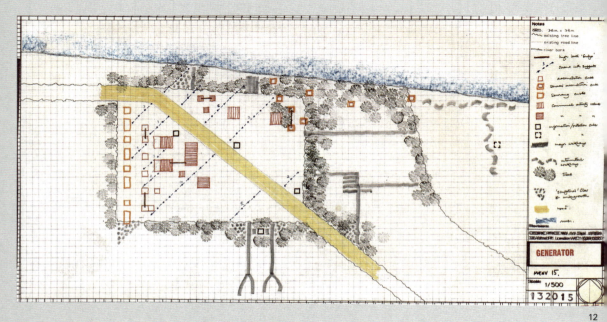

12 Cedric Price. Generator, site plan, c. 1976. Coloured pencil, porous-point pen and stamp-pad ink on diazotype on paper, 70 x 35.7 cm. Cedric Price fonds (AP144), CCA. DR1995:0280:406

space and how they would be served. Network diagrams show information coming in and being transmitted to teleprinters. At this time computers did not have monitors, so Price proposed using a number of teleprinters, cameras and screens. Information runs up the network diagram and is then distributed through the building. This is a massive information undertaking. Price identified the need for an 840,000-pound computer run by IBM, which would require between twenty and fifty operators to pull up information for a user in a moment. Price and Lyons studied screen placement for maximum information use. The information flows structured what happens in architectural space. Price also believed that the floors should move. Elevators would move swimming pools and the floors would create modular spaces depending on the uses and requirements.

He used information charting techniques in a number of projects. The network charts for Generator and the Fun Palace are probably the best known. In the one for the Oxford Corner House, you see factors requiring physical definition and total design elements for a feasibility study, and factors determined by supposition (fig. 10). Each of these goes with a probability chart that shows the likelihood not just of completion, but also of the knowledge that might be gained. There's something playful about these charts, and yet they are serious at the same time. They seem to map to things like critical path management and other 1950s-era project management tools. Price owned a copy of William R. Martin's *Network Planning for Building Construction*. A diagram in this book demonstrates the way that this kind of model can work, showing the contingencies and the critical path for completion of the project (fig. 11).

Price was a great categorizer of everything. For him, taxonomizing the world was a way of understanding architecture in it. In one information-storage project, everything has a specific number. The first number is the general classification; the second is the type of process. But these inputs are not architectural in the traditional sense. Price worked through an entire ontology in this process and, using a big computer system, identified the possibilities of turning the process out to the world at large to provide information. But ultimately they used punch cards. You stick a needle through all of the cards and the ones that you're looking for fall out. You could use this method to find "trends in ground-level concentration of smoke," for example. EAT (Experiments in Art and Technology) used something like this for their artist-matching system. It was very inexpensive, and vital to Price's process.

Generator, which Price developed between 1976 and 1979, is the visualization of a different set of approaches. Here he shows the possibilities of distributed computing, distributed interaction, playfulness and the continual return to indeterminacy (fig. 12). In an interview with Hans Ulrich Obrist in 2003, Price said that defining architecture does not necessarily define the consumption of it. There is no built form in the Generator project—as is the case with almost all of Price's projects—so there are no easy start and end points. Generator is a reconfigurable responsive architectural project for the White Oak Plantation in Georgia, on the Georgia–Florida border, commissioned by Howard Gilman. It is a kit of parts with 150 twelve-foot-by-twelve-foot recombinable cubes with off-the-shelf panels. There are springs and catwalks, and the idea is that, with this grid, you would wander around and have whatever art and leisure experiences you might desire. It started with a number of plans, but then users could request what they wanted of Generator.

Later in the project Price realized that getting people to move Generator's parts around might prove difficult. So he contacted John Frazer and started working with him on ways to get people to do something different. Frazer suggested outfitting all the pieces of Generator with sensors—micro-controllers—and one program tracked all of the pieces to provide a method for modelling. These are what Frazer called intelligent beer mats (fig. 1). You could move them around and the location of each part would be plotted on the screen with a comment. If Generator wasn't moved around enough, it would get bored and would run what Frazer called a boredom program. If the site was not being organized for change for some time, the computer would start generating unsolicited plans and improvements. In a hand-written postscript to Price, Frazer wrote, "If you kick a system, the very least that you would expect it to do is kick you back. You seem to imply that we were only useful if we produced results that you did not expect. I think this leads to some definition of computer aids in general. I'm thinking about this. But in the meantime, at least one thing you would expect from any half-decent program is that it should produce at least one plan that you did not expect."

The work of Nicholas Negroponte and the MIT Architecture Machine Group (AMG) raises some further questions related to formatting architectural problems. It's important to note the institutional context of AMG. It represents a strange moment that corresponds to what Paul Edwards calls the "closed world": the flows of funding from the United States Department of Defense, to private defence contractors, to certain schools and back again. Nicholas Negroponte was born into a very wealthy Greek shipping family. His brother is John Negroponte, who is a career diplomat in the United States and was director of national intelligence. Nicholas Negroponte studied at MIT, and the title of his thesis is "The Computer Simulation of Perception During Motion in the Urban Environment." He worked with Stephen Coons, who oversaw the Sketchpad project once Ivan Sutherland left MIT for the University of Utah.

It was never Negroponte's interest to work with computers. He wanted to find a field of research within architecture. In his 1966 thesis he wrote, "As a profession we've done little research. All this work must take place within the academic world as we have no General Motors or NASA to sponsor philanthropic research. However, schools of architecture are still trade schools by nature and not compatible at this moment with the process of research." His approach to architectural research would be to have architects and engineers collaborate in a process that looks less and less like architecture but that has an architectural logic. Negroponte needs the broader focus of architecture in order to run AMG and later the Media Lab.

In his book *The Architecture Machine: Toward a More Human Environment*, Negroponte discusses the URBAN 5 project. This is his software for designing a set of ten-foot-by-ten-foot blocks and applying programmatic features to them. He wanted URBAN 5 to change in its interaction with users. He was using the notion of symbiosis, which was the 1960s version of interactivity; computer scientist J. C. R. Licklider coined the term *symbiosis* around 1960. Negroponte thought that the machine would grow to be very flexible over time. The way that this would work is that the user would draw with a light pen on the screen and choose programmatic attributes. But URBAN 5 didn't work very well. Although Negroponte designed it in concert with students and with AMG co-director Leon Groisser, it was a lot of talk and it wasn't capable of doing much. URBAN 5 was a system of top-down control and limited environments—"blocks worlds," as they were called—and in reality it didn't produce what the architects and designers said it was producing.

SEEK, a project developed by Negroponte involving the interaction between gerbils and a machine, is another project that is relevant here. The gerbils would nudge blocks around, make homes, run around and fight with each other. The machine would try to stack the blocks, using computer-visioning tools to see where the edges of blocks were. These were blocks-worlds tools developed by MIT's Artificial Intelligence Laboratory and AMG. The machine would run one of six programs and try to organize the tools. SEEK was a tremendous failure; it tended to kill the gerbils.

Another project that Negroponte includes in *The Architecture Machine* is an experiment done by an MIT undergraduate named Richard Hessdorfer. He put three African American residents of Boston's South End in front of a computer and had them respond to questions about urban life: How do you feel about your housing? How do you feel about your tenants, schools et cetera? Negroponte writes, "First, the three residents had no qualms about talking with the computer in English about personal desires. They did not type uncalled-for comments, but they said things they probably never would have said to another human, particularly a white planner or a politician. To them the machine was not black, it was not white,

Molly Wright Steenson

13 Put That There experienced in the media room at MIT, c. 1980

208

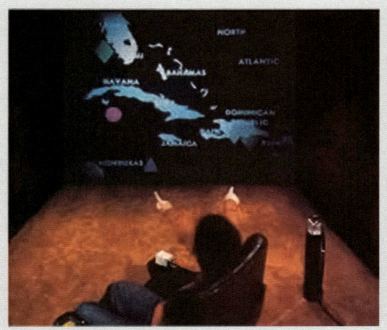

13

and surely had no prejudices." But actually they were interacting with the white man at the other end of the telephone line. I'm not sure that Negroponte and others in AMG gave much consideration to some of the political issues that were going on in the outside world.

In the 1970s, AMG began a set of projects in the media room, which was a space with cameras, a large light-dot screen in front, two touch screens on the side and an Eames chair for the user to sit in. It was a place where AMG wanted to start envisioning what they would call "supreme usability." They started referring to computing as something like a place, a milieu or a state of mind, and they claimed that a state of mind is a comfortable place to be with computers. The Aspen Movie Map is one of the most famous projects developed for the media room. It involved an interactive map of Aspen, Colorado, including street views and satellite images.

The media room was also used to develop the Spatial Data Management System for the management of ship fleets for the US Department of Defense. This involved zooming through satellite maps and touching icons. AMG was trying to figure out the navigation and information interfaces as a key to understanding information spatially. They were working on issues that informed the desktop computing models that we are familiar with today. A user could zoom in on Landsat satellite images to get to a large set of Boston landmarks. There was also a set of architectural slides that had been put on video disc and that could be accessed in the same way. The body becomes important here; within this space with cameras, sitting in the chair or perhaps standing up, you could begin to point to things and use voice and gesture to interact.

In another project, called Put That There (fig. 13), a user says, "Pay attention," and the system says, "Okay." And then the user says, "Make a pink circle," and it says, "Where?" and the user says, "There," and then it makes the circle. The system models some manner of abstraction, so you can say, "Put the yellow circle there. Put that there," and you see circles, but otherwise the video displays only fleets of ships, so it's clear what kind of context this is in. These military contexts were necessary for the funding of projects during this period.

AMG developed the project Mapping by Yourself in the late 1970s. They started talking about the computer creating a reality that is indistinguishable from the real thing. They say, "We are reminded of the prompt from Bell [the telephone company]. It is the next best thing to being there. This proposal is about being there." What they begin to imagine is that this is not a substitution. It's not virtual. It *is* the thing. A Westinghouse twelve-inch-by-twelve-inch screen from 1978 was to be used for mapping (fig. 14). It's basically an early proposal for augmented reality and transparent maps. These are maps with haptic feedback that you could run your fingers over to get the feel of the

Molly Wright Steenson

14 Mapping by Yourself, touch-sensitive display, 1977

15 Mark Dorf. Plate 3 from the series *Axiom and Simulation*, 2011

14

15

terrain below. Eventually AMG moved away from military models and toward media.

These were Negroponte's teething rings: broadcasting, publication and computers. He used these three things together to form the Media Lab. He received forty million dollars from forty different companies and started the Media Lab in 1985 with ten different groups, which AMG folded into. The Media Lab was funded by automotive, broadcasting, electronics and toy companies among many others, by movie studios, by newspapers, by money from Japan and by the National Science Foundation of the United States. The advantage, of course, is that the Media Lab could be used as a place to develop media, and this is where a research budget should go.

There are five key points in this set of other archaeologies: formatting architectural problems, visualizing information paradigms in architecture, generating solutions, architecture as a mediating process and spatializing data. These examples present other modes of architectural information and architectural formatting. Where do we go from here? I don't think that you can separate the virtual and the real. There is no longer a distinction between online and offline.

The New Aesthetic is relevant here (fig. 15). According to Matthew Battles, this is "a collaborative attempt to draw a circle around several species of aesthetic activity, including but not limited to drone photography, ubiquitous surveillance, glitch imagery, Streetview photography, 8-bit net nostalgia. Central to the New Aesthetic is the sense that we're learning to wave at machines and that perhaps in their glitchy, buzzy, algorithmic ways, they're beginning to wave back in earnest."

Processing language can present something that is beautiful or algorithmic; it can also teach somebody how to draw online, and it is developed especially for designers to learn. These technologies affect our streets in different ways. Flash mobs are an example, but so are the Arab Spring uprisings. People in San Francisco organized to develop parklets in part because of access to social media and in part because their lifestyles allow them to be outside and mobile frequently. We begin to see things like the Wiggle, an area that didn't have an identity until recently, but, thanks to bicycles, young people and social media, an entire neighbourhood has been developed. (It's called the Wiggle because of the way that you bike through San Francisco in order to avoid hills.) I think the future is one in which online is not offline, and in which we see these formatting problems as looking architectural and not quite so technological. And I think there is fertile ground for architects, historians and theorists to be involved in this.

Andrew Witt

Approaches to design based on quantification, computation and networks intensified <u>around 1970</u>, with a strong presence in projects developed for Expo '70 in Osaka. Behavioural computation and scripting, as they were refined in projects like Yona Friedman's Flatwriter and Frei Otto's Olympic Stadium in Munich, became pivotal for future use of digital technologies in design.

ANDREW WITT

1 Arata Isozaki & Associates. Deme, a demonstration robot, during a performance at Expo '70

THE MACHINIC ANIMAL: AUTONOMIC NETWORKS AND BEHAVIOURAL COMPUTATION

Andrew Witt

In 1949, the electrical engineer Claude Shannon republished two unassuming papers together as *The Mathematical Theory of Communication*. Though oriented toward telecommunications scientists and centred on problems of signal measurement, Shannon's book had as its true subject nothing less than the organization and transmission of collective information, intelligence and meaning. In these papers, Shannon introduced a new lexicon of encoders and decoders, channels and information, and transmitters and receivers to describe networked systems of symbolic message exchange. More fundamentally, he proposed new metrics for the semantic quantification of those messages and thus, in effect, created a mathematics of communicative meaning. The striking generality of his formulation allowed exchangers of these symbols to range from

Andrew Witt

2 Claude Shannon at the Bell Telephone Laboratories with Theseus, an electromechanical mouse capable of learning to navigate a maze, 1952. Hulton Archive

autonomic machines to human minds. As a consequence, Shannon's work implicitly reframed fields as diverse as social science and cryptography in terms of relational communication. An enduring implication of Shannon's work is that apparent behaviour—even of complex systems—was cast in part as an epiphenomenal quality of transactional information networks (fig. 2).

Shannon's conceptual construct of information networks decisively shaped the emerging use of digital computers in design over the twenty years following the publication of *The Mathematical Theory of Communication*. While popularly consumed within the architectural profession as a merely utilitarian development, or even as inimical to creativity, the computer was seen by a specific cadre of experimental designers as something more. They understood the computer not as a machine for making drawings and artifacts but as a tool for planning behaviours. They adopted or replicated Shannon's model of transactional networks as an epistemic armature for this behavioural digitization. During the period around the year 1970, these experimentalists formulated a radically new way of thinking about the role of the designer and the representation of operational and relational design knowledge.

This sophisticated network approach required specialized techniques which ultimately demanded that designers begin to develop software commensurate with their conceptual ambitions. The role of scripting—the custom programming of computer software—was key in the emergence of the network approach and computational aesthetic around 1970. Whether in collaboration with computer scientists or through their own entrepreneurial initiative, a few designers of this period promulgated a new language of design—the language of code—and transformed the tools of architecture.

3   Claude Shannon and Warren Weaver. Diagram of a general communication system, in *The Mathematical Theory of Communication* (Urbana, IL: University of Illinois Press, 1963), p. 7

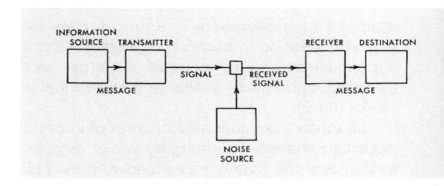

3

Networks and the Quantificational Turn

Although the two developments were closely linked, the adoption of network and information-theoretic ideas in design preceded design digitization chronologically and epistemologically. While digital experiments developed in earnest from at least the mid-1960s, network approaches were characteristic of a broader tendency toward quantification in design that had deep historical roots and had already accelerated and intensified by the 1950s. New mathematizations and quantifications were integral parts of design discourse at least a decade before digital tools could fluidly explore their consequences. During the 1950s, computational tools, far from being catalysts of conceptual innovation, were often the manifestations of earlier evolutions in disciplinary thinking. We might call this inclination toward mathematical methods in design the *quantificational turn*.

This quantification is manifest in developments that range from the Hochschule für Gestaltung Ulm's broad teaching of mathematical topics (including Shannon's information theory) to Luigi Moretti's definition of parametric design for architecture and planning in 1960. It is apparent in the crystallographic fascinations of Buckminster Fuller and Louis Kahn, and in the combinatorial experiments of Leslie Martin and Lionel March. It is clear from the first experiments with formal languages, distinct from but closely related to the language of code. Indeed, if anything, this turn is characterized by a promiscuous interest in all things scientific that might relate to the human experience of space. But in this bricolage of topics, the notion of the network—informational, behavioural, spatial and operational—has a certain recurring primacy that marks it as a linchpin of early computational thinking.

Network research in design intensified greatly around 1970. Although it receded from architectural conversation shortly thereafter, work from this period shaped latent dimensions of design computation that are often unacknowledged. I propose here a partial archaeology of networks of design computation, tracing their lineage from the informational, cybernetic and behavioural graphs modelled by Shannon and his contemporary Norbert Wiener (fig. 3). I consider three specific projects that constituted novel and fundamental developments of these ideas: Yona Friedman's Flatwriter, the 1976 group exhibition *Architect and Computer: A Man-Machine-System* and the resolution of the complexly curved roof structure for the Olympic Stadium in Munich. Each project documents incipient tendencies in design computation that proved deeply anticipatory of our own moment of design.

Certain commonalities connect the networks that designers elaborated during this period. First, they exhibit a persistent optimism about the communicative potential of the computer. Not merely a neutral information processor, the computer is an actor in a communications network, at once source, channel and receiver. Second, these projects are among the first serious and recurring attempts by designers to use networks as simulations of forces. These forces are often physical, although just as frequently they could be organizational forces endowed with quasi-physical action. Finally, and perhaps most fundamentally, in each of these projects there is a commitment to the possibility of the operative network to endow design systems with a certain capacity for autonomic behaviour. Thus networks became an early tool for thinking through self-organization at an architectural or urban scale.

Network methods could naturally be associated with parallel formal developments in design, such as a new language of structural spaceframe networks or fluid transformations and deformations of topology. And ultimately networks produced tangible artifacts through broad experimentation with articulated and discretized shell and spatial structures. But beyond superficial formal traces, the network played a more visceral, almost analogical role; the behavioural network became a tangible framework for man–machine symbiosis. With it, the machine, or the systems simulated by the machine, could take on the characteristics of a living organism. Machines could react and interact. With these new synaptic networks, the machine, and architecture, could *live*.

A Bioelectrical Frame

The rich associations that behavioural networks might have evoked for mid-century designers emerge from the biological and telematic roots of the concept. Since Luigi Galvani's eighteenth-century discovery of the bioelectrical basis of the nervous system and his attempts to breathe life into the dead with its power, humanity has been understood to share a kind of fundamental electrical equipment with machinery. If our own organism, so intimately bound to consciousness, is articulated though an electromechanical nervous system, might machines be endowed with the same life-giving networks of behavioural response? If our machines for living in were themselves living machines, what would their networks of choice and action be?

Bioelectrical networks took on a dramatically extended scope of association with the development of the telegraph, which meant that electrical networks transmitted information as well as power. Not only was this a significant advancement of the geographic extension of technology, but it also became a powerful new analogy for our animal bioelectrical systems. Could these biological and mechanical networks be used identically for communication, control or even consciousness? Shannon's research on the transmission of information moved this durable fantasy of the feeling machine toward tangible possibility. It introduced the notion that machines were not only computing but also *behaving*. But it was left to a second researcher to translate that possibility into specific theory.

The mathematician Norbert Wiener, at the Massachusetts Institute of Technology (MIT), took Shannon's information theory in a radical new direction by considering systematic feedback loops within networks. He synthesized and extended Shannon's information theory through his own formulation of cybernetics, which foregrounded the epiphenomenal behaviour that was possible through a feedback process. Through this mechanism Wiener also directly addressed the possibility of machine adaptation, both by learning and self-reproduction. Wiener's formulation of the feedback system and its role in control and behaviour sparked the imagination of a wide range of thinkers. Designers, artists and architects found particular resonance in this possibility of self-organizing or emergent machines. In fact, Wiener became something of a celebrity in progressive design circles. He was invited to lecture at Ulm, and his ideas found ready acceptance among those interested in design's digital frontier. Wiener's cybernetics became a theoretical point of departure for a new kind of autonomic architecture.

The Computer as Animal and Automaton

Of course, the notion of autonomous architecture, though informed by Wiener, was already one of modernism's preoccupations. Here, Pierre Jaquet-Droz's autonomous draftsman, completed in 1774, assumes outsize importance as both reference and model (figs. 4–5). An Enlightenment invention of a Swiss watchmaker, the draftsman was a mechanical doll that could automatically draw four distinct images, including frolicking dogs and royal portraits. The Jaquet-Droz automaton was known to Sigfried Giedion, who cited it in *Space, Time and Architecture* as a kind of archetypal evidence for the culture of invention that enabled modern material production. Giedion further qualified this automaton as fundamentally communicational, "anticipating the principle of the modern automatic telephone."[1] It became an iconic cipher not only for autonomous action but also for the more nuanced state of autonomous behaviour through feedback and communication. It was cited

4   Pierre Jaquet-Droz. Autonomous draftsman, 1774. Musée d'art et d'histoire, Ville de Neuchâtel. Inv. AA 3

5   The mechanics of the autonomous draftsman, programmed to produce four images. Musée d'art et d'histoire, Ville de Neuchâtel. Inv. AA 3

4

5

by figures from Nicholas Negroponte to Tomás Maldonado as a kind of precursor to the autonomously behavioural computer. Maldonado, in particular, gives it a key role in his 1964 essay "Science and Design," a manifesto for the engagement of objective methods by designers. In this essay Maldonado defines a program for design that includes an intimate connection with the conception of "man–machine systems," of which the automaton is a paradigmatic example. By Maldonado's time, discussion of automata was in fact a coded consideration of the computer. In the figure of the computer, the designer is confronted with an agent to which the very human capacities of choice, communication and perhaps even creation can be delegated. It is this strange dualism of the computer—both its animalistic potentials and its rational efficiencies, each summarized, embodied and embedded in certain kinds of networks—that created a dynamic frisson for design innovation.

The computer is more than mere technology; in its capacity to adopt and adapt human functions, it is a mirror for and a test of our own ambitions, capacities and flaws. In fact our contemporary understanding of the computer and its role in design is inseparable from the notion that the computer itself behaves and is a repository for behavioural and epistemic regimes that, as Nicholas Negroponte has suggested, have an evolutionary relationship to us. At the same time, machine behaviour endows a certain power—sometimes mysterious and often considered dangerous—that has had a fraught association with autonomic machines since their inception. It was this kind of existential conflict that informed much of the theoretical work of design computation in the 1960s.

1970

In this context, 1970 marked the beginning of a period of heightened visibility for and intensive interest in the theoretical possibilities of computation and behavioural networks, which crystallized into specific technologies, practices and projects. It represents a pivot point, a moment of phase change in the role of the computer from mere calculator of rules to behavioural actor, a transition enabled in part by increasingly specialized network structures. It also represents a moment of stark contrast between an idealized future of behaving machines and a more conservative perspective from design practice.

6 *Overleaf:*
Festival Plaza at Expo '70, showing Kenzo Tange's Big Roof and Taro Okamoto's Tower of the Sun. Bill Cotter, photographer

One undeniable sign of the enthusiasm for these new cybernetic and networked processes was the explosion of inventive experimentation manifest in the universal exposition of that year, Expo '70, in Osaka. The exposition was master-planned by Kenzo Tange and realized through the specific architectural visions of designers such as Arata Isozaki, Kiyonori Kikutake and Fumihiko Maki (figs. 6–7). A significant number of the pavilions integrated computer-assisted behavioural feedback systems or even completely autonomous robots. The largest of these were Isozaki's towering megarobots Deme and Deku, which used audio-sensing systems to create performances that would respond to a crowd's applause (figs. 1, 8–10). Both imposing and inviting, Deme and Deku became symbols of optimism around the new animism of the computer.

Perhaps even more significant was the Pepsi Pavilion, the multimedia magnum opus of the art and engineering collective EAT (Experiments in Art and Technology) (fig. 11). A collaborative work of over two hundred artists and engineers, the remarkable faceted dome of the pavilion was cloaked in a mechanically generated fog. Surrounding the pavilion itself, a terrace hosted artistic director Robert Breer's swarm of autonomous interactive robots, which he called Floats. The Floats moved slowly, covering about half a metre each minute, and emitted a range of whale-like sounds. They would reverse direction when encountering obstacles or the edges of the terrace. They created a strange new dynamically reconfigured space that was both responsive and sensorial.

Despite the almost hallucinatory possibilities of Expo '70's behavioural approach, a much more prosaic view of computation prevailed among practitioners at the time. The view from practice is summarized in Murray Milne's essay "From Pencil Points

Andrew Witt

230

7

8

7 View of Expo '70. Bill Cotter, photographer
8 Arata Isozaki & Associates. Deme in a light performance by the Gutai group of artists at Expo '70
9 Arata Isozaki & Associates. Deme, axonometric

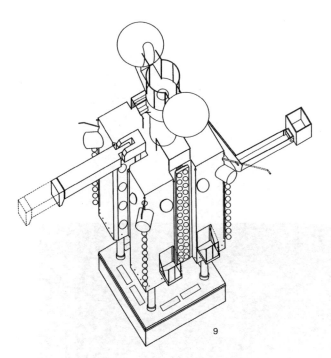

Andrew Witt

232

10 Festival Plaza and the Big Roof with Deme. Bill Cotter, photographer

11 EAT (Experiments in Art and Technology). Exterior view of the Pepsi Pavilion at Expo '70. Harry Shunk and János Kender, photographers. Shunk-Kender Archive, Getty Research Institute, Los Angeles. 2014.R.20

to Computer Graphics," published in the June 1970 issue of *Progressive Architecture*: "As costs plummet, competition promises to motivate even the smallest firms to computerize." The appearance of the computer in everyday practice was met with some poetically epochal nostalgia, even resignation: "It is pleasing to the senses to pull soft lead across clean vellum, to hear the squeak of a felt tip, to smell the dust of a pencil sharpener.... It is jarring and distasteful to realize that some day soon, almost all of this may be replaced by the chatter of teletypes, the hum of electric equipment, and the blue penumbra of great blinking tubes. Unfortunately, this is the price architects must pay for technological progress."[2] The virtual identification of architecture with drawing betrays a bias that all but ignored the new language of the computer: scripted code. During the 1960s, the practice of programming or scripting the computer became a radically new way for operative networks to be embedded in design processes. Any design technique that could be represented procedurally could be transcribed into coded scripts. The painstaking strictures of code demanded the categorization, prioritization and transcription of not only the designer's epistemic faculties but also the faculties of desire, taste, sensation and even neural responsiveness—in effect, all of the designer's human and animal capacities. Rendered in code, these capacities were made entirely portable, to potentially be copied, used and modified in a perpetually expanding scope of contexts by ever-newer machines. The capacities of the computer forced a reflective atomization and deconstruction of human capacities, a kind of immortality in code.

    In a prelude to the developments of the 1970s, Negroponte published "Toward a Theory of Architecture Machines" in 1969, while working in the Urban Systems Lab at MIT. The essay confronted the fundamental questions of autonomy, action and architecture raised by the computer. The dual challenges of heuristics and behaviour are clear: "Whenever a mechanism is equipped with a processor capable of *finding a method* of finding a method of solution, the authorship of the answer probably belongs to the machine. If we extrapolate this argument, eventually the machine's creativity will be as separable from the designer's initiative as our designs and actions are from the pedagogy of our grandparents. The partnership of an architect with such a device is a dialogue between two intelligent systems—the man and the machine— which are capable of producing an evolutionary system."[3]

Networks, Behaviour, Code: Three Cases

It is possible to identify three projects that characterize the critical developments of the early and mid-1970s and presage architects' assumptions about the computer in design. While each project is revealing in its own right, the preconditions and anticipatory work that made these events possible are just as important and will be examined in turn. First, Yona Friedman's Flatwriter proposed a remarkably prescient system for "design by search" that used network simulations of spaces and urban contexts as intelligent filters, warnings and aids in the evaluation of combinatorial space. Designed as a customized interactive software–hardware system, the Flatwriter anticipated expert systems, the democratization of design knowledge through the Internet and the introduction of hardware as essential to design evolution. Second, the exhibition *Architect and Computer: A Man-Machine-System*, curated by Helmut Emde and held at the Goethe-Institut in

Berlin, presented a selection of contemporary projects to make explicit the methodological impact of network ideas. The exhibition catalogued the broad new software tools that designers were producing in the service of progressive research. Finally, Frei Otto and Günter Behnisch's Olympic Stadium in Munich took an almost muscular approach to the understanding of operational networks. The stadium also became the catalyst for the development of industrial software to enable ambitious formal design as well as for the emergence of the parallel discipline of design computation. Collectively, the Flatwriter, *Architect and Computer* and the Olympic Stadium suggest a coalescing of specific strains of behavioural design research that reverberate in the discourse of computation today.

Design by Search: Yona Friedman's Flatwriter

The evolution of design computation during the 1960s and 1970s was a symptom of broader attempts to harness calculational techniques for the negotiation of exploding information, populations and economies. These underlying demographic developments pushed architects to design with an intention of massive scalability. Whereas the designer of the nineteenth century could draw for a single client, the designer of the twentieth must design for ten thousand. Moreover, any specific design is no longer the concern only of the owner but also of all the neighbours; a new paradigm of design demanded a broader understanding of stakeholders. Yona Friedman saw these problems of design, information and production as interdependent and considered the challenges of scale to be incompatible with the classical atelier approach. His solution

12 Yona Friedman. "About the Flatwriter," 1967. Reprinted in *Pro Domo* (Barcelona: Actar, 2006), p. 136. CCA. BIB 180433

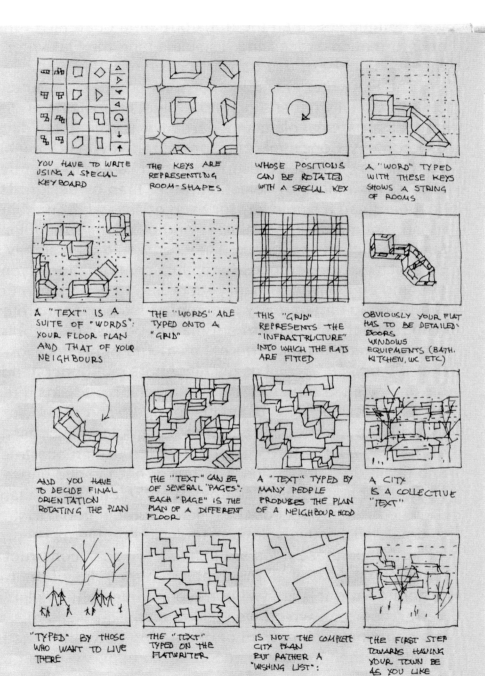

was nothing less than the transformation of architecture into an information-processing discipline, and the Flatwriter was the key catalyst of this transformation (fig. 12).

The Flatwriter was Friedman's theoretical computer for combinatorially generating and evaluating millions of distinct options for spatial plans in a particular dwelling, building or city context. Consisting of a specialized keyboard and associated display, it allowed users to directly enter their preferences and realize spaces by selection rather than by design. The keyboard had a single key for each of several room connectivity arrangements, room shapes and positions for equipment such as kitchen appliances. The user would then simply specify, by keystroke, preferences for spatial configuration, eventually defining an ideal apartment. According to Friedman, "Each future inhabitant of a city can imprint his personal preferences with respect to his apartment (flat) to be, using symbols which put in visual form the different elements of his decision so that the builder as well as his neighbors can understand what his choice is. In other words, this machine contains a repertoire of several million possible plans for apartments, knows how to work out instructions about the characteristic consequences of the way each future inhabitant would use an apartment, and finally, can determine whether or not the site chosen by a future inhabitant will risk upsetting the other inhabitants."[4]

Friedman proposed an explicitly combinatorial system to create alternative solutions to design problems programmatically: "Once these rules are defined, we shall construct a combinatorial list of all the things that the rules of the mapping generate. And this list will correspond, element by element, to the repertoire which we wish to establish."[5] His rule set is a combinatorial method of generating network structures, which are then evaluated according to edge-weighted traversal matrices. These evaluations produce a certain kind of topographic map of fitness which Friedman calls *isoefforts*. Isoefforts parallel the more modern concept of the heat map, which is ubiquitous in the evaluation of urban form. A set of isoefforts is a visible ranking of possibilities that are more or less suitable for a specific user. According to Friedman, "The effort map is a sort of meteorological map that shows the fluctuations of the urban mechanism, and I think that it is as much a matter of public interest to everyone as is the weather report. All the applications cited here are based on this analogy with the weather map, from which the effort map differs only in that the city mechanism can be influenced by the acts and choices of the inhabitants while the weather, at least so far, is not subject to human will."[6]

Originally conceived as a means to enable a more direct facilitation of clients' aims without the intermediary of the architect, the Flatwriter marshalled a range of ideas and methods that proved even more radical and remarkably prescient. Since the architect was increasingly a medium for information, Friedman saw the whole notion of design epistemology as essentially interchangeable with information theory. Thus the challenge of architecture in an information age was to recast it as a communicable—and thus encapsulatable—process. The architect is a channel, the client a transmitter and the architecture a receiver. The telephone system becomes an explicit analogy for Friedman. Within this framework, he saw the architect as the fundamental bottleneck in the scalable creation of built form satisfying to the client, as the architect's human capacities were simply not scalable to the speed and size of the client's demands or construction's complexities. He therefore proposed design through selection from vast libraries of combinations. "Instead of an architect, the future user encounters a repertoire of all possible arrangements that his way of life may require. This repertoire, which is necessarily limited, must be presented to him in a form he can understand," he writes.[7] Thus design becomes less an act of divination and more a kind of systematic and ordered search.

The proto–"big data" tendencies of Friedman do not end there. He proposes a system of urban observation that is almost exactly the kind of sensor networks that are routinely used today: "I would like to examine the way we observe a larger complex, such as a city, adhering to the postulates concerning objective descriptions which I established.... To begin with, I must put forth the improbable hypothesis...that we may observe a city as if through the eye of God.... Naturally, such vision is impossible. Instead, we could consider using a television camera that films the city, night and day, from a helicopter. This camera would not see inside the heads of people or microorganisms, but it would record all the movements of the people of the city. This record would show who went where, when."[8] Through this observational apparatus, a feedback cycle is established that accelerates and intensifies the work of the architect as one component of an engineered ecology of knowledge.

An essential dimension of the Flatwriter was Friedman's proposed custom software and hardware for an open-ended and non-authorial design interface. This machine then supplants the architect as epistemic transmitter between client and building, and the architect is elevated to the designer of an extensive menu of combinatorial options. For Friedman, choice was an essential aspect of the Flatwriter's power; in fact, he explicitly describes the Flatwriter as a choice machine. He suggests that not only would it immediately enable the end user to design by selection, but that it would also allow immediate

13 Yona Friedman. The Flatwriter,
inhabitant survey, 1967

communication with the building department for permit purposes and other construction automation tasks (fig. 13).[9] Thus the design of a new role for the architect also implied the development of new heuristic and communication technologies.

The Flatwriter was a well-developed concept by the time of Expo '70, where Friedman intended to allow visitors to interactively design and print their own customized apartment from a reportoire of three million to five million generated flats. While it would have been an appropriate addition to the exposition, unfortunately the Flatwriter was never executed and it remained a theoretical project. It nevertheless became a touchstone of Friedman's ambitions and he elaborated on its basic concepts and algorithms in his March 1971 article in *Progressive Architecture*, "The Flatwriter: Choice by Computer," and in his book *Toward a Scientific Architecture*. The project influenced Friedman's interlocutors, students and colleagues, including Nicholas Negroponte, who was struck by its computational qualities. The Flatwriter marks an expansive and ambitious attempt to use networks—operational and communicational—to create an entirely new design ecology, and with it a new kind of architecture.

Moretti and the Behaviour of Surface

It is instructive to compare Yona Friedman's approach with Luigi Moretti's work a decade earlier on the parametric design of buildings and cities. In hindsight, Friedman's work has striking similarities with Moretti's formulation of parametric design; both address architecture and urbanism as analogous problems on a continuous spectrum of probability and performance maps. Friedman's isoefforts quantifiably graph

14 Luigi Moretti. Studies in arena design based on variable parameters of visibility, in *Exhibition of Parametric Architecture and of Mathematical and Operational Research in Town-Planning* (Rome: Istituto nazionale di Ricerca Matematica e Operativa per l'Urbanistica, 1960), p. 25. CCA. ID:86-B14621

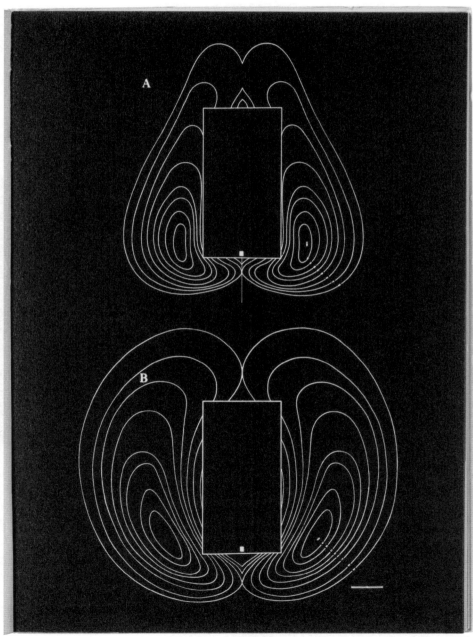

Andrew Witt

244

15 Luigi Moretti. Model of a parametrically designed stadium, in *Exhibition of Parametric Architecture and of Mathematical and Operational Research in Town-Planning* (Rome: Istituto nazionale di Ricerca Matematica e Operativa per l'Urbanistica, 1960), p. 17. CCA. ID:86-B14621

15

variations while Moretti maps variations directly on parametric forms, but the graphic languages of both hinge on topographies of parametric spaces and on gradients of performance functions (fig. 14).

As early as 1942, Moretti investigated the possibility of mathematical control of families of building forms, and by 1960 this research culminated in an exhibition on parametrics in architecture and urban design. In fact, Moretti's work contains the first published appearance of the term *parametric architecture.* Moretti's proposal for a parametric architecture is strikingly contemporary. Drawing on game theory and the military operations research of the Second World War, Moretti's work defines objectivity in the face of analogy and optima directed by the will of the architect. Inspired by the work of mathematicians such as Hermann Weyl and Évariste Galois, Moretti outlines three stages of a parametric methodology:
(1) the definition of a theme; (2) the definition of parameters governing the theme; and (3) the definition of analytic relationships between the quantities depending on the parameters.[10]

Moretti's investigation proceeds typologically, through a taxonomized generative method for event spaces and particularly for arenas (fig. 15). Here he conscripts an archetypal architectural parameter: the view. Using the continuously changing field of values of visibility for the spectator, he implicates the form of the building itself in the analysis and begins to elastically deform it according to visibility from the seats. He encapsulates a range of interdependent variables such as visibility of the entire venue and visibility of specific areas of interest. The result is a series of four parametric permutations of arena design generated by their distinct spectacles: soccer, swimming, tennis and cinema. Each arena is a supple surface gently articulating a kind of optimal spectatorship for its associated event. Moretti then goes beyond the architectural implications of these parametric functions to the consequences for school districting, traffic optimization and ultimately the spatial distribution of the city. At the root of Moretti's parametric design is a challenge to the foundations of modernism. Moretti saw in the technical advances of science and mathematics "extraordinary instrumental possibilities" for architecture.[11] Mathematics provided a way to render objective the avowed aims of modernism, and therefore to put them on a secure and cumulative foundation.

Moretti's work corroborates the significance of projects like the Flatwriter, which were specifically engaged in the documentation and design of fields of forces shaping design. The Flatwriter and Moretti's parametric design address architecture as a specific instance in a definable parameter space, and both use similar mathematical tools such as implicit performance functions and level sets to graphically define these parameter spaces. The approaches of both Friedman and Moretti are clear manifestations of the quantificational turn in design.

The Man–Machine Organism

The Flatwriter was by no means alone in its exploration of custom-optioneering software to confront design challenges. The early 1970s saw expansive and systematic research into software as an architecture project. In 1976, a remarkable exhibition organized several bespoke software systems developed by designers in a collective statement on the future of design method. Curated by the German structural designer Helmut Emde, *Architect and Computer: A Man-Machine-System* comprised a selection of network approaches to design

16 Joachim Luther. Variations on a facade design responding to set criteria of relationships between dwelling units and their terraces, in *Architect and Computer: A Man-Machine-System*, ed. Helmut Emde (n.p., 1976), p. 52

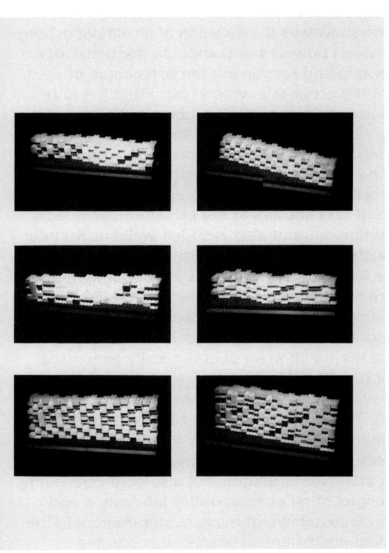

and revealed the command of software coding that designers had embraced.

Implicitly responding to the more widely known *Cybernetic Serendipity* exhibition held at London's Institute of Contemporary Arts in 1968, *Architect and Computer* confronted many of the same themes but with specifically architectural motivations. Central to the show was the question of an almost cyborg-like symbiosis between human and computer, the behaviours of one complementing and reinforcing the behaviours of the other. Many of the proposals were in fact intended to be systems for the automated testing of stochastically generated design alternatives—a project closely related to Friedman's work. The visual structure of these projects was as remarkable as it was broad, and it provided a snapshot of design computation at that moment.

The collection of contributors to the exhibition included a strong German contingent, but also included well-known international figures such as Eric Teicholz, from Harvard's Laboratory for Computer Graphics, and Nicholas Negroponte, founder of the Architecture Machine Group and the MIT Media Lab. Perhaps most striking was the range of design problems that were engaged algorithmically as well as combinatorially. The exhibition featured the first known parametrically generated modular wall structure (fig. 16), as well as experiments in three-dimensional cellular systems for constrained growth and adaptation (fig. 17). The modular variation of spaceframes was also a common theme. Emde's own entry to the exhibition (figs. 18–19) not only engages the generative possibility of the computer for non-standard structures but also confronts some of the basic challenges of rationalization for fabrication and assembly that are characteristic of mass-customization. Emde writes, "The building costs depend essentially upon the

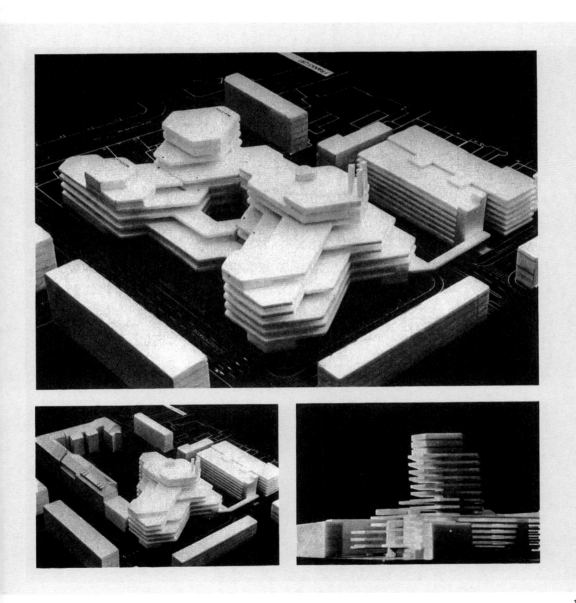

17 Pöhlmann and Hanisch. Model for an office building designed with Joachim Luther's RES (Grid-Oriented Design System), in *Architect and Computer: A Man-Machine-System*, ed. Helmut Emde (n.p., 1976), p. 12

Andrew Witt

250

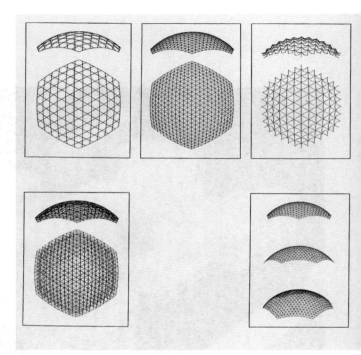

18 Helmut Emde. Spatial lattice frameworks for a hexagonal dome, in *Architect and Computer: A Man-Machine-System*, ed. Helmut Emde (n.p., 1976), p. 19

19 Helmut Emde. Conic lattice framework for the Olympic Stadium, Berlin, in *Architect and Computer: A Man-Machine-System*, ed. Helmut Emde (n.p., 1976), p. 23

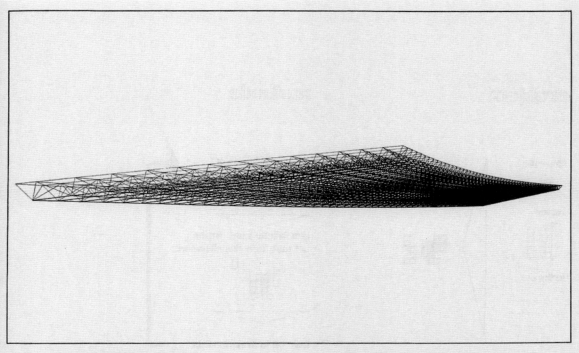

Andrew Witt

20 Joachim Luther. RES (Grid-Oriented Design System) spatial criteria flowchart, in *Architect and Computer: A Man-Machine-System*, ed. Helmut Emde (n.p., 1976), p. 5

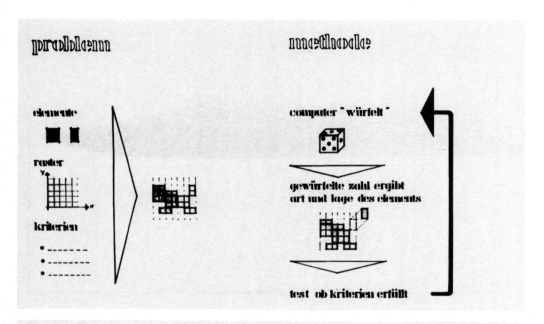

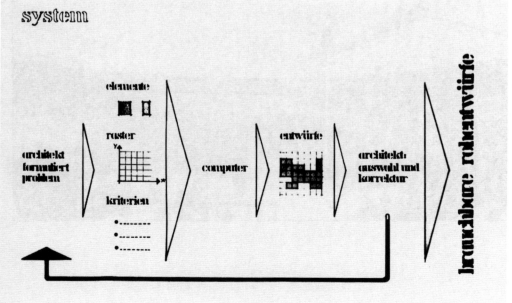

number of different types of elements, since different production equipment would normally be required. Aside from preliminary considerations of the geometrical arrangements, special modular investigations have to be made to minimize the number of types of elements and optimize the generated structures.... This minimization of types influences first, the topological structure of the lattice, i.e. the design of its geometrical arrangement. Second, it determines the metrics of the lattice elements, i.e. its modular execution."[12] Multi-objective optimization through computation of networked lattices was thus a core concern for Emde.

The exhibition served as a remarkable showcase of designer-developed software tools. Rule-based constraint solvers, embedding nuanced design criteria, took on the design of everything from modular construction components to buildings, cities and landscapes. For instance, Joachim Luther's RES (Grid-Oriented Design System) deployed a combinatorial system which stochastically produced a user-specified number of grid-based layouts conforming to user-defined criteria, a system that was strikingly similar to the Flatwriter (fig. 20). According to Luther, "The individual determines [the] grid, building elements, and the explicit criteria determining spatial structure. Consequently the machine generates solutions for the proposed design tasks in [the] form of floor plans, perspectives, gross estimates of buildings costs, etc. Finally the architect selects from these designs a solution which satisfies all his demands."[13] Eric Teicholz's GRASP (Generation of Random Access Site Plans) system was a kind of urban planning–scale version of the same idea (fig. 21). Teicholz proposed a stochastic layout process which defined building elements and found an optimal placement for them. "In this way, it is hoped that the computer, given a vocabulary of architectural units from which to choose, can produce as

Andrew Witt

254

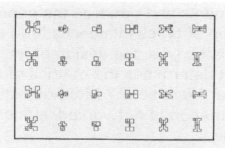

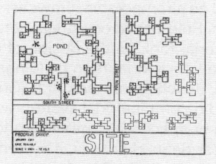 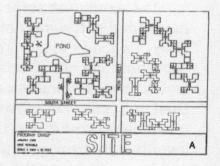

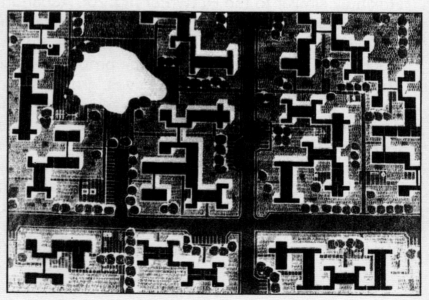

21 Eric Teicholz. GRASP (Generation of Random Access Site Plans) for the production of modular architectural units, in *Architect and Computer: A Man-Machine-System*, ed. Helmut Emde (n.p., 1976), p. 27

22 Willis and Associates. CARLA (Computer-Aided Residential Land Analysis) for finding optimal site plans, in *Architect and Computer: A Man-Machine-System*, ed. Helmut Emde (n.p., 1976), p. 31

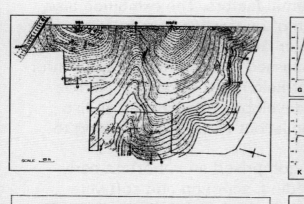
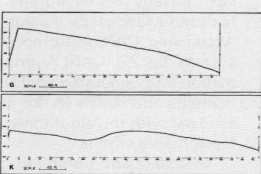
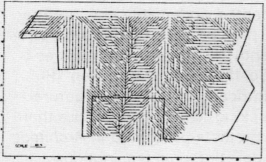
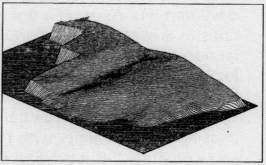

many random solutions to a plan as desired, evaluate each solution according to the specified criteria, and draw the appropriate 'best fit' solutions." The solutions produced by GRASP integrated constraints around density, development cost, privacy and environmental factors. The exhibition also featured a landscape version of generative layout: Willis and Associates' CARLA (Computer-Aided Residential Analysis) system (fig. 22). CARLA processed digitized topographic information and generated vector-field maps of results such as drainage and suitability for development purposes. It also assisted with the algorithmic layout of units conforming to topographic criteria.

Architect and Computer comprised an important early collection of designer-led coding, scripting and software development. As such it documented undeniably new approaches to archetypal architectural problems. But Emde's curatorial frame was informed significantly by his previous work as a lecturer at the Hochschule für Gestaltung Ulm between 1961 and 1968. There he developed intricate spatial and structural systems based on polyhedral packing, which had a more than passing formal affinity with the projects presented in *Architect and Computer*.[14] But beyond Emde's personal fascinations, the methodological dimension of Ulm is in conspicuous evidence in *Architect and Computer*. It is worth noting that the title of the exhibition itself, in its invocation of man–machine systems, directly refers to the writing of Ulm rector Tomás Maldonado, who had previously theorized the same symbiosis between human and machine. Thus these computational experiments can be understood as an organic extension of pre-existing numeric approaches to design with deep roots at Ulm.

23 Tomás Maldonado lecturing at the Hochschule für Gestaltung Ulm, 1956

Andrew Witt

24 The Sierpinski triangle, a programming problem posed to students at the Hochschule für Gestaltung Ulm

Ulm and Computable Knowledge

During its existence from 1953 to 1968, the Hochschule für Gestaltung Ulm was a staging ground for the development of proto-computational design methodologies, as well as a theatre for vibrant discussion of questions of objective design epistemology. Arguably the kernel of Ulm's scientific approach emerged from Maldonado's own perspective on the design–science relationship. Maldonado taught at Ulm from 1954 until 1966, a significant part of that time as rector of the school. With the help of a number of younger faculty members, he implemented a more scientifically oriented program than that of his predecessor Max Bill. The new scientism that flowered under Maldonado's direction was one of Ulm's lasting legacies (fig. 23).

In part, Ulm was an experiment in institutional propagation of mathematical knowledge within a design context. It questioned who should teach designers, what they should teach and how this teaching should be applied. Ulm's lecturers were some of the most progressive thinkers in systemic design, including Konrad Wachsmann, Buckminster Fuller, Frei Otto and Norbert Wiener. Kenneth Frampton writes that the core design course was supplemented by "a course in 'operational research,' comprising group theory, statistics, and linear programming; and...in courses dealing with the 'epistemology of science,' branching out into behavior theory and theory of machines."[15] Further mathematical courses included topics such as fractal geometry (through the Sierpinski triangle) (fig. 24), combinatorics, curve theory, set theory, probability, game theory and information theory.[16] Frampton sees these techniques as encouraging "a logical approach to the organization and generation of basic form, with the intent of applying such procedures to actual design problems." He goes on to say that "these operations varied from simple projections to three-dimensional transformations, from matrices to the manipulation of lattices, from the progressive deformation of regular grids to the rotation of ellipses centred on such grids, from the application of graph theory to topological studies, from exercises in solid geometry to the development of three-dimensional modular components which were capable of being combined in alternative sequences."[17]

The Ulm curriculum was particularly committed to a network approach or, in this approach's more technical guise, graph theory in design. This commitment stemmed from Maldonado's interest in topology as the network understanding of form. Maldonado writes: "In 1937 the British scientist J. D. Bernal was one of the first to draw attention to the future importance of topology for architecture and town and regional planning. (In this case the combinatorial or algebraic form of topology is meant, and not the set-theoretic general topology.) Bernal's prediction has been confirmed, at least in one of them: the theory of linear graphs possesses a considerable instrumental value in the design of buildings where extremely complex circulation problems must be solved—hospitals, airports, stadiums, factories, theatres, and exhibitions.... Flexible architecture, which has been hailed so often, could become a reality if this architecture of transformations could be realized with the aid of the geometry of transformations, i.e. if this 'rubber' architecture would be expressed in a 'rubber' geometry. But that is a hypothesis, the validity of which must first be proved—in other words a hypothesis which cannot be confirmed yet."[18] The faith in the network as an organizational armature for design was buttressed by numerous exercises that diagrammed architectural spaces not as plans or sections but as abstract graphs of nodes and lines. For instance, in design exercises for airport terminals, the graph structure of the spaces was developed in detail prior to any architectural proposal.

An Ulm perspective on the emerging computer, still in its gestation phase, was an organic extension of the school's predisposition to mathematical methods. The journal *Ulm* records conversations on the role of computation in design, highlighting the relevance of operational network representations in the formulation of machine-readable and communicable design problems. Martin Krampen's "Computers in Design: A Survey," the lead essay in *Ulm* 19/20, considers such questions. Krampen, though not well known to designers today, was an influential theorist of visual structure and semiotics. For Krampen, communicational issues are of primary importance in the "man-machine conversation": "In order to bring the capacities of man and computer together into a synergism it is necessary that man can directly converse with the computer, using all forms of communication which are most comfortable for him.... Man tends to develop anthropomorphic concepts about all action centers, which he perceives as capable of capricious, unpredictable, mobile responses.... The style of conversation made between man and machine should... include expressions of reinforcement for competent performance of the human operator. Man and machine should exist in a veritable symbiosis."[19] Krampen goes on to characterize a kind of ideal framework for the network representation of design problems, following the lines that Christopher Alexander had set out in his HIDECS software tools in the early 1960s.

At Ulm, Krampen was far from alone in his interest in behavioural computation. If anything, his colleague Horst Rittel more thoroughly considered these questions. Rittel was professor of design methodology at Ulm from 1958 to 1963 and became one of three directors of the school from 1959 until his departure. He was trained as a mathematician and was intimately familiar with early research in information theory, signal processing and cybernetics. His design methodologies were thus shaped to a large degree by the work of Shannon and Wiener, and his own research grew out of precisely these militarized planning approaches. This was inevitably reflected in his Ulm course, which had significant roots in war games and simulations that were intended to refine tactical and strategic approaches. Rittel also directly engaged the dual question of design communication and design rationality. At Ulm, he "argued that dichotomies purporting to distinguish systematic versus intuitive, and rational versus non-rational design are untenable. Rather, he asked, to what degree can and should design processes be made explicit, and to what extent can and should they be made communicable to others. For only communicable processes can be taught, and only explicitly formulated processes can be critically scrutinized and improved upon."[20] Rittel formulated a very specific definition of design: "an activity that aims at the production of a plan, which plan— if implemented—is intended to bring about a situation with specific desired characteristics without creating unforeseen and undesired side and after effects."[21] Design and planning were thus interchangeable.

There is a palpable lineage of early information theories that passes through Ulm and lands at a wide range of theoretical experiments in design computation. Ultimately, the experiments showcased in Emde's *Architect and Computer* reflected these earlier, and perhaps even more foundational, investigations. Moreover the Ulm project created an expectation of technical literacy in the designer, which made scripting and custom software development a feasible—indeed an inevitable—part of architecture's future.

Munich's Olympic Stadium and New Disciplinarities

While Friedman's Flatwriter and the projects included in *Architect and Computer* probed the theoretical implications of network approaches and custom software programming, these trends were also beginning to transform the progressive professional practice of design. The development of Munich's Olympic Stadium, completed in 1972, is specific evidence of this transformation: a singular moment at the intersection of design, engineering and computation (fig. 25). The stadium's sensuous, curving canopy was a revelation of a new kind of formal vocabulary. But more than being just a realization of Frei Otto's physical modelling methods, its execution in fact reveals a relationship between design, geodesy, network simulation and the reciprocity between empirical and computational tools. Moreover, the stadium would have been impossible to realize without the reorganization of the design enterprise around customized software tools, such as those introduced to use the newly developed force density method of dynamic relaxation. The Olympic Stadium revealed the need for a unique kind of technically synthetic discipline at the boundary of design, engineering and computation that would be capable of marshalling novel digital techniques for new architecture. It was not merely a grand formal experiment; it was also a prototype of a new professional synthesis of design and calculation.

Even more fundamentally, the Olympic Stadium marks a specific shift from physical modelling of form to digital representation of behaviour that took place around 1970. This was not necessarily deliberate; in fact, the Olympic Stadium's early development dramatically pushed and significantly redefined the possibilities of physical simulation. Yet ultimately it

also definitively exposed the limitations of physical models, and in doing so delineated more precisely the future role of the computer in design development and construction.

The initial project for the Olympic Stadium was the result of a 1967 competition won by Behnisch & Partner with Juergen Joedicke. The jury was skeptical of the practicality of the project. To allay some of these concerns, Frei Otto and Fritz Leonhardt, then professors of civil engineering at the Universität Stuttgart, joined the team to design the remarkable canopy more systematically. The stadium's roof consists of several anticlastic, cable-stayed tents clad with rigid transparent acrylic sheets. These tents were to be suspended by large compression masts that punctuate the elevation. The entire effect is one of a thin and diaphanous shell, hovering above and lightly shading the stadium stands.

The challenge of the canopy was twofold. First, its structural performance required an unprecedented precision of form finding. A cable-net structure had never been seriously proposed, let alone built, at this scale, and the viability of such a structure was a basic unknown. Second, its construction demanded equally precise information to cut thousands of non-standard acrylic panels. Such patterns could only derive from extremely accurate measurements of the static state of the canopy, which had never before been extracted for such a large dynamic form. These two problems hinged on the common challenge of the indeterminate quality of the canopy's tensile net. Each node in this net was interdependent; a small change in the tension of one of the net's cables would have a cascading impact on all others and would also alter the panel-cutting pattern. The project is analogous to tailoring a bespoke suit while the client is in constant motion.

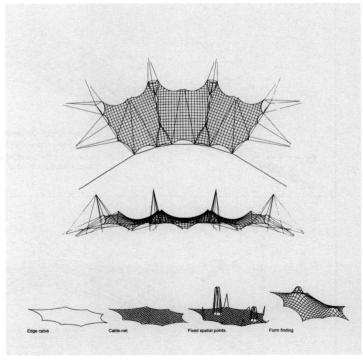

26 John Argyris. Form-finding method for long-span net structures with finite elements. Drawings by Marios C. Phocas, in "John Argyris and His Decisive Contribution in the Development of Light-Weight Structures: Form Follows Force." Lecture at the *5th Greek Association of Computational Mechanics*, Limassol, Cyprus, 29 June–1 July 2005

[27] John Argyris. ASKA (Automatic System for Kinematic Analysis) software. Reprinted in R. Goos, "The ASKA Finite Element System," in *Finite Element Systems: A Handbook*, ed. C. A. Brebbia, (Berlin: Springer-Verlag, 1985), 55–79

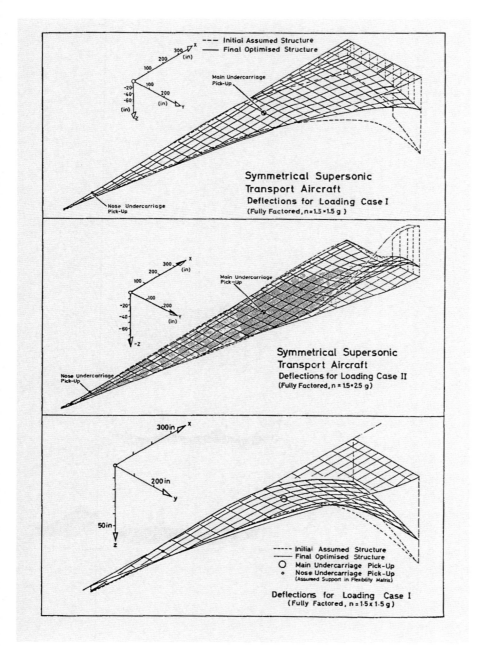

These two challenges were the catalysts for the development of two distinct but related computation methods, each drawing on the expertise of different specific disciplines. The first method is finite element analysis, the then-new procedure of indeterminate structural calculation, which was adapted from techniques used for more dynamic structures such as airframes. The finite element method had been elaborated in the late 1960s by, among others, John Argyris, a professor of aerospace structures at the Universität Stuttgart who ultimately also contributed to the Olympic Stadium (fig. 26). Finite element analysis depends on the discretization of a designed shape into a network of smaller finite parts. A solid shape is thus represented as a web of interdependent cells. Calculationally, the method actually represented an evolution of matrix-based displacement methods which embedded notions of elasticity and plasticity into massive matrices of simultaneous equations. (Interestingly, these methods are distantly related to Friedman's isoeffort maps and matrices.) Argyris encapsulated this method in customized software, ASKA (Automatic System for Kinematic Analysis), which became the foundation of his work on the Olympic Stadium (fig. 27). While the fundamentals of the finite element method predate the Munich project, Argyris was compelled to substantially enhance the technique in response to the unique demands of the canopy. Most significantly, he introduced a novel iterative approach that allowed for a continuously adaptive convergence toward increasingly stable solutions.

    The second novel computation method rationalized the cut pattern for the acrylic panels and cables from the global canopy geometry. Initially, the challenge of the panel discretization of the Munich canopy was treated as a classically cartographic problem. Otto's intricate 1:125 scale models were surveyed in exactly the same way as landscape terrain, through the use of highly precise photogrammetric cameras and numerical reconstruction. Unfortunately the models, as careful as they were, proved insufficiently exact to generate the cut patterns for the acrylic cladding panels. Thus the team developed computational methods to smooth, reconstruct and interpolate the resulting scanned data using least squares–fit splines. Like the finite element method, this interpolation method hinged on an iterative convergence. Although it is less commonly known among designers today, least squares is still in use as a key rationalization method and has been used extensively on contemporary projects such as the glass facade of Frank Gehry's Fondation Louis Vuitton.

The development of the stadium was not only a design and construction project but also a true software enterprise that involved two separate teams building what were in effect two custom software packages. The results of this work straddled the boundary between architecture, engineering and software development. While the Olympic Stadium may have been the most public example of the adaptation of custom software tools and network methods for construction, other designers were also developing digital applications specifically for the mass customization of componentized assemblies. Many of these projects also developed novel approaches to shape discretization particular to specific formal ambitions.

Knowledge, Networks and the Evolving Machinic Animal

The advent of scripting culture in design is commonly understood as a relatively contemporary development, fused inseparably to specific formal projects. Behavioural simulation is often associated with even more recent work. But in fact both of these developments were broad and relatively early consequences of the information-theoretic and cybernetic research of the late 1960s applied to emerging computational forms. In each of the case studies considered here, behavioural networks became proxies for new systems of knowledge and operational organization. Each application-specific behavioural network in turn became a coded repository for specific techniques and validation practices, embedded in new software. Ultimately, this was made possible by the emergence of scripting: the organization of knowledge through an explicit literature of operations.

    These developments also shifted the existing relationship between design and science in subtle but definitive ways. This was a moment at which design's epistemic preoccupation with science was gradually supplanted by a preoccupation with computation. In fact it was not always so clear that the computer was not simply an extension and manifestation of scientific epistemologies. The positivist and scientistic proclivities of design had emerged early in modernism, and were apparent even to outside observers. Rudolph Carnap, the famed physicist turned philosopher of science, was highly influenced by the implications of axiomatic mathematical unification and specifically by the work of mathematicians Bertrand Russell and Alfred North Whitehead. He saw the scientistic approach of the Bauhaus as something of an analogue to the new rationalism of the Vienna circle, a positivist frame for design. Within design, there was a similarly strong attraction to science as an epistemic model. Max Bill famously treated the connection between geometry and design at length in his 1949 essay "The Mathematical Approach in Contemporary

Art": "I am convinced it is possible to evolve a new form of art in which the artist's work could be founded to quite a substantial degree on a mathematical line of approach to its content.... Like those models at the Musée Poincaré in Paris where conceptions of space have been embodied in plastic shapes...they undoubtedly, provoke an aesthetic reaction in the beholder."[22] Here Bill anticipates the influence mathematical models and visualizations would have on designers in the twentieth century —not only as visual organizations of formal elements, but also as knowledge systems to be admired and perhaps emulated.

Perhaps in part because of its threat to the unique capacity of humans to process information and even to articulate knowledge, in the 1960s the computer replaced science as the key epistemic conundrum of design, and the behavioural network was a catalyst in this transformation. Or perhaps *replaced* is too strong a term; in part, the computer promised to subsume questions of scientific knowledge in design by allowing the encapsulation of entire domains of scientific method, such as structural analysis, circulational optimization and optical simulation, as componentized software.

An inicipient need for custom software drove demand for a new kind of design specialist, already recognizable in these case studies: the computational designer. An archetypal early practitioner of this new discipline was Ron Resch, particularly in his work after 1970. While within architecture Resch is probably best known for his intricately patterned folded structures undertaken during the 1960s (fig. 28), he later substantially contributed to methods of fabrication automation that parallel those of Munich's Olympic Stadium. Moreover, his techniques were a direct application of topological network armatures in the development of complex rationalization systems. Ultimately, Resch's work in folded shells led him to ambitious new

28 Ron Resch. Paper-folding study produced at the University of Utah during the 1960s

Andrew Witt

274

29 Ron Resch. Algorithmically designed Easter egg, 9.5 metres in length, comprised of 1108 congruent equilateral triangles and 524 concave hexagons, Vegreville, Alberta, 1975

29

experiments in computer graphics and the parametric simulation of these shells.

Resch was among the first to propose a fully automated approach to large-scale construction of complex geometry structures facilitated by scripting. Although Resch's work was not widely known, Robin Evans was sufficiently convinced of its implications such that he included an image of Resch's mass-customized sculpture in Vegreville, Alberta, appropriately known as the "Easter egg," in *The Projective Cast* (fig. 29). Resch details these scripting innovations in his 1973 paper "The Topological Design of Sculptural and Architectural Systems." In it, he joins many others in defining communication as the point of departure for computational methods: "The introduction of the computer into this complex set of relationships, as the greatest and fastest of machines, may only lengthen and slow down the communications process. Its introduction as a medium of communication, however, could bring together the maker, the object, and the user into a cohesive whole once more."[23] In many ways Resch was convinced of the possibility of computer-aided systems to enable direct-to-fabrication structures selected and configured by clients. In this sense his work was not so far in spirit from Friedman's Flatwriter, and indeed his language echoes this: "My work in the area of structure design, having been coupled with the computer as a medium of design and production, seems to suggest its possibility as a communications medium.... I believe from present experience that it is possible to reintroduce a 'soft prototype'; to pay attention to the subtle variations of user needs; to conceive of objects as a continuously varying class of solutions to a continuously varying set of needs; and to use these needs as input to a transformation upon this topologically conceived object class such that it determines a specific set of instructions that will work within the variations made possible by automatic machines and process."[24]

Pragmatically, Resch saw the development of networked systems as essential to the evolution of architectural form beyond convention: "The geometric surfaces employed in architectural design are typically the plane and the sphere. When one wished to build a network approximation to these ideal surfaces, or more complicated ones, a generating system is required." To move beyond these forms, Resch proposed the notion of a topological transform: "The distinction between geometric and topological generating systems is in the rule for part definition; the rule for connections being held constant. A generating system is topological if the rule for part definition is a continuous mapping of the geometry of some or all parts. It is geometric if the rule for part definition produces a unique part geometry for each of the parts. The discriminating question here is: Does the system define a continuous transformation which varies the geometry of some parts while maintaining connectivity?"[25] Resch's notion of topological form is fundamental to the entire project of contemporary parametric design and therefore to the infrastructure of encapsulated design knowledge. Indeed, Resch embodies more generally the disciplinary shifts characteristic of our case studies.

The development of new knowledge systems and knowledge practices in design around 1970 paralleled the increasing entanglement of behavioural rules in software and hardware machines. Seen only as a shadow of possibility, these bold insights suggest a trajectory on which we still find ourselves today, with a destination yet unknown. Computing machines are not yet agents unto themselves, not least because a construct of machine selfhood, its interests and its desires, remains elusive. But the animal state first grasped during the period around 1970 became a way station between the inanimate and the conscious, the mechanical and the artificially sentient. It was the potential of autonomous action and the creation of machine behaviour which were most exciting, puzzling and dismaying to these design experimentalists. These qualities are not entirely at odds with the architectural techno-formalism of the last twenty years, but they are profoundly more projective. If the computer is not simply a factory for form but is instead a mind for searching, comprehending, creating and responding to space, then the most profound transformations of design at the impetus of digital technology are still dim shadows on the horizon.

Greg Lynn

In 1987, Peter Eisenman used custom software for the design of his project for the Biozentrum at the Goethe-Universität in Frankfurt. Faxes of computer code and printed plots provide material evidence of Eisenman's working process. The Biozentrum project marks the beginning of a period, from the late 1980s to the early 2000s, in which architecture practice was transformed by the adoption of digital tools into existing, established working methods. Studying the digital and physical record of working processes from this period forms an archaeology, which can in turn provide solid ground for a history of the digital in architecture.

GREG LYNN

1   Peter Eisenman, Eisenman/
    Robertson Architects. Biozen-
    trum, Goethe-Universität,
    Frankfurt am Main, drawing
    showing the process of trans-
    cription through fractal geometry
    using the DNA code of collagen,
    1987. Technical pen on trans-
    lucent paper and graphic
    appliqué film, with correction
    fluid, 21.5 x 28 x cm. Peter
    Eisenman fonds (AP143), CCA.
    DR1999:0356:005

GOING NATIVE: NOTES ON SELECTED ARTIFACTS FROM DIGITAL ARCHITECTURE AT THE END OF THE TWENTIETH CENTURY

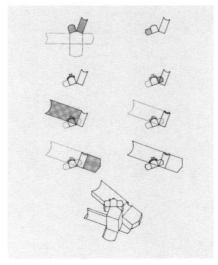

Greg Lynn

It cannot be affirmed too often that bad scholarship in the field generally involves the fruitless and final obliteration of evidence.

Mortimer Wheeler,
Archaeology from the Earth

The nearly decade-long foray into archaeology of the digital began innocently enough, with a simple question to the CCA: "Would you like a hard disk with all of the digital files related to the Embryological House, along with the models, drawings, photographs, videos and sketches?" I had asked this question many times before to other institutions, and the answers were always constrained by concerns about how to fit animations, renderings and plots into the existing categories of film, prints and drawings. But no one ever wanted the actual files; they didn't know what to do with them. What has made this such

Greg Lynn

an adventure is that the CCA asked for the files even though they too didn't know what to do with them.

The Archaeology of the Digital research program and the digital archive that it forms address two questions simultaneously. First, the question of when digital technology began to transform architects' creative process and conceptual design work was posed to identify a specific period of time and to guide a selection of twenty-five projects for the CCA to collect and study. The fundamental assumption that, in order to understand projects developed with digital technology, researchers must rely on digital archival material leads to the second critical question: how can archives that include digital content be studied, conserved, exhibited and published?
In fact, the second question prompted the initial search for twenty-five projects developed with digital technology. But regardless of which came first, these two questions formed the starting point for the CCA's digital archive and provided the direction, rather than simply the subject, of Archaeology of the Digital.

An archaeologist is not a historian. The focus of archaeology is not on coherent narratives but on the collection and organization of material artifacts. There is no continuous historical narrative structuring the Archaeology of the Digital program. The history of digital technology in architecture is already being written and it spans decades—some would say centuries—but if it is written without a foundation in archaeology, it is necessarily a limited history. It is certainly possible to write a history of the computer, the algorithm or the numerical machine and to include examples from the present within a longer temporal narrative. This has been done exceptionally well, and in the context of an exhibition, in *Architectures non standard*, organized and curated by Frédéric Migayrou and Zeynep Mennan at the Centre Georges Pompidou in 2003 and 2004. But if the work of the 1990s is defined only by earlier developments, much will be overlooked in both the legacy and the inheritance of digital technology in architecture. For example, the work of Nicholas Negroponte and the Architecture Machine Group at the Massachusetts Institute of Technology was of course deeply influential for architects using digital tools in the 1990s. One cannot write a history of digital architecture without relation to Negroponte, but neither can one simply trace Kas Oosterhuis's work with interactivity, software programming, mechatronics and transformable structures to the Architecture Machine Group. Before imposing legacies and defining influences, it is essential that historians have access to an archaeology that draws from an archive of digital material.

Inferences about the role of digital tools can be made by looking at completed buildings; the physical materials derived from digital design files; the claims made by designers, engineers, builders and clients; and off-the-shelf software. But to write a lucid history of digital architecture, scholars must consult the physical and digital archival materials specific to a project. It is impossible to fully understand Bernini's elliptical colonnade and trapezoidal plaza of St. Peter's Square without the ability to use a drafting compass. Similarly, it is impossible to fully understand Michelangelo's distorted oval of the Campidoglio without this same facility with a compass and the ability to construct a one-point perspective drawing. Just as historians and critics were trained in the conventions of drawing and measure, they now need access to digital tools and files.

The advent of the computer produced a cottage industry of futurists who predicted innovations that would follow the adoption of digital tools; texts written by theorists and architects from the period often make unreliable sources for historians. Designers frequently claimed that software and hardware could do things that in fact they only hoped would soon be done. Too often the word *digital*, in architecture, was followed by the promise of "in the future." The theoretical tone surrounding digital media in architecture was primarily promissory and, worse, often a thin futuristic proclamation. Archaeology of the Digital assumes that digital technology can no longer be discussed *in the future* but instead must be discussed in the recent past. Mirko Zardini defines this principle as a difference between a projective historical narrative and an archaeological expedition into the recent past, and it has guided the collection, exhibition and publication of archival material over the course of the research program. In the late 1990s, thematic exhibitions on the digital in architecture began with a formal or cultural assumption to situate the digital impact on architecture and focused on architectural traits or formal language that could be understood as a consequence of digital technology. These exhibitions included *Folds, Blobs, and Boxes: Architecture in the Digital Era*, curated by Joseph Rosa at the Carnegie Museum of Art in 2001; *Skin + Bones: Parallel Practices in Fashion and Architecture*, curated by Brooke Hodge at the Museum of Contemporary Art in Los Angeles in 2007; *Digital Real: Blobmeister, First Built Projects*, curated by Peter Cachola Schmal at the Deutsches Architekturmuseum in 2001; and the Venice Biennale's 7th International Architecture Exhibition, *Less Aesthetics, More Ethics*, curated by Massimiliano Fuksas in 2000. These exhibitions proclaimed the innovation brought about by digital technology and projected this innovation into the future. With the exception of *Digital Real*, which claimed a first qualitative evaluation of buildings designed with digital tools, the exhibitions announced a new digital regime pioneered by their participants.

Archaeology of the Digital addresses the 1980s, the 1990s and the early 2000s as a specific period in the past, rather than as the harbinger of things to come. Instead of promising a digital future, the archaeological approach intends to collect the recent past before it disappears. The term *archaeology* is especially appropriate, as the digital files for several projects selected for study had been lost and all that remained were printouts of software programming code, plots, printed renderings, audio recordings, videotape footage and photographs. And for almost all of the twenty-five projects, there are files that cannot be opened using contemporary software. The archaeological method uncovered an acute problem of access, for the purposes of both study and display. Several reconstructions were undertaken, including building Karl Chu's Catastrophe Machine, 3D-printing a model of Preston Scott Cohen's Eyebeam Atelier Museum from stereolithography (STL) files, machining an Objectile wall panel through computer numerical control (CNC) from Bernard Cache's G-code and reanimating ONL's Festo muscles using original proximity sensors. The Archaeology of the Digital exhibitions were conceived as tools to understand the nature of the materials entering the archive for cataloguing and preservation. Although many of the projects are familiar to critics, theorists and historians, the digital archival materials have never been available for research before. It is unlikely that anyone would be able to write a full history of the digital before gaining a technical and creative understanding of its role through study of these materials.

This method often challenged assumptions about the tools and the period. The ideas that designers were late adopters of off-the-shelf software and that they had no interest in

Greg Lynn

2 Chuck Hoberman, Hoberman Associates Expanding Sphere, calculations and geometrical analysis of the movements of the expanding structure, 1988. Graphite on paper, 21.6 x 27.9 cm. Chuck Hoberman fonds (AP165), CCA. Gift of Chuck Hoberman

3 Objectile (Bernard Cache, Patrick Beaucé). Objectile, screen capture of the interface of TopSolid version 5 showing variations of surfaces through the manipulation of a parametric equation, 1998. Original file: ondul6.jpg, 139 KB, last modified 29 September 1998. Objectile fonds (AP169), CCA. Gift of Bernard Cache

288

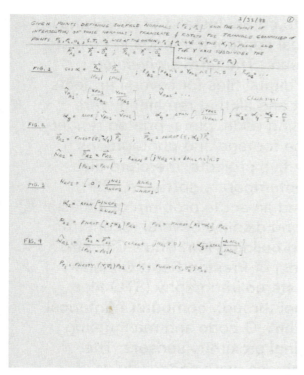

2

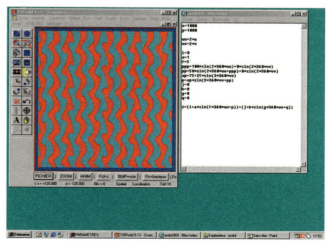

3

coding and programming were disproved by archival material. In 1987—the earliest point in this archaeological survey— Peter Eisenman worked with Chris Yessios at the Ohio State University to develop the first industry-standard 3D solid modeller, called FormZ, during the design of his project for the Frankfurt Biozentrum competition. The digital plots, faxes of coordinates fed into the computer and examples of notations of the hidden line perspectives show how Eisenman's office had written custom software for the design of the project. According to Yessios, Eisenman thought and designed like a computer, using procedural operations that could be coded and scripted numerically (fig. 1). Similarly, Chuck Hoberman's archive of the Expanding Sphere project revealed numerous software programs that he had written to study complex mechanical motions as well as some of the earliest 3D prints and building components manufactured through CNC (fig. 2). And for his Objectile panels, Bernard Cache worked directly with software developers, often writing code for the programs themselves, as off-the-shelf solutions either did not exist, were too exotic or were unknown to him (fig. 3).

An archaeology of digital tools from the late 1980s through the early 2000s can be divided into three stages according to architecture's changing concerns with respect to digital technology. A first stage addresses architecture's initial encounter with digital technology, which articulated a set of questions for the discipline. A second concerns the integration of interactive media and robotics into architectural projects. A third stage provides a thematic grouping of developments that could be used to build a history of the digital. Archaeology of the Digital articulates this sequence with a series of three exhibitions that address four, six and fifteen projects respectively.

Greg Lynn

Archaeology of the Digital

The first exhibition, called *Archaeology of the Digital*, offered a chronological selection of projects that were among the first to use digital technology. There was a general assumption that, in the late 1980s and early 1990s, the first architects to use digital tools were the young designers who congregated around the paperless studios initiated by Dean Bernard Tschumi at Columbia University's Graduate School of Architecture, Planning and Preservation and at new media art institutions such as the Ars Electronica Center and V2_ Institute for the Unstable Media. But, in fact, important design work with digital technology during this period was carried out by Peter Eisenman, Frank Gehry, Chuck Hoberman and Shoei Yoh— established architects who incorporated digital tools into their design repertoire. Each architect had already clearly formulated a role for digital technology in their way of working. Each knew what he wanted and either sought out specific hardware and software or engaged programmers to invent the necessary tools to realize a design. Although the architects were using technology in ways that were unfamiliar to them, their work was always guided by a creative and critical mandate that allowed for qualitative evaluation. The projects are not a collection of happy accidents produced by dilettantes and amateurs, but rather thoughtful developments by designers with great insight into digital tools. Eisenman, Gehry, Hoberman and Yoh approached the digital medium with a perspicacity and an intelligence that made the digital not merely a tool but a new creative medium integral to their design process. The projects did not spring fully formed from a software program, and in each case the digital tools were put to guided use and were compared to alternative methods. The four architects articulated

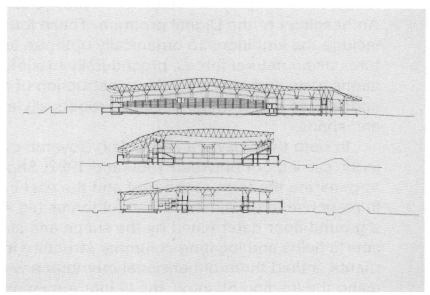

4 Shoei Yoh + Architects. Municipal Sports Complex, Odawara, Kanagawa, Japan, sections, 1990–1991. Electrostatic print on paper, 42 x 29.7 cm. Shoei Yoh fonds (AP166), CCA. Gift of Shoei Yoh

Greg Lynn

four directions for the use of digital technology that would reappear in the projects studied in subsequent phases of the Archaeology of the Digital program. These four directions include the ambitions to organically optimize and form structures using natural forces, procedurally execute formal operations, gain authority over the construction of complex forms and spaces and animate buildings robotically to change size and shape.

In both the Odawara and Galaxy Toyama gymnasium projects, carried out between 1990 and 1992, Shoei Yoh aspired to generate the form of the roof and the vast interior space in response to physical and natural forces (fig. 4). By defining a ground floor determined by the shape and size of different sports fields and locating columnar structure in these alignments, a fluid three-dimensional membrane was developed using the loading of snow, the height requirements for the various functions below and the spans. Digital tools were used for form finding and optimization to generate shape as well as lightweight, inexpensive structure. Acquiring a textile-like quality, the roof of the Odawara Municipal Sports Complex is in fact a non-standard wireframe structure composed of individual steel rods and joints, a system that had evolved from previous research Yoh conducted with prefabricated assembled construction techniques. The different length and angle of each individual rod allowed Yoh to modify the depth of the roof itself to create, in his own words, a "3D topology" that is both sustainable and economical (fig. 5). The dimensioning of roof elements responds to certain external factors, calculated and verified by the computers of the consulting engineering company Taiyo Kogyo. Yoh used the computer to give the buildings a sense of forces in nature and his digital modelling and simulation, done in collaboration with structural engineers

5 Shoei Yoh + Architects. Municipal Sports Complex, Odawara, Kanagawa, Japan, computer-generated images for structural analysis of the roof, 1990–1991. Electrostatic print on plastic, 36.4 x 25.7 cm. Shoei Yoh fonds (AP166), CCA. Gift of Shoei Yoh

6 Peter Eisenman, Eisenman/Robertson Architects. Biozentrum, Goethe-Universität, Frankfurt am Main, schematic representation of a DNA sequence, 1987. Electrostatic print on paper with ink notations, 21.5 x 28 cm. Peter Eisenman fonds (AP143), CCA. DR1999:0646

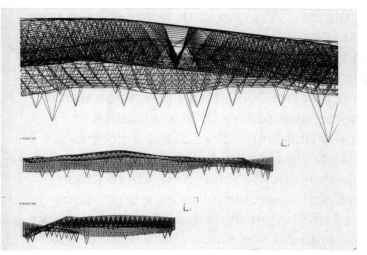

5

6

and contractors, resulted in complex geometries of space-frames. The physical phenomena of light, form and material defined the ambition of Yoh's designs and he integrated digital technology into his working method as the medium for creation as well as for calculation. Working with both German and Japanese engineering software, he used digital tools for analysis, form generation and one of the first-ever instances of a direct-to-manufacture construction method.

For the Biozentrum project of 1987, Peter Eisenman used iterations of pairs of figures resembling DNA molecules to define four- and five-storey building blocks along a central spine (fig. 6). A fractal-like technique to duplicate these figures at varying scales and oblique orientations along shared faces was developed, using a Cray supercomputer as a procedural modelling tool capable of drafting predefined figures at varying alignments and scales in endless sequences based on logical statements in code. These chains of figures were designed by revising coded sequences that were faxed daily to a computer lab at the Ohio State University, where custom software was written and plots were made. Using the newly available overnight delivery service of Federal Express, these plots were later marked up and revised in Eisenman's New York office, and new codes were transmitted back to Ohio (fig. 7). Eisenman was looking for a digital counterpart to his vision for a rational linguistic tool capable of creating complex overlapping figures with intricate alignments, connections and scales scripted using logical statements that could be revised and repeated endlessly. The oscillation between written code and algorithms, between plotted arrays and plans drafted with adjustable triangles, and the ability to visualize the spine space using layers of objects based on their iterative generation was a hybrid between digital and analog design.

Whereas Eisenman looked to the digital as a tool to execute formal operations according to a logical and procedural method, Frank Gehry, with the Lewis Residence, sought both the expressive potential of digital technology and a way to regain control over intricate shapes and structures, which would put the architect back in a position of authority during the process of engineering, bidding and construction. The incessant feedback loops between sketches, three-dimensional computer simulations, built models and engineering drawings caused the Lewis Residence project to undergo many creative leaps and transformations during its seven-year period of design, between 1989 and 1995 (fig. 8). The design evolved rapidly in conjunction with the development of digital tools for scanning, building and describing physical models. Gehry's office had already been working with computer-aided three-dimensional interactive application (CATIA) software on the fish sculpture in Barcelona, but in the house for Peter Lewis, modelling, scanning and manufacturing technologies were used in the formal expression of surfaces and their underlying structure and not simply for documentation (figs. 9–10). The point-scanning hardware for digitizing physical models was aligned with 3D-printing techniques such as stereolithography and laminar object modelling. Technical innovations and formal and construction languages that matured in Gehry's later projects were first developed in the Lewis Residence. Moreover, many of the issues uncovered at this time became the core competence of the independent software and services company Gehry Technologies. The sequential changes to the design of the Lewis Residence show that the computer was not only a tool used to document and deliver the project, but also a partner in the development of an expressive formal and spatial design language.

Greg Lynn

296

7 Peter Eisenman, Eisenman/Robertson Architects. Biozentrum, Goethe-Universität, Frankfurt am Main, study plan, 1987. Electrostatic print on paper with black and red ink and graphite notations, 27.9 x 21.6 cm. Peter Eisenman fonds (AP143), CCA. DR1999:0573:001

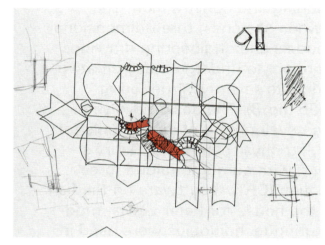

7

8

8 Frank O. Gehry & Associates. Lewis Residence, Lyndhurst, Ohio, United States, model showing the west elevation view of the conservatory and pool, 1994

9 Frank O. Gehry & Associates. Lewis Residence, Lyndhurst, Ohio, United States, perspective from a CATIA 3D model, 1994. Electrostatic print on paper, 127 x 91.4 x cm

10 Frank O. Gehry & Associates. Lewis Residence, Lyndhurst, Ohio, United States, model of the conservatory made from 3D surfaces, showing the structural support, 1995

9

10

Greg Lynn

11 Chuck Hoberman, Hoberman Associates. Iris Dome, rendering of the structure, 1990–1994. Dot matrix print on paper, 21.7 x 28 cm. Chuck Hoberman fonds (AP165), CCA. Gift of Chuck Hoberman

12 Chuck Hoberman, Hoberman Associates. Expanding Sphere, collage, 1991. Electrostatic prints on paper, adhered to paper, 43.2 x 28 cm. Chuck Hoberman fonds (AP165), CCA. Gift of Chuck Hoberman

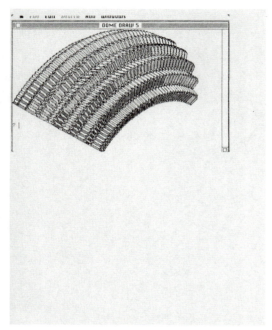

11

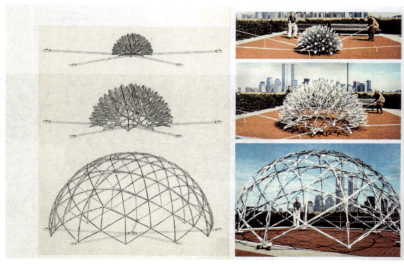

12

In his Expanding Sphere and Iris Dome projects, carried out between 1988 and 1994, Chuck Hoberman used digital technology to design objects and structures that can change size and shape through coordinated mechanical movement. The use of computers—in particular of AutoLISP, customized commands for CAD drawings, which Hoberman coded himself—was crucial for solving the complex mathematical and geometrical calculations necessary to control the design and engineering of each moving component. Hoberman drafted the principles of transforming geometric motion and then wrote AutoLISP scripts to test for collisions (fig. 11). The mechanisms were manufactured at small scales using the earliest 3D printing technology and at larger scales using CNC milling router tables and lathes. Large-scale mechanical connections were made by cutting solid aluminum billet into custom shapes and profiles. The Expanding Sphere and Iris Dome are mechatronic prototypes that can be adapted for multiple uses—from toys to buildings that become giant robots (fig. 12).

An archaeology of the selected projects by Yoh, Eisenman, Gehry and Hoberman broadly defines a set of concerns for architects working with digital technologies, including custom software, high-fidelity 3D models for fabrication and construction, point scans and complex-curve geometries, structural and environmental data and algorithmic procedures for form generation. The second stage of Archaeology of the Digital and the exhibition that accompanied it, called *Media and Machines*, addressed the extension of the architectural object beyond a building through an intensive use of digital technology and the integration of media into space to create interactive environments.

Greg Lynn

Media and Machines

The projects chosen for the second phase include Asymptote Architecture's New York Stock Exchange Virtual Trading Floor and Command Center, Karl Chu's Catastrophe Machine and X Phylum, Bernard Cache's Objectile panels, dECOi Architects' HypoSurface, ONL's NSA Muscle and NOX's H_2Oexpo. The creative breadth of this group of architects extends from the design of buildings to the design of interactive media, interactive robotic mechanisms, dynamic drafting machines, generative algorithms, websites, digital 3D models, digital animation files, CAD drawings and renderings, physical models, sketches and architectural and cultural theories. The difficulty in collecting and displaying material from these projects echoes the questions that the projects posed for architecture in the 1990s. At the time, architects and artists rethought the edges and centres of their fields in light of the immersion, interaction and immateriality made possible through digital media. As architects expanded the scope of their design work into art and media practices, they explored ways to engage people in intelligent, interactive environments along with the proposition that buildings should be active rather than passive. These projects resulted from a desire to create interactive spaces, to enrich environments with media and machines, and they remain the most relevant examples of architecture's engagement with the experience of digital technology.

Architects and artists working in Europe in the 1990s defined new interactions between digital media and digitally designed structures. In particular, the thriving digital media art culture in Austria and the Netherlands fostered these interactions through galleries, museums, festivals and generous grants for projects. In this context, Lars Spuybroek and his

13 NOX (Lars Spuybroek). H$_2$Oexpo, Neeltje Jans, the Netherlands, 3D model of the pavilion, 1996. AutoCAD file converted to scalable vector graphics format for publication. Original file: 3D model maybe metal skin with layers.dwg, 1.8 MB, last modified 24 January 1996. Lars Spuybroek fonds (AP173), CCA. Gift of Lars Spuybroek

14 NOX (Lars Spuybroek). H$_2$Oexpo, Neeltje Jans, the Netherlands, interior view, 1997. Original file: Bokay.tif, 8.5 MB, last modified 7 August 1997. Lars Spuybroek fonds (AP173), CCA. Gift of Lars Spuybroek

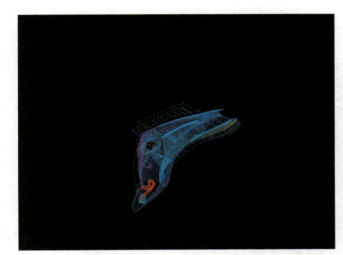

13

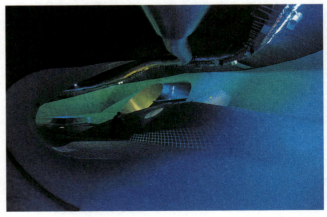

14

Greg Lynn

302

15 Asymptote Architecture (Hani Rashid and Lise Anne Couture). New York Stock Exchange Virtual Trading Floor, digital rendering, 1997. Original file: 3nyse.jpg, 125 KB, last modified 7 February

2001. Asymptote Architecture New York Stock Exchange Virtual Trading Floor and Command Center project records (AP184), CCA. Gift of Asymptote

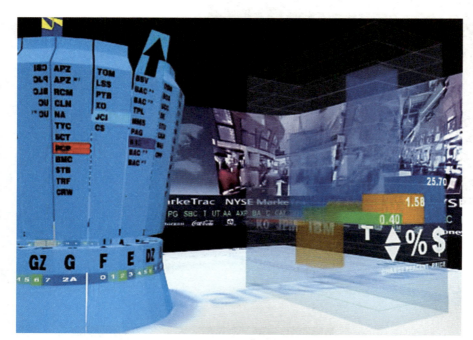

15

office, NOX, collaborated extensively with V2_ Institute for the Unstable Media, an international centre for media art, technology, music and architecture in Rotterdam. NOX's H$_2$Oexpo pavilion, a visitors' centre in the Netherlands dedicated to water, was an immersive, interactive digital environment that synthesized the experience of physical and digital media through sloping ground planes, dynamic lighting, projected patterns and images, sound and other kinesthetic elements (fig. 13). The pavilion, completed in 1997, was the first building to convincingly combine topological surfaces designed with computer software with digitally projected and controlled interactive media (fig. 14). Spuybroek was deeply engaged with philosophies of perception, balance, kinesthesia and motion, and the space and geometry of the H$_2$Oexpo pavilion reflect his interest in immersive multidisciplinary media. Interactive sound, images, light and moisture throughout the space engaged both individual and group movement.

The interest in media and interactivity extended to virtual environments. Architecture begins with the virtual definition of a building through drawings and models, and in the 1990s the virtual model was exploited for its ability to be experienced through digital media. An extreme example of this is the New York Stock Exchange Virtual Trading Floor, a virtual-reality environment that parallels the physical New York Stock Exchange in order to visualize real-time numerical and statistical data. Hani Rashid and Lise Anne Couture of Asymptote Architecture had been experimenting with photography, collage and image projection, and they were among the first architects drawn to three-dimensional texture-mapped digital environments for their spatial consequences. For the virtual trading floor project in 1997, Asymptote worked with Softimage and Alias software for modelling, rendering and animating and with VRML (virtual reality modelling language) and Macromedia Flash in order to integrate real-time data into a navigable three-dimensional environment. Virtual versions of the circular booths where traders are stationed on the floor integrate dynamic graphic elements that display data and allow the user to zoom in on a particular stock (fig. 15). Other elements communicate trends in individual stocks and the atmosphere of the entire market through colour and motion. Web-based applications, such as MarkeTrac, were also proposed and developed. The virtual trading floor and these later proposals have proven to be prescient about how we navigate the world today, whether it is in virtual environments or with augmented reality devices.

Whereas Chuck Hoberman used digital technology to design, simulate, engineer, fabricate and control robotic structures for the Expanding Sphere, other architects looked to the dynamism of robotics not as an architectural and structural paradigm but rather in terms of its potential to create interactivity and a new form of engagement with built objects, in which the movement of people relates to the movement of the space in a reciprocal relationship of influence. The NSA Muscle by Kas Oosterhuis and Ilona Lénárd of ONL and Hyposurface by Mark Goulthorpe's dECOi Architects use robotics rather than digital media to create interactive spaces. Both projects integrate environmental sensors with mechanical control systems to move dynamic building components in relation to the movement of people.

ONL's NSA Muscle is a pneumatic paradigm for a malleable, dynamic and deforming room. It was designed and constructed in 2003 and 2004 for the *Architectures non standard* exhibition (fig. 16). Fluidity of form is achieved through the use of pneumatics for a soft inflatable envelope and for hydraulic robotic actuation. The moving room is controlled with Virtools

16 ONL [Oosterhuis_Lénárd] (Kas Oosterhuis, Ilona Lénárd). NSA Muscle, installation view at the *Architectures non standard* exhibition, Centre Georges Pompidou, 2003. Original file: DSC02769.jpg, 1.7 MB, last modified 10 December 2003. ONL [Oosterhuis_Lénárd] NSA Muscle project records (AP167), CCA. Gift of Kas Oosterhuis

17 ONL [Oosterhuis_Lénárd] (Kas Oosterhuis, Ilona Lénárd). NSA Muscle, Virtools simulation showing changes in shape, 2003. Original file: configurations.jpg, 85 KB, last modified 1 April 2004. ONL [Oosterhuis_Lénárd] NSA Muscle project records (AP167), CCA. Gift of Kas Oosterhuis

16

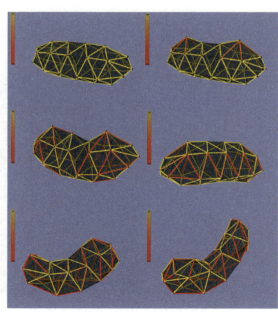

17

Greg Lynn

18 dECOi Architects (Mark Goulthorpe). Hyposurface, installation view, 2004. Original file: Oblivion.jpg, 2.3 MB, last modified 7 May 2007. Mark Goulthorpe Hyposurface project records (AP170), CCA. Gift of Mark Goulthorpe

19 dECOi Architects (Mark Goulthorpe). Hyposurface, screen capture of an interface prototype, 2001. Original file: DOS interface.jpg, 45.8 KB, last modified 10 November 2013. Mark Goulthorpe Hyposurface project records (AP170), CCA. Gift of Mark Goulthorpe

18

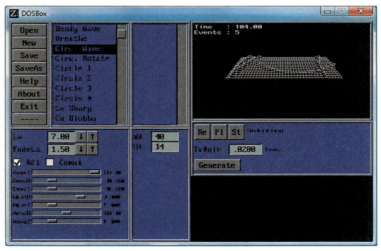

19

software, owned by Dassault Systèmes. Virtools combines 3D virtual space with programmed interactivity in real-time relationships between sensor input and the devices that control the behaviour of the muscle (fig. 17). The movement of people near the muscle is measured by sensor input and then fed to the controller, triggering preset behaviours including tensing and relaxing of the robotic muscles as well as sounds. ONL programmed the muscle to behave as if it had a will of its own in order to stimulate spontaneous interactivity between human and architecture machine.

Goulthorpe's Hyposurface has the spatial character of digitally modelled polygonal surfaces that create visual effects, commonly called "bump" or "displacement" mapping. Goulthorpe brought this digital texturing tool into physical construction at the scale of a building—not as a frozen force in static sculpture but as a dynamic machine. The Hyposurface is a wall, a "skin" divided into pixel-like metallic facets and manipulated by a network of actuating pistons in order to create images, texts and patterns in dynamic relief (fig. 18). The Hyposurface features sensors that allow people near the wall to influence its movement; this interactivity then generates the visual effects displayed on the wall. Prototypes of the project have explored mechatronics, sensor systems, sound design, image projection and lighting techniques, involving multiple teams of collaborators. Under Goulthorpe's direction, computer programmers, architects, engineers, composers, mathematicians and manufacturers from Australia, the United Kingdom, France and Canada worked together on the project through its various iterations, a collaboration made possible because everyone involved could speak the language of computer code. The teams developed a custom software program called AC/DC and then Aegis Hyposurface, which could operate the physical wall in real space using a virtual simulacrum on a computer screen (fig. 19). Virtual collaboration around the world through email was carried out in parallel to the design, engineering and prototyping of the physical wall, and the first prototype was exhibited at the Venice Biennale's 7th International Architecture Exhibition in 2000.

Coding and programming were created during the course of the design and execution of every one of the projects mentioned so far. Some architects made the algorithm itself the subject of design. Karl Chu and Bernard Cache used a mathematical approach to software that led to algorithmic design processes for the definition of geometry and, in Cache's case, an entirely new and expanded role for the architect that involved controlling the cost estimation and fabrication of building components, thereby eliminating the role of the construction manager.

Karl Chu's X Phylum and Catastrophe Machine were treated as one conceptual project. Like many other architects in the 1990s, Chu was immersed in the way the disciplines of biology and physics used computation to visualize structure and growth. The use of mathematical topological models to describe non-linear behaviours in these fields drew architects like Chu to the Santa Fe Institute and to the work of epigeneticist René Thom, whose catastrophe theory had a profound impact on many disciplines in the 1990s. Thom's mathematical principles described changes in both state and position that are non-linear but continuously calculable through the use of topological models with inflection points called cusps. The dynamic behaviours described by these topological models were depicted by the mathematician Christopher Zeeman through devices made of wheels and rubber bands, machines reminiscent of the pantographs and compasses used for drafting and measurement by architects, only with non-linear behaviour. Chu's Catastrophe Machine and X Phylum display the interaction between drafting and digital modelling that was common in the 1990s. The Catastrophe Machine is a drafting machine that exhibits the variation and unpredictability of stochastic mathematics. The CCA reconstructed this machine for the *Media and Machines* exhibition, following the archives of Chu's design (fig. 20). X Phylum is one of the first projects to explore spline-based topological digital modelling and it involved the most powerful digital technology available for the geometric visualization of mathematical principles. Chu was deeply committed to technology and was the first architect to purchase a Silicon Graphics Indigo workstation and a licence of Alias software, which allowed him to generate spline surfaces with a Lindenmayer system of branching lines in three-dimensional space (fig. 21). His focus was not on buildings but on systemic research into serial families of topological surfaces. Chu's approach indicates a wider trend. In the 1990s, architects used editing tools in software like Alias, Softimage, Wavefront and Maya to write scripts to perform modelling exercises. For the Embryological House project, carried out between 1997 and 2001, I generated scripts for more than fifty thousand houses in Microsoft Excel and then exported the code into an expression editor to generate geometric surfaces. This approach to modelling using animation software later inspired the development of software like Grasshopper for Rhinoceros 3D and Bentley's GenerativeComponents, and heralded a new wave of research on parametricism in architecture, as theorized by Patrik Schumacher and others.

Among the twenty-five projects selected for study, the most ambitious paradigm for regaining a more expansive role for the architect that encompasses the conception and the

Greg Lynn

310

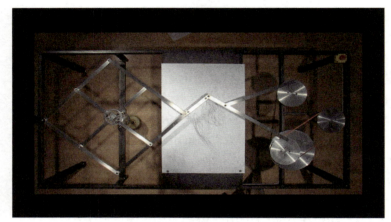

20 Metaxy (Karl Chu). Catastrophe Machine, reconstruction for the exhibition *Archaeology of the Digital: Media and Machines* at the CCA, 2014. Karl Chu X Phylum and Catastrophe Machine project records (AP176), CCA. Gifts of Karl Chu and Afsheen Rais Rohani

20

21 Metaxy (Karl Chu). X Phylum, translation in plan of a rule-set into splines (*upper right*), orthographic projection of splines (*upper left*) and lofted and rendered transparent views of splines (*bottom*), 1997–1998. Original file: 620_Phylom_ego2.tif, 42 MB, last modified 1 June 2001. Karl Chu X Phylum and Catastrophe Machine project records (AP176), CCA. Gifts of Karl Chu and Afsheen Rais Rohani

22 Objectile (Bernard Cache, Patrick Beaucé). Objectile, decorative wooden panel manufactured by a computer numerical control machine, 1998. Original file: OBJE_999_01_183.jpg, 87.1 KB, last modified 7 February 2014. Objectile fonds (AP169), CCA. Gift of Bernard Cache

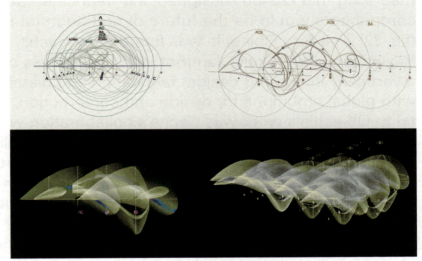

21

22

execution of buildings was proposed by Bernard Cache with his Objectile panels. Cache was a critical figure in the discipline of architecture in the 1990s. He wrote the canonical book *Earth Moves* and collaborated with Gilles Deleuze, contributing to the book *Le pli*. He was the first to establish the connection between native-digital design software and CNC machines, theorizing that custom-designed and -fabricated building components would be the future of architectural production (fig. 22). The firm Objectile was founded by Cache, Patrick Beaucé and Jean-Louis Jammot in 1996 and was conceived as a vertically integrated design, fabrication and distribution office with global ambitions for design and construction. Fundamental to Objectile's work was Cache's collaboration with Missler Software for the design and development of TopSolid software. Objectile established partnerships not only with software companies but also with manufacturers and distributors in France, the Netherlands, the United Kingdom, Singapore, New Zealand and the United States. With a software platform for the design of endless variations of families of elements and a network of machines around the world, an architect could send a file to Singapore, New York or New Zealand and have it made, just as a document is sent to the printer. Objectile was one of the first architecture firms to have a website, through which users could order decorative panels from six families of patterns and even manipulate an online interface to determine their own unique patterns (fig. 23). Cache's radical proposition to link parametric design software directly to robotic manufacture might explain the rapidity with which his work was consumed, imitated and reproduced by both experimental and corporate practices. His design influence could be seen in elevators, hotel lobbies, airports and restaurants around the world only a decade later, just as he proposed it should be. Using the

23 Objectile (Bernard Cache, Patrick Beaucé). Objectile, website showing six choices of panels, 1998. Screen capture for publication. Original file: pane.htm, 5.3 KB, last modified 21 February 1999. Objectile fonds (AP169), CCA. Gift of Bernard Cache

[Objectile](#) : other operations   switch to : [French](#)

Decorative wooden panels

manufactured by numerical command machine tools
(Copyright Objectile)

Thanks to its knowledge in surfaces calculation and machining programms generation, Objectile developed six ranges of decorative panels the design of which can vary on demand. Objectile panels have won the golden medal for innovative products at the international trade fair of building components Batimat in November 1997

OBJECTILE'S SIX RANGES OF PANELS CATALOGUE

incisions   acousticals   screens   grooved   patterns   surfaces

Technical customization:

A wide variety of purposes: particular references   Objectile designs can be machined in many types of materials : MDF, plywood with colored veneer or not, plainwood, stone, metal, glass, etc.
These panels can be adapted on demand to all types of sub-divisions with no constraints other than the size of the available boards.

Design customization:

Objectile proposes a catalogue of designs which can be used as shown or re-interpreted
- geometrical adaptation: catalogue designs can easily be widened, repeated, densified, etc, on demand.
- interactive design: Objectile also enable their customers to generate their own design by simply moving sliders which modify a video image.

Customized contouring, rebates, grooves on demand. Finishing on demand: rough, varnish, laquer or rough, with natural or colored veneers.
Fireproof : solutions for all types of requirements (specially for high building regulations)
Acoustics : Objectile provides very good designs for both absorbtive and diffusive effects
Delocalization : Objectile machining programms can adapted to all types of machines and be excuted anywhere in the world.

other Objectile operations

original archival machine code to run a CNC router, the CCA reconstructed an Objectile panel in Montreal and displayed it alongside an original panel from the permanent collection of the Frac Centre—a testament to Cache's numerical, mathematical and algorithmic approach to design and fabrication.

In the current age of the internet of things and the Fourth Industrial Revolution of manufacturing on demand, the six projects selected for *Media and Machines* seem highly relevant for their concern with smart buildings, interactive environments and direct-to-manufacture approaches to design. But the discipline of architecture has delegated these concerns to what have become the largest and most profitable companies in the world, notably Google and Microsoft. Cache's comprehensive rethinking of the role of the architect through CNC fabrication has not been carried through seamlessly in subsequent years, and the majority of contemporary architects focus their creativity on CNC craftsmanship of complex structures and enclosures on much narrower algorithmic and cultural terms.

Complexity and Convention

By the late 1990s, digital tools had been broadly integrated into architecture practice. The fifteen projects that comprise the third phase of Archaeology of the Digital were carried out in this period, and each project often involved several digital processes or approaches. For earlier projects, many of the native-digital files had been lost, hardware to open files had ceased to exist, data storage formats had become obsolete and custom or commercial software programs were no longer compatible with archived data. The opposite is true for the last group of projects; there is a vast quantity of digital material and the hardware and software used more than a decade ago is often still operational.

    The third exhibition, called *Complexity and Convention*, groups specific digital content from individual projects into categories, emphasizing commonalities and cross-pollinations of the digital medium and digital methods. The projects selected are the Erasmus Bridge (1990–1996) by Van Berkel & Bos Architectuurbureau; the Chemnitz Stadium (1995) by Peter Kulka with Ulrich Königs; the O/K Apartment (1995–1997) by Kolatan/Mac Donald Studio; the Yokohama International Port Terminal (1995–2002) by Foreign Office Architects; *Interrupted Projections* (1996) by Neil M. Denari Architects; the Kansai-kan, National Diet Library (1996) by Reiser + Umemoto; the Hypo Alpe-Adria Center (1996–2002) by Morphosis; the Jyväskylä Music and Arts Centre (1997) by OCEAN North; the Witte Arts Center (2000) by Office dA; the Phaeno Science Centre (2000–2005) by Zaha Hadid Architects; Villa Nurbs (2000–2015) by Cloud 9; the Eyebeam Atelier Museum (2001) by Preston Scott Cohen; Carbon Tower (2001) by Testa & Weiser; BMW Welt (2001–2007) by Coop Himmelb(l)au and Water Flux (2002–2012) by R&Sie(n). Shared approaches and tools across projects include the creation of high-fidelity 3D models to coordinate across scales and between teams; digital information supplied directly to CNC machines for fabrication, construction and assembly; 3D printing for model building; data visualization tools using simulated physics for the optimization of structure, energy and infrastructure systems; conflict-detection software to identify areas needing coordination; and the use of algorithms, programs and scripts for the procedural modelling of form, structure, fenestration, shading and organizational diagrams. Material from the projects was therefore presented according to five categories: high-fidelity 3D, topology and topography, photorealism, data, and structure and cladding.

Before digital tools, three-dimensional relationships were described by correlating two-dimensional drawings and specification documents. Changes in the scale of drawings allowed architects to increase detail and dimensional accuracy, but the coordination across scales of drawing was a time-consuming task that was fraught with potential for human error. The development of high-fidelity 3D digital models made it possible to describe a building, from its smallest detail to its overall organization, in a single three-dimensional file. Physical drawings could be updated in correlation with the three-dimensional model. Construction drawings were thus no longer two-dimensional documents, but rather slices of the three-dimensional model. Architects could generate these drawings easily and in vast quantities, as Van Berkel & Bos Architectuurbureau did for the Erasmus Bridge (fig. 24). High-fidelity 3D models allowed architects to achieve greater complexity, higher efficiency, faster realization and more control of the building process. In some cases, models, mock-ups and even finished building elements were fabricated using CNC by machines with tool paths generated directly from high-fidelity 3D content. For example, R&Sie(n) used three-dimensional data to work directly with manufacturers for the on-site CNC milling process for Water Flux, eliminating the need for an intermediary contractor and gaining greater control of fabrication (fig. 25). A high-fidelity 3D model contains the full range of data related to the project, from basic information about the site to measurement details. In addition, metadata and performance criteria were associated with geometric entities, which would eventually lead to building information modelling (BIM).

24 Van Berkel & Bos Architectuurbureau. Erasmus Bridge,
Rotterdam, construction drawing
for the stairs at the bridge
landing, with annotations in red,
1995. Ink on paper, 118.6 x 84.1
cm. UNStudio Erasmus Bridge
project records (AP175), CCA.
Gift of UNStudio

25 R&Sie(n). Water Flux, Évolène,
Switzerland, five-axis CNC
prototype of a spike facade
element, 1:1, c. 2007. Larch
wood, 129.5 x 152.4 x 66 cm.
R&Sie(n) project records (AP193),
CCA. Gift of New-Territor-
ies/R&Sie(n) by François Roche
and Stéphanie Lavaux

26 Kolatan/Mac Donald Studio.
O/K Apartment, New York,
screen capture showing texture
mapping of the bed/bath element
across construction lines, 1996.
Original file: BEBA5.1.7.tif, 316
KB, last modified 1 July 1996.
KOL/MAC project records
(AP185), CCA. Gift of KOL/MAC

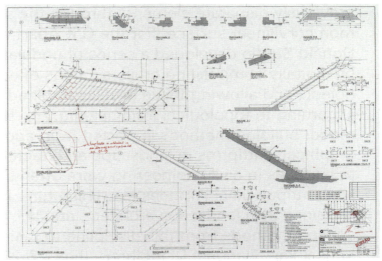

24

25

26

Digital curve networks, such as non-uniform rational B splines (NURBS), suggest continuities across surfaces rather than lineaments between x-y-z coordinates. Topology became the geometric reference for new connections between previously disparate elements through the sharing of a common curvilinear surface. For the O/K Apartment, Kolatan/Mac Donald Studio developed a series of undulating profiles by digitally compositing cross-sections of everyday domestic objects and allowing these profiles to blend and propagate according to topological affinities (fig. 26). The drawing and model-building methods imported from approaches to topographical landforms in landscape architecture and approaches to surfaces in civil engineering were often employed to describe topological surfaces in architecture. Nanako Umemoto is trained as a landscape architect, and she and Jesse Reiser applied methods from this discipline to their project for the Kansai-kan, National Diet Library (figs. 27–28). Geometric topology and tools associated with topography created new affinities between building mass, ground and landscape. For the Hypo Alpe-Adria Center, Morphosis used FormZ to impose a new landscape in a context that was shifting between urban and rural, merging a 3D-modelled sphere with the existing topography to create a new landform (fig. 29). In their project for the Jyväskylä Music and Arts Center, Johan Bettum and Kivi Sotamaa of OCEAN North define the "flow space" between the concert hall and the galleries and offices, through which the urban fabric could enter the design (fig. 30). In a range of projects, sloping and undulating surfaces were imported from the exterior landscape into the interior of buildings. The use of topological tools for describing movement and flow across curved surfaces and the interest in landscape and contour lines produced a consistent focus on new archi-

27 Reiser + Umemoto. Kansai-kan, National Diet Library, Kyoto, roof plan and structural diagrams, 1996. Ink, coloured pencil, adhesive label and pressure-sensitive tape on paper, 55.9 x 41.8 cm. RUR Architecture Kansai-kan, National Diet Library project records (AP177), CCA. Gift of RUR Architecture

28 Reiser + Umemoto. Kansai-kan, National Diet Library, Kyoto, model of the topological *roofscape*, 1:500, 1996. Cardboard, foam, graphite, adhesive and pressure-sensitive tape, 49.5 x 16.2 x 5.1 cm. RUR Architecture Kansai-kan, National Diet Library project records (AP177), CCA. Gift of RUR Architecture

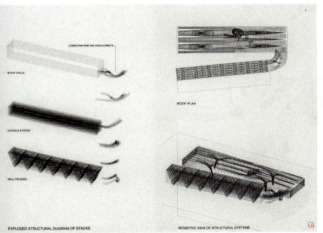

27

28

Greg Lynn

29 Morphosis. Hypo Alpe-Adria Center, Klagenfurt, Austria, diagram of deforming building mass, 1997. Original file: hypo final4.tif, 3.2 MB, last modified 29 June 1997. Morphosis Hypo Alpe-Adria Center project records (AP192), CCA. Gift of Morphosis

30 OCEAN North. Jyväskylä Music and Arts Centre, Jyväskylä, Finland, digital cloud model to describe interior geometry, 1997. Original file: jyv.virmod.peel.allcol.aer.jpg, 969 KB, last modified 3 May 1998. Johan Bettum OCEAN North project records (AP194), CCA. Gift of Johan Bettum

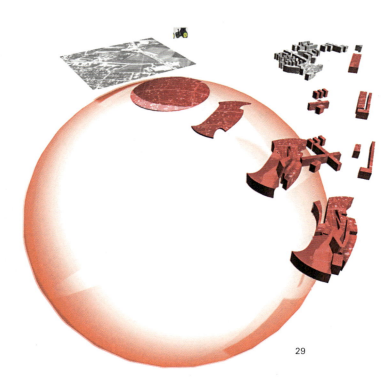

29

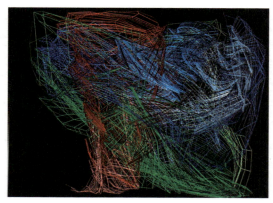

30

31 Foreign Office Architects. Yokohama International Port Terminal, rendering of a fluid space for public and passenger use, 2002. Original file: bifurcation8.tif, 1.3 MB, last modified 30 April 2002. Foreign Office Architects fonds (AP171), CCA. Gift of Farshid Moussavi and Alejandro Zaera-Polo

32 Foreign Office Architects. Yokohama International Port Terminal, presentation model, 1:400, c. 1995. Plastic, silver wire, metal and glue, 175.9 x 62.9 x 8.9 cm. Foreign Office Architects fonds (AP171), CCA. Gift of Farshid Moussavi and Alejandro Zaera-Polo

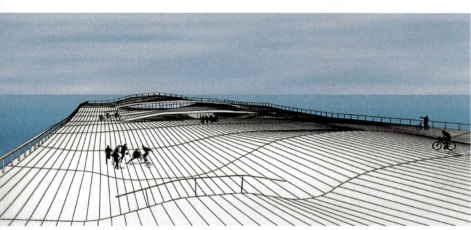

31

32

tectural types—such as passenger ship terminals, bridges and parks—that had previously been within the domains of civil engineering. The Yokohama International Port Terminal, by Foreign Office Architects, is one of the strongest examples of the conversation between landscape and infrastructure in the new language of complex curved surfaces. The architects developed their design not as a monumental piece of infrastructure but rather as a project that is topographically continuous with the landscape (figs. 31–32).

Digital technology enabled easy access to perspective views, hidden line drawings, shaded surfaces and projected shadows. This reduced labour in the design process—producing these drawings manually was arduous. Digital visualization of three-dimensional models added a new window to the architect's desktop, as the conventional screen layout became plan window, front window, side window and perspective window. The perspective view could act like a camera moving through the space, which gave rise to fly-through animations. Design software included texture libraries of materials, as well as lighting libraries to be used for rendered scenes. In some cases, the architecture was informed not only by the formal vocabulary implicit in the design tools but also by the look of the rendering styles particular to the software. With photorealistic renderings, architects could closely simulate the built result in the digital rendering, as the animation that Imaginary Forces made for Coop Himmelb(l)au's BMW Welt clearly demonstrates (fig. 33). The renderings produced for the design of Neil Denari's *Interrupted Projections* exhibition at TOTO Gallery MA in Tokyo bear a strong resemblance to the photographs of the built space (figs. 34–35). Similarly, Kolatan/Mac Donald Studio chose glossy fibreglass as a building material for the O/K Apartment to establish a close affinity between the rendering and the built project (fig. 36). Some architects combined previous methods of representation with digital tools. Zaha Hadid and Patrik Schumacher used paint as a rendering surface on digitally generated perspective drawings (fig. 37). Others reacted against the materials libraries of new digital software. In his renderings and animations for the Eyebeam Atelier Museum, Preston Scott Cohen did not make use of these libraries, instead focusing exclusively on lighting studies (fig. 38).

With digital tools, designers could visualize shapes and forces and the impact of these forces on form and space. In the case of Carbon Tower, Peter Testa and Devyn Weiser wrote a custom script to generate geometry dynamically, through patterns and densities of 3D-modelled structural tubes (fig. 39). Methods of finite element analysis (FEA) enabled architects and structural engineers to collaborate on solutions that produced more complex structural concepts due to the visual presentation of load paths and areas of stress. This is particularly evident in the design for the Chemnitz Stadium, developed by Peter Kulka and Ulrich Königs in close collaboration with Cecil Balmond and Robert Lang of the structural engineering firm Ove Arup & Partners (figs. 40–41). The method of computational fluid dynamics (CFD) was used to simulate the effects of wind load, thermal transfer, air flow, drainage, traffic and pedestrian movement through space and around forms. Notably, Coop Himmelb(l)au developed the design for BMW Welt through digital structural testing with the engineering firm Bollinger + Grohmann (fig. 42). In some cases, CFD was used to generate paths and curves for massing. The ability to render shade and shadows with a moving light source facilitated digital solar studies, in which form was studied with the impact of a moving sun that simulated daily and seasonal change. CFD

Greg Lynn

324

33 Coop Himmelb(l)au. BMW Welt, Munich, animation by Imaginary Forces, 2004. Still for publication. Original file: BMW_Imaginary_Forces_050414_divX.avi, 175 MB, last modified 14 April 2005. COOP HIMMELB(L)AU BMW Welt project records (AP181), CCA. Gift of COOP HIMMELB(L)AU

33

34 Neil M. Denari Architects. *Interrupted Projections*, Tokyo, digital rendering, 1996. Photographic slide, 5 x 5 cm. Neil Denari *Interrupted Projections* project records (AP168), CCA. Gifts of Neil Denari and Mr. Koz

35 Neil M. Denari Architects. *Interrupted Projections*, Tokyo, installation view, 1996. Photographic slide, 5 x 5 cm. Neil Denari *Interrupted Projections* project records (AP168), CCA. Gifts of Neil Denari and Mr. Koz

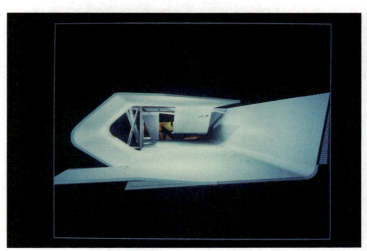

34

35

Greg Lynn

36 Kolatan/Mac Donald Studio. O/K Apartment, New York, view of the bed/bath element from the master bedroom, 1997. Michael Moran, photographer

37 Zaha Hadid Architects. Phaeno Science Centre, Wolfsburg, Germany, painting of surface lighting over wireframe lines, 2001. Acrylic paint on paper

36

37

38 Preston Scott Cohen. Eyebeam Atelier Museum, New York, still from the animation by KDLAB, showing the cutting plane through floors, 2001. Original file: Interior11.jpg, 16 KB, last modified 12 May 2007. Preston Scott Cohen Eyebeam project records (AP190), CCA. Gift of Preston Scott Cohen

39 Testa & Weiser. Carbon Tower, ramp segments with weave applied, 2003. Maya 3D model. Screen capture for publication. Original file: 20030226 woven_tubes.mb, 3.5 MB, last modified 26 February 2003. Testa & Weiser project records (AP174), CCA. Gift of Peter Testa and Devyn Weiser

38

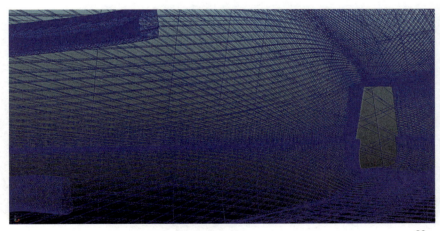

39

Greg Lynn

328

40 Peter Kulka with Ulrich Königs. Chemnitz Stadium, elevation view, 1995 Alias 3D model converted to scalable vector graphics format for publication. Original file: draetchen.wire, 3.5 MB, last modified 7 February 1996. Ulrich Königs Chemnitz Stadium project records (AP183), CCA. Gift of Ulrich Königs

41 Cecil Balmond. Chemnitz Stadium, structural diagram indicating loads, 1996. Graphite and ink on drafting film, 29.7 x 41.9 cm

42 Coop Himmelb(l)au. BMW Welt, Munich, screen capture of a digital 3D model highlighting collisions in structural elements, 2006. Original file: 060331_Rauschutzwand_kollision_1.jpg, 436 KB, last modified 31 March 2006. COOP HIMMELB(L)AU BMW Welt project records (AP181), CCA. Gift of COOP HIMMELB(L)AU

43 Cloud 9. Villa Nurbs, Empuria-brava, Spain, simulated solar path animation, 2004. Still for publication. Original file: 21MARZO TIMELINE.mov, 3.2 MB, last modified 15 July 2004. Cloud 9 Villa Nurbs project records (AP186), CCA. Gift of Enric Ruiz Geli

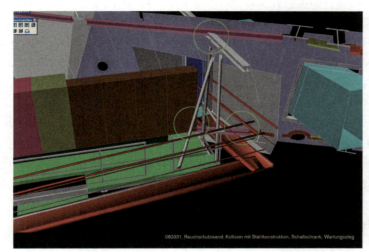

42

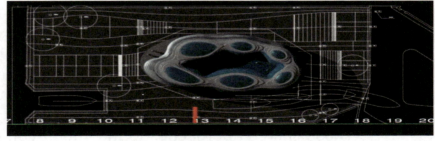

43

and solar studies, such as those that Cloud 9 carried out for Villa Nurbs, allowed designers to investigate building mass and form through a dynamic rather than a static environment (fig. 43).

Before digital technology, structure played a primary role in the geometric and spatial development of a building design. Often, all the dimensions, from the smallest detail to the position on the site, were referenced to the centreline of structure. Digital technology allowed for a new freedom and complexity, and had important effects on structure and cladding. First, data visualization tools such as finite element analysis showed stresses and load paths graphically during the design process, rather than afterward in purely analytic terms. Second, the ability to refer to elements abstractly in three-dimensional space reduced the role of structure as a dimensional reference for building. Third, digital tools allowed designers to use scripts to design procedurally at all scales. Scripts were also used for form finding and optimization; curvature and variation and standardization of components could be studied during the design process in relation to spatial and volumetric decisions, as well as to structure, cladding and envelope design. For example, for the Witte Arts Center, Office dA used digital technology to define complex curves and apertures for a structure built in brick, a conventional construction material. The architects used an algorithm to stack the bricks in a highly accurate way (fig. 44). Similarly, for Villa Nurbs, Cloud 9 used digital fabrication to configure the skin elements—in this case tiles in ceramic, another conventional material (fig. 45).

These shared approaches to the integration of digital technology attest to the transformation of the design process and of the role of the architect at a moment when architecture crossed a digital threshold, after which many of these pioneering technologies became standard. The archival material

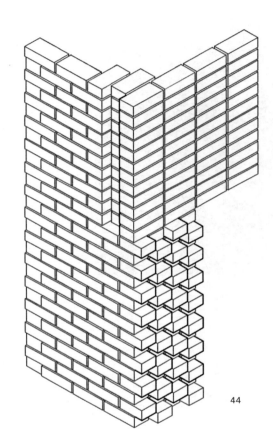

44 Office dA. Witte Arts Center, Green Bay, United States, axonometric drawing of brick configurations, 2000. Original file: CornerStipple FINAL.tif, 501 KB, last modified 30 November 2000. Office dA project records (AP179), CCA. Gift of Mónica Ponce de León and Nader Tehrani

Greg Lynn

45 Cloud 9. Villa Nurbs, Empuria-brava, Spain, photograph of ceramic skin elements, 2006. Original file: DSC01056.jpg, 3 MB, last modified 28 July 2006. Cloud 9 Villa Nurbs project records (AP186), CCA. Gift of Enric Ruiz Geli

collected by the CCA shows how a digital approach to design proved that buildings could be delivered in a functional, timely and fiscally responsible way while allowing for more complexity, ingenuity and innovation than would have previously been possible. Indicating a diversity of practices and developed at a wide range of scales, the fifteen projects included in the third phase of Archaeology of the Digital represent the period during which digital technology moved from experiment to acceptance.

An archaeology of twenty-five projects dating from the late 1980s through the early 2000s reveals the transformation of architecture through digital technology in real material terms. A history of this pivotal moment must rely on a survey of software, hardware, scripts, scans, digital models and machine code alongside built work, drawings, models, interviews and writings. Archaeology of the Digital is therefore the initiation of a critical and historical project, rather than a summation. Only through this archaeological method can a more complete, more confident history of the digital begin to be written.

The challenge of archiving native-digital content, to make it available to researchers along with physical materials, is now just beginning to produce coherent questions: Were architects adopting technology from other fields or inventing it themselves? What new uses for digital tools did architects discover and what opportunities were overlooked? What new media entered the built environment along with digital design tools? How do digital tools change the role of the architect relative to the builder? What is the expressive potential of digital tools, and do they delimit or unlock the creativity of designers? It was through an archaeology of hard disks, crates and tubes that these questions were formed to address a recent past, before the explosion of native-digital files in architecture. The interest

Greg Lynn

of uncovering selected artifacts from digital architecture at the end of the twentieth century extends beyond the disciplinary boundaries of architecture. It is fundamentally a media archaeological project, an active listening to artifacts and fragments to give us insight into how things were done, and to help us ask the right questions.

Nathalie Bredella

The Ars Electronica Festival <u>in 1991</u> was held just after the end of the Gulf War, a conflict that, in the West, seemed to unfold on television screens. The war prompted artists participating in the festival to rethink the relationship between space, information and media. This led to collaboration between architects and artists that produced media-rich environments and new approaches to digital interaction.

NATHALIE BREDELLA

1 Jeffrey Shaw. *The Virtual Museum*, installation view at the Landesmuseum Linz during Ars Electronica, 1992. This work allows users to navigate virtual spaces by moving in a chair attached to a motorized, rotating platform. The virtual spaces are replicas of the physical room in which the user is seated and contain exhibitions of painting, sculpture, cinema and digital art.

IN THE MIDST OF THINGS: ARCHITECTURE'S ENCOUNTER WITH DIGITAL TECHNOLOGY, MEDIA THEORY AND MATERIAL CULTURE

1

Nathalie Bredella

During the 1990s, significant discussion about architecture and media took place at newly founded media art institutes, focusing on the expanding impact of media technologies on perception and experience, as well as on representation and communication (fig. 1). This discussion led to the recognition of architecture as a form of media, and to the recognition of inter-media processes in architectural design. In this context, institutions such as V2_ Institute for the Unstable Media in Rotterdam, the Institut für Neue Medien at the Städelschule in Frankfurt, the Zentrum für Kunst und Medientechnologie (ZKM) in Karlsruhe and the Ars Electronica Center in Linz dealt with questions of technology and the transformation of social structures in theory and practice.[1] These institutions created trans-disciplinary environments, bridging the arts, sciences and humanities, while also making the technology of interactive new media art more widely available. By producing, exhibiting, archiving and publishing research, they fostered a dialogue at the intersection of art, architecture, technology and society. As architects examined media systems, with these institutions

Nathalie Bredella

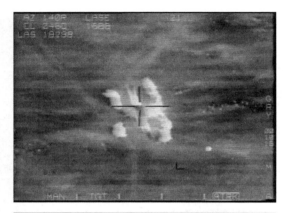

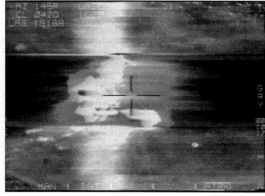

2 Still images from a video showing a laser-guided missile striking a building in Kuwait during Operation Desert Storm, 1991. Images like these were shown on television during the Gulf War.

as incubators, architecture became a more prominent site for negotiating the spatial, political and social implications of digital media and communication technologies.[2]

V2_ Institute for the Unstable Media was one of the leading sites for interdisciplinary research in the emerging field of media technologies, and the work of V2_ provides a good opportunity to understand the media, art, theory and design context of the 1990s. Founded as an art collective in 1981, V2_ was dedicated to the development of multimedia work.[3] In opposition to existing exhibition practices, artists at V2_ moved across media to combine music, video, sound and visual art. The happenings at V2_ pointed toward the multi-disciplinary nature of media practices, and how perception was related to social, economic and environmental change. By the 1990s, in response to the development and proliferation of digital technologies, V2_ acted as a site where practitioners and thinkers grappled with the role of digital media in design, while continuing to foreground architecture's relationship with other media and with other disciplines and fields of knowledge. Architects at V2_ reflected on how technology underpinned architectural thinking. They focused on visualization and communication techniques, and on the way in which technological change affected design strategies and the relationship between human and non-human actors. When architects connected with media theory and art at V2_, they questioned the politics and aesthetics of technological systems and addressed architecture's participation in the social and spatial transformations of the 1990s.

In this period Paul Virilio's writings offered a critical commentary on technology's impact on the organization of territory, on the human body and on the perception of reality. In V2_'s first publication, *Book for the Unstable Media*, Virilio

Nathalie Bredella

342

3 Christine Meierhofer. *In den Mund gelegt: The Media Is Not the Message*, 1991. In this interactive video art installation, the newscaster's messages could be manipulated by keyboard inputs. It was nominated for the Prix Ars Electronica in interactive art in 1991.

3

4 V2_ Institute for the Unstable Media. "Manifesto for Unstable Media," published in *de Volkskrant* on 31 December 1986

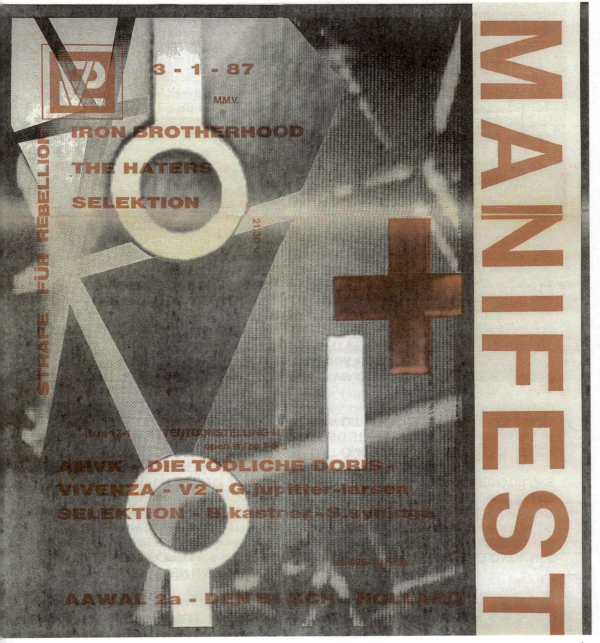

Nathalie Bredella

[5] V2_ Institute for the Unstable Media. "Manifesto for Unstable Media." "We do not want to bring existing art to the public. We want new art, and a new public."

WIJ WILLEN DE BESTAANDE KUNST NIET NAAR HET PUBLIEK BRENGEN.
WIJ WILLEN NIEUWE KUNST EN EEN NIEUW PUBLIEK.

ONS DOEL IS STREVEN NAAR EEN CONSTANTE VERANDERING.
WIJ WILLEN DE VOORTDURENDE REVOLUTIE PROPAGEREN IN EEN WERELD VOL MET ZOGENAAMDE ZEKERHEDEN EN MET DEZE ZEKERHEDEN WILLEN WIJ BREKEN.
HET IS DE KUNST HET INSTITUTIONELE EN HET ZEKER WETEN TE VOORKOMEN. DE QUANTUMTHEORIE EN DE RELATIVITEITSTHEORIE HEBBEN ONS DUIDELIJK GEMAAKT DAT DE AANSCHOUWELIJKE VOORSTELLING VAN ONZE ERVARING SLECHTS GELDT VOOR EEN BEPERKT GEBIED. EN DAT ZIJ IN GEEN GEVAL TOT EEN ONOMSTOTELIJKE STELLING VAN DE WETENSCHAP BEHOORT.
WIJ WILLEN STEEDS BLIJVEN ONTDEKKEN. NIET OMDAT WIJ ALLES WILLEN WETEN MAAR OMDAT WIJ HOUDEN VAN HET IDEE DAT WIJ STEEDS ZULLEN ONTDEKKEN, OMDAT WIJ HOUDEN VAN DE EINDELOOSHEID VAN DIT UITZICHT. EN ONS DEZE EINDELOOSHEID ALS DOEL STELLEN.

WIJ MOETEN VORMGEVEN AAN HET NIEUWE, WAARBIJ WE ERVAN UIT GAAN DAT NIEUWE VORMEN SLECHTS UIT EEN NIEUWE INHOUD KUNNEN ONTSTAAN EN NIET OMGEKEERD. NIEUWE KUNST MAKEN BETEKENT EEN NIEUWE INHOUD ZICHTBAAR, VOELBAAR EN HOORBAAR MAKEN.

KUNST MOET FUNCTIONEEL ZIJN. WIJ ZIEN DE KUNST ALS EEN VORMGEVEND PRINCIPE IN DE SAMENLEVING. KUNST MOET DE MATERIALEN, MEDIA EN DE MOGELIJKHEDEN VAN HAAR TIJD BENUTTEN OM ZO DE TIJD MEDE TE BEPALEN.
WETENSCHAP EN KUNST MOETEN EEN REVOLUTIONAIRE KRACHT BINNEN DE SAMENLEVING ZIJN EN GEEN VERFRAAIING VAN EEN ELLENDIG BESTAAN OF EEN ECONOMISCHE FACTOR.
KUNST MOET DESTRUCTIEF EN CONSTRUCTIEF ZIJN.

KUNST, WETENSCHAP OF WELK MEDIUM DAN OOK IS GEEN DOEL OP ZICH MAAR EEN MIDDEL TER REALISERING VAN EEN TE VORMEN IDEE. HET MOET GEEN AUTONOMIE BINNEN ONS MAATSCHAPPELIJK BESTEL VORMEN, MAAR ER DEEL VAN UIT MAKEN. NIET OM DE HEERSENDE MORAAL EN POLITIEK TE BEVESTIGEN MAAR OM DE VERANDERING TE PROPAGEREN. DE KUNST MOET NIET PLAATSVINDEN IN DE AUTONOME WERELD VAN GALERIES EN MUSEA OMDAT DEZE DE VERANDERING JUIST TEGENWERKEN. DE KUNSTHANDEL IS NIET GEBAAT BIJ EN DAARDOOR NIET GEÏNTERESSEERD IN VERANDERINGEN. ZIJ WILLEN HET EINDPRODUCT EN NIET DE WEG ERHEEN. ZIJ VERONDERSTELT DE AFWEZIGHEID VAN DE DRANG TOT HET OMVERWERPEN VAN HET RESULTAAT. HAAR MOTIEVEN WORDEN LOS DAARVAN AANGEREIKT DOOR DE MAATSCHAPPELIJKE CODE WAARIN VOLGENS EEN INTERESSANT PROCES DE KUNSTKENNIS OOIT TOT MACHT EN DAARDOOR TOT INVLOED EN PRESTIGE GEWORDEN IS.
ONZE MENTALITEIT HEEFT TEN DOEL DEZE HOUDING TE BEKRITISEREN EN ONMOGELIJK TE MAKEN.
WIJ HOUDEN VAN DE ONZEKERHEID EN DE CHAOS.

WIJ STREVEN NAAR DE OPTIMALE VERWEZENLIJKING VAN DE MOGELIJKHEDEN VAN HET INDIVIDU EN HET COLLECTIEF ALS SCHAKEL NAAR EEN NIEUWE CULTUUR. WIJ GELOVEN IN DIT LEVEN NU EN NIET IN DE VERWEZENLIJKING VAN DE MOGELIJKHEDEN BUITEN DIT LEVEN. WIJ RICHTEN ONS OP HET NU EN NIET OP DE TOEKOMST OF OP EEN ANDERE TIJD IN DE GESCHIEDENIS. DE MOGELIJKHEDEN MOETEN NU GEREALISEERD WORDEN ZONDER COMPROMIS.
WIJ STIMULEREN DE VERGANKELIJKHEID IN DE KUNST.

V2 ORGANISATION   MUNTELSTRAAT 23   5211 PT   s-HERTOGENBOSCH   NETHERLANDS writes on modern warfare and perception, addressing the transmission of images and sounds that facilitated the monitoring of the geographical landscape in war.[4] This dynamic was not new, but it attained a new magnitude as a result of the "live" broadcast of the Gulf War (fig. 2). The televised conflict delivered a distorted relay of images and sounds, putting viewers in direct contact with the war via their televisions.[5] Virilio emphasized that new technologies introduced ways of monitoring and carrying out war on a local and on a global scale. In this media reality, warfare and its representation became technologically mediated events that provoked questions regarding media's power and its mechanisms of operation and control.

Similarly, at the 1991 Ars Electronica festival, the Gulf War proved to be a crucial turning point of the digital era (fig. 3). The 1991 festival became the "festival after"—that is, a festival after the first total electronic war during which electronic media operated on the battlefield and also regulated worldwide media coverage of the war. According to Hannes Leopoldseder, co-founder of Ars Electronica, media produced a war in people's minds.[6] Drawing attention to the emerging conditions of virtual reality and artificial life, the Ars Electronica Center, with a special focus on the exploration of interactive scenarios within virtual space, was inaugurated in 1996. And the Ars Electronica Future Lab, a part of the Ars Electronica Center, offered another testing ground, where the outlines of digital art could be defined, and the growing information technology industries and their impact on globalization could become subjects of debate.[7]

In this discourse on media technologies, certain new modes of inquiry were clearly apparent, as architects began to consider information-technology networks and emphasized

Nathalie Bredella

INSTABIELE MEDIA IV

Wanneer wij ons bezighouden met de vraag hoe ruimte en tijd onder invloed van nieuwe media en technologieën in de architectuur gestalte krijgen, dan is het goed om te beseffen welke richtingen en stromingen op het ogenblik in het denken over architectuur in zwang zijn. Het gaat voornamelijk om drie stromingen namelijk, kritisch regionalisme, postmodernisme en deconstructivisme.

Het kritisch regionalisme, met als belangrijkste vertegenwoordiger Kenneth Frampton, wordt gekenmerkt door het zoeken naar het streek- of stadseigene, is daarom dialektgebonden, wordt gedragen door een zeker heimwee, en is erop uit om de oorspronkelijke plek te herstellen en tegen de dwaalwegen van de moderniteit in bescherming te nemen. Het kritisch regionalisme beschouwt architectuur, echte architectuur, als daad van verzet tegen het kapitalisme en tegen de daarbijbehorende mono-cultuur. Het is op zoek naar niet-arbitraire criteria voor architectuur, dat wil zeggen dat het probeert niet op basis van de toevallige creativiteit van de architect of van een door functionaliteit dwingend voorgeschreven eisenpakket te ontwerpen. In plaats daarvan probeert deze stroming om de in de eigen stad of streek aangetroffen beeldtaal kritisch te reflecteren en voor nieuwe ontwerpen vruchtbaar te maken.

Het postmodernisme, met als belangrijkste vertegenwoordigers critici als Charles Jencks en Paolo Portoghesi, en filosofen als Jean-Francois Lyotard en Gianni Vattimo, wordt gekenmerkt door de kritiek op het moderne subjectbegrip. Het maakt een einde aan de mythe van het autonoom ontwerpende ik, en benut zonder schuldgevoel de geschiedenis van de artistieke vormen om ze te herhalen en voor eigen doelen te benutten. Het gaat hier om een bij uitstek internationale stroming, met dien verstande dat zij tendeert naar etnocentrisme voorzover het het oude Europa is, dat men als reservoir van stijlvormen benut. Dat hoeft overigens niet altijd op een eclectische manier te gebeuren, maar kan ook zoals bij Leon Krier worden gedragen door de wil tot reconstructie van het oude Europa in het algemeen en van de antieke polis in het bijzonder.

Het deconstructivisme is de meest recente stroming in de architectuur. Zij wordt vertegenwoordigd door de filosoof Jacques Derrida (recentelijk versterkt door Lyotard) en door met hem samenwerkende architecten als Peter Eisenman en Bernard Tschumi of zich mede op zijn ideeën beroepende architecten als Daniel Libeskind. Sinds kort heeft deze stroming echter zo'n hoge vlucht genomen dat vele andere architecten zich ook tot deze stroming rekenen of ertoe gerekend worden.

Deze stroming wordt vaak een elitaire mentaliteit en een hoogdravend intellectualisme verweten, maar in werkelijkheid gaat het hier voor het eerst sinds de avant-gardes weer om de poging tot een echte internationale beweging te komen, waarvoor Europa en de Europese geschiedenis niet meer het enige referentiepunt vormen. Veeleer gaat het om een planetaire stroming die een artistiek antwoord wil geven op de ontheeming van de mens en die de verworvenheden van de moderniteit, inclusief de negatieve aspecten ervan zoals de ontworteling, wil integreren in het architectonisch ontwerp.

Het beste kan men daarom deze drie stromingen met elkaar vergelijken door te kijken hoe ze omgaan met de plek. Voor het kritisch regionalisme moet de architectuur bij de plek aansluiten en de oorspronkelijke staat ervan zo niet herstellen dan wel respecteren. Het postmodernisme realiseert zich dat dit onmogelijk is geworden en tovert met behulp van de geschiedenis van de stijlvormen de plek om tot een theater waarop de historische vormen een maskerade opvoeren. Het deconstructivisme verwacht tenslotte van de architectuur een antwoord in termen van een ontwerp op de oplossing en de ontbinding van de plek, en wil aan de plaatsloosheid en het dolen van de moderne mens een concrete en geldige gestalte geven. Tussen het heimwee naar het wonen en de ontheeming van de mens, tussen het onkritische verzet tegen de moderniteit en de kritische bevestiging ervan, verloopt het spectrum van het huidige architectuurdebat.

Het deconstructivisme neemt binnen dit debat zo'n belangrijke plaats in omdat het hier om een echte democratische stroming gaat die niemand uitsluit. Daar zij afrekent met de notie van de oorspronkelijke plek en van de eigen plaats, wordt in haar ogen de mensheid niet langer verdeeld in autochtonen en vreemdelingen, maar wordt erkend dat iedereen in onze wereld een balling is. De ontheeming wordt als condition humaine geaccepteerd, en strekt zich uit van de letterlijk dakloze tot aan de rijke jet-set toe, die niet minder ontheemd is, daar zij iedere oriëntatie heeft verloren. Het deconstructivisme wordt dan ook voornamelijk gedragen door Joodse intellectuelen als Jacques Derrida, Peter Eisenman, Stanley Tigerman en Daniel Libeskind voor wie het Jood zijn niet zozeer iets is, dat met ras of gezindte heeft te maken, maar veeleer het dolen door de woestijn en de oorspronkelijk verwonderbare en welhaast ongeneeslijke geaardheid van de mens tot uitdrukking brengt.

Deze stroming zoekt dan ook geen nieuwe synthese, maar ontvouwt verschillen om ze tot een nieuw wereldspel te laten komen. Dit nieuwe wereldspel is niet gebaseerd op harmonie of consensus, maar is erop uit om verschillen en geschillen te laten bijdragen tot het stellen van de wezenlijke problemen waar wij nu voor staan. Dat het daarbij niet langer kan gaan om het vinden van oplossingen, maar om het op de juiste wijze stellen van de problemen, is de belangrijkste boodschap van deze stroming voor het cultuurbeleid.

Een ander opvallend punt is dat het deconstructivisme erop is gericht om gevestigde denkpatronen en hiërarchieën te doorbreken. Gewoonlijk is ons denken gestructureerd in termen van vorm en stof, mens en wereld, idee en materie, subject en object, binnen en buiten enz. Deze structuur is niet neutraal, maar van dien aard dat steeds de eerste term de tweede onderwerpt en aan zich toeëigent: de vorm wordt aan de stof opgelegd, de mens heerst over de wereld, de materie is slechts afglans van de idee, het object is slechts object voor een subject, het buiten wordt door het binnen gekoloniseerd enz. De operatie van de deconstructie bestaat er nu in de rechten van de onderdrukte pool te herstellen door de hiërarchie om te keren en plaats te maken voor wat voorheen werd verdrongen.

De centrale vraag van het deconstructivisme luidt dan ook: hoe ziet een denken eruit waarin de vorm aan de stof ondergeschikt wordt gemaakt, waarin het onbewuste veeleer de mens overheerst dan dat de mens over de wereld heerst, waarin de idee slechts een bijverschijnsel van de materie is, waarin het soevereine subject afstand doet van zijn troon, en waarin het denken wordt uitgeleverd aan een buiten dat het niet in kaart kan brengen?

Voor het architectuurdebat impliceert deze vraagstelling dat men zich buigt over de wijze waarop het deconstructivisme het institutionele karakter van de architectuur ter discussie stelt, het opneemt voor de onderdrukte pool en de verdrongen ervaring, er als het ware een minderhedenbeleid in de architectuur zelf tot stand brengt. De wijze waarop de individuele vertegenwoordigers van deze stroming datgene in de architectuur proberen in te voeren, wat de architectuur altijd heeft proberen te verdringen, en ik denk daarbij in eerste instantie aan de ontheeming en de ontworteling van de moderne mens, maakt deze stroming tot zo'n grote intellectuele uitdaging.

6   V2_ Institute for the Unstable Media. *Manifestation for Unstable Media 4*, newsprint featuring installations by Kees Christiaanse (*upper left*) and Lebbeus Woods (*lower right*), 1992, p. 1

7   V2_ Institute for the Unstable Media. *Manifestation for Unstable Media 4*, newsprint featuring, (*from top to bottom*) work by Steina Vasulka, Jeffrey Shaw, Jem Cohen and Christina Kubisch, 1992, p. 10

architecture's mediating role in discussions of communication technology and its impact on space. Architecture became understood as an interface, as a space for information access and communication. This position extended from theory to built form. In built projects, sensory experiences caused by interactions with media aimed at augmenting perceptual skills and at making social interactions between the individual and the group visible. While a democratic vision of media dominated initial discussions, theorists and architects also pointed toward authoritarian modes of interaction pursued by marketing and governmental agencies.

What follows is a reflection on how architecture participated in the cross-disciplinary art context of the 1990s. By tracing a number of prominent projects and exhibitions in the media art context, I focus on architects' concern with communication networks and with the protocols of informational networks that configured the built environment. In addition to discussing installations and performances, this essay also investigates inter-media networks in built forms. In the H_2Oexpo pavilion, designed by NOX, questions of perception provided a point of departure for a building that addressed ecological concerns. I then turn to the relevance of the work of Frei Otto and Buckminster Fuller for 1990s discourses and for the more synthetic approach to material, form and information that accompanied them. The final part of the text focuses on projects that deal with the politics of informational networks and with visualization techniques on an urban scale. Taken together, these projects explore design strategies across disciplines, and reveal how technologies and new media affected architectural design and its relationship to social and economic life.

Media Environments: Architecture and Communication Networks

In 1986 V2_ published a first manifesto, which called for new exhibition practices that would be better suited to dealing with the constant change inherent in electronic media (figs. 4–5).[8] In response to the revolution in information technology, V2_ considered instability as characteristic of new media, and focused its research on making temporal changes and interactions productive in cultural practices. Rather than working with known categories of art, artists at V2_ saw the potential of the changing dynamics of space-time relations as a means to establish new hierarchies based on interactions that could only stabilize temporarily. To manifest their manifesto, so to speak, between 1987 and 1993 V2_ carried out a program of "manifestations" intended to stimulate interaction between architecture, technology and society. In this context the impact of technology on communication, the configuration of space and the challenges these posed for design became part of a debate that brought together media theory and architecture.[9]

A growing interest in communication and visualization techniques inspired many of the works shown at the *Manifestation for Unstable Media 4* at V2_ in 1992 (figs. 6–7),[10] in particular two exhibitions with a special focus on urbanism and architecture: *Interactive Art Works* and *Scale Models: Architectural Ballistic, Fire and Forget*. Artist Jeffrey Shaw's *Legible City* (fig. 8), installed in *Interactive Art Works*, probed different possibilities for action within a virtual environment. The work made use of a three-dimensional structure within which the viewer could move, navigating multiple relationships between images and thus defining architecture as malleable. This

Nathalie Bredella

8   Jeffrey Shaw. *Legible City*, installation view at World Design Expo, Nagoya, 1989

interactive space, a dimensional database of the virtual image, revealed itself in relation to the specific position and orientation of the user and, depending on actions, could be repeatedly reconstructed.[11] In a similar vein *Scale Models: Architectural Ballistic, Fire and Forget* addressed the tension between the materiality of architecture and its transformation via projected images. In cooperation with TU Eindhoven, architects displayed models that aimed at destabilizing the architectural object. Using different media, the models in the exhibition interwove concrete spatial situations and visual projections, resulting in space-melding installations. This relationship between communication technology and physical space was also the subject of a symposium that focused on the interdependency of the visible and invisible networks of the city.[12] In his lecture at this symposium, "The Secret of the White Box," Lebbeus Woods presented his concept of "free spaces" and "free zones," highlighting architecture's role as an instrument for social transformation. Woods addressed urban "conflict zones," exploring systems in cities, particularly Berlin before and after the fall of the Wall.[13] He identified spaces that provided evidence of social and political conflict, and that had been marked by either the division or the destruction of the urban fabric. Imagining a new type of space, his drawings and collages of dynamic architectural forms were intended to introduce spaces within the strictures of existing buildings. Woods characterized these spaces as being "functionally ambiguous" and in order to preserve their independence, they had to remain hidden from the "controlling gaze of authorities."[14] Electronic telecommunication knots connected these "free spaces," forming interstitial networks of communication within the built environment. Manifestation events such as Woods's lecture were central to V2_'s attempts to frame architecture's

Nathalie Bredella

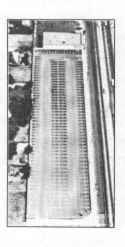
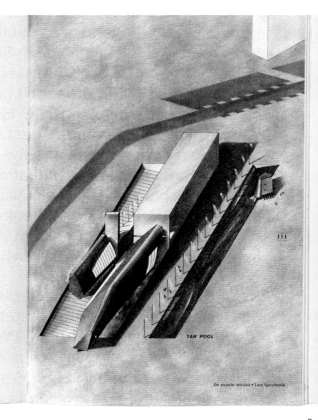

Actiones in distans

De zwarte secties • Lars Spuybroek

9 Lars Spuybroek. "De Zwarte Secties," in *NOX: Actiones in distans* (Amsterdam: Stichting Highbrow, 1991), p. 110–111. CCA. BIB 226487

10 Lars Spuybroek. Image published in *NOX: Biotech* (Amsterdam: Stichting Highbrow, 1992), 52–53. CCA. BIB 226488

relationship to politics and communication, as well as architecture's intersection with electronic media.

The work of architect Lars Spuybroek and his office, NOX, is essential to understanding the happenings at V2_ and, more generally, the dialogue on architecture and media that was shaped by collaborative projects at media art institutes in the 1990s. NOX played a crucial role in V2_'s activities, fostering debate on both the cultural potentials and the stakes of architecture's engagement with digital technology. NOX grew out of the magazine *NOX*, which Spuybroek and Maurice Nio edited between 1991 and 1995.[15] The magazine was created when the interests of formerly distinct disciplines as diverse as architecture, biology and neurophysiology began to overlap. Consequently, the magazine's subjects were tackled from many angles, and its content included stories, visual essays, facts and speculations about culture and technology. The issues—*Actiones in distans* (1991), *Biotech* (1992), *Chloroform* (1993) and *Djihad* (1995) (figs. 9–12)—introduced readers to media theory and included texts by Jean Baudrillard and Paul Virilio in Dutch translation. NOX's involvement with V2_ brought architecture more directly into dialogue with media discourse, and the resulting knowledge practices framed new inter-media relationships within architecture.

In 1993 NOX and V2_ carried out the event *Prosthetics: From Extensions to Ecstasy*, which included an exhibition, lectures and a performance. The exhibition featured work by architects Elizabeth Diller and Ricardo Scofidio, who used audio, video, sound and film projections to reveal how social, technological and economic forces governed daily behaviour. They presented their video installation *Soft Sell* (fig. 13), which had originally been shown in an abandoned pornographic theatre on 42nd Street in New York. *Soft Sell* addressed "the production of 'desire' in relation to several forms of 'urban currency' specific to the site: bodies, real estate, and tourism."[16] Diller also gave a lecture, entitled "Designing in Architecture and Industry," which dealt with the interdependence of economic and mechanical production, as well as with methods of transportation and how these methods impacted design.[17] Diller + Scofidio's work across media and disciplines engaged with questions of instability by drawing attention to the cultural diffusion of architecture, as well as to architecture's mediating power. Through collaborative projects such as these, V2_ drew wider attention to the social significance of architecture as media.

Beyond V2_, artists and architects collaborated to address the transformation of the urban sphere in relation to electronic media. The Zurich-based group Knowbotic Research proposed the exploration of information and knowledge structures through an art practice that focused on communication and visualization techniques.[18] Knowbotic Research examined the possibilities of collaboration in local and networked spaces. In their work IO_Dencies, different megacities were analyzed in order to develop mapping interfaces that would allow users "to rethink urban planning and construction and arrive at a notion of process-oriented collaborative agency" (fig. 14).[19] The Shimbashi area of central Tokyo was studied, and different "zones of intensities" were selected and recorded, addressing the movement of capital, information and traffic flows. Knowbotic Research's mapping of these urban movements resulted in a notation system in which the interference and interaction of flows were digitally coded. When this code was displayed on the Internet, users could probe scenarios by intervening within representational flow charts. At the same time, users with similar interests were connected with each other in order

Nathalie Bredella

Stamers knikte. 'Uhhuh. Gloria Tremayne. Haar ware naam was Emma Slack. Overigens, iedereen uit de buurt weet het, maar zegt u alstublieft nooit dat u het van mij heeft. We houden het zo lang mogelijk stil. Als we de naam Gloria Tremayne lieten vallen, zou niemand het huis zelfs maar willen bezichtigen.'

'Gloria Tremayne,' herhaalde Fay piekerend. 'Dat was toch de filmster die haar man had doodgeschoten, niet? Hij was een beroemde architect – Howard, heb jij niet met dat proces te maken gehad?'

Terwijl Fay doorbabbelde draaide ik me om, keek langs de trap naar het zonneterras, en verplaatste me in gedachten tien jaar terug naar een van de beroemdste processen van die tijd – een proces dat door zijn verloop en vonnis uitgroeide tot een van de grote symbolen die het einde van een hele generatie markeerde en de onverantwoordelijkheid van de wereld in de periode vóór de Grote Crisis aan de kaak stelde. Hoewel Gloria Tremayne vrijgesproken was, wist iedereen dat ze haar man, de architect Miles Vanden Starr, in koelen bloede had vermoord terwijl hij sliep en dat ze alleen maar gered was door de fluwelen tong van Daniel Hammett, haar verdediger, die geassisteerd werd door een jongeman genaamd Howard Talbot. Ik zei tegen Fay: 'Ja, ik heb haar helpen verdedigen. Wat lijkt dat lang geleden. Engel, wacht jij even in de wagen. Ik wou even iets nakijken.'

Voor ze me kon volgen rende ik de trap op naar het terras en sloot de glazen deuren achter me. De witte muren rezen, thans roerloos en onaandoenlijk, aan weerskanten van het bassin omhoog. Het water was rimpelloos: een transparant blok gecondenseerde tijd waarin het beeld van Fay en Stamers, zittend in de auto, verdronken lag. Ik staarde naar dit tafereel gedurende een moment dat mij, toen ik aan Gloria Tremayne dacht, een gebalsemd fragment van mijn toekomst scheen.

Tijdens haar proces, tien jaar geleden, had ik drie weken lang op enkele passen van Gloria Tremayne vandaan gezeten, en net als alle andere aanwezigen in de propvolle rechtszaal zou ik nooit haar koele, maskerachtige gezicht vergeten, noch de onbewogen blik waarmee ze de getuigen opnam als ze hun getuigenis aflegden – de chauffeur, de politiedokter, de buren die de schoten hadden gehoord. Het bleef net een briljante spin die, aangeklaagd door haar slachtoffers, nimmer een sprankje emotie of reactie toonde. Haar web werd uit elkaar getrokken, draad voor draad, maar zij bleef onberoerd in het midden zitten, moedigde Hammett op geen enkele wijze aan en vertrouwde zelfgenoegzaam op het beeld van zichzelf ('De IJspegel') dat de voorgaande vijftien jaar over de hele aardbol op het doek was geprojecteerd.

Misschien was dit uiteindelijk haar redding: de Sfinx knipperde niet met haar ogen en de jury kon daar niet tegenop. Eerlijk gezegd had ik in de laatste week wel interesse voor het proces verloren. Ik gaf Hammett de nodige adviezen, opende en sloot zijn koffertje van rood hout (Hammetts uithangbord en uitstekend geschikt om jury's van de wijs te brengen) wanneer dat vereist werd, maar besteedde mijn aandacht verder uitsluitend aan Gloria Tremayne, in wier masker ik een kiertje probeerde te ontdekken waardoor ik een glimp van haar persoonlijkheid kon opvangen. Ik neem aan dat ik gewoon, als talloze andere naieve jongemannen, verliefd was geworden op een mythe die door duizenden publiciteitsagenten in elkaar was gezet – alleen golden mijn gevoelens de

11 *CHCl33* (*left*). J. G. Ballard. "De Duizend Dromen van Stellavista" ["The Thousand Dreams of Stellavista"] (*right*). In *NOX: Chloroform* (Amsterdam: Stichting Highbrow, 1993), p. 66–67. CCA. BIB 226489

12 Chidi Onwuka. "Ik Ben de Hemelpoort" (*left*). Maurice Nio and Lars Spuybroek. Image from the *Comsat Angels* series (*right*). In *NOX: Djihad* (Amsterdam: Stichting Highbrow, 1995), p. 22–23. CCA. BIB 226490

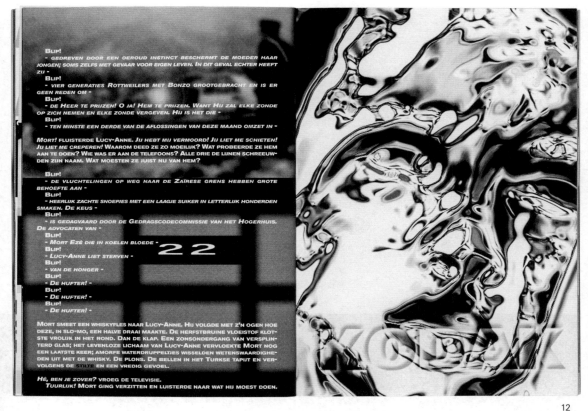

Nathalie Bredella

13 Alex Adriaansens, co-founder of V2_, at the installation of Diller + Scofidio's *Soft Sell* as part of *Prosthetics: From Extensions to Ecstasy*, 1993. Jan Sprij, photographer

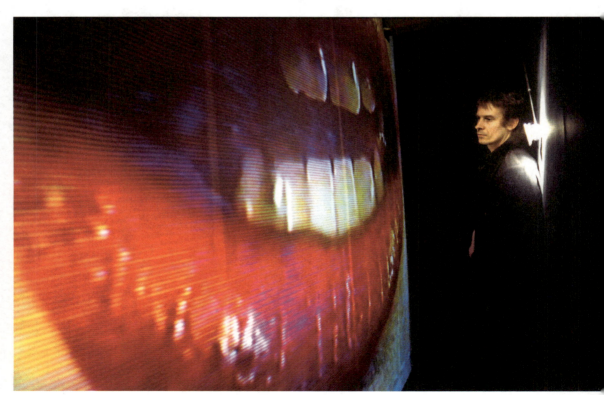

to suggest the possibility of collaboration. Maps and diagrams coordinated the urban activities, and this game-like atmosphere allowed users to simulate different modalities of control.

The Institut für Neue Medien (INM) in Frankfurt offered a forum for artists and scientists to experiment with inter-media relationships.[20] By the mid-1990s the institute had acquired extensive experience with the use of software and hardware. Architect Bernhard Franken developed the Netzstadt project at the INM with the *Fliessgleichgewicht* ("flow equilibrium") interactive computer installation, which explored the possibilities of virtual architecture and network technology (fig. 15). With Frankfurt as a site, a net-like structure was created to integrate an assemblage of high-rise buildings. The dynamic features of the animation software were tested, such that under the influence of turbulence and gravity the "liquid" topography of the architectural objects was constantly changing. The installation was transformed into a model in virtual reality modelling language (VRML) and put on the Internet, where it acted more as a metaphor for a space of communication than a buildable structure.[21] The user could navigate through these spaces, in which hyperlinks allowed for the exploration of nested environments in the digital model.[22] At the same time that dynamics between urban forces were visualized and controlled in the digital realm, physical objects within the city were fitted with sensors that allowed for the registration and regulation of their conditions.[23] As these examples show, media art institutes offered architects the possibility to probe design, visualization and communication strategies based on relational information systems, while making the interdependency of media and architecture more tangible.

Nathalie Bredella

14 Knowbotic Research. IO_Dencies, at the Dutch Electronic Art Festival (DEAF), 1998. In this project, urban forces were coded and visualized as a network of flows.

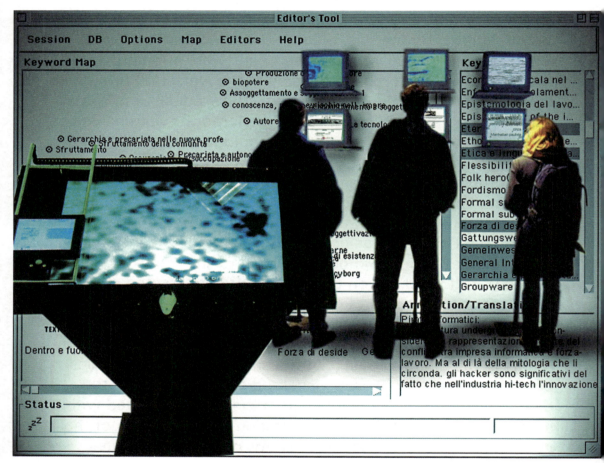

Inter-Media Relationships and Built Form

In discussions of communication technology and its impact on space in the early 1990s, Vilém Flusser emphasized architecture's mediating role, arguing that architecture had become an interface technology for people and their environment.[24] Flusser suggested that architects needed to design the architecture of information spaces as well as new points of access to these spaces, and he advocated for thinking about relationships, rather than objects, in design. At first, most of the architectural projects exhibited in the media art context took the form of installation art, but some architects began to explore inter-media relationships in built form.

In 1992, NOX received a commission from the Dutch government to realize a pavilion devoted to fresh water in Water-Land Neeltje Jans (figs. 16–17), a theme park that also included an adjacent pavilion by architects ONL (Kas Oosterhuis and Ilona Lénárd) devoted to salt water.[25] The WaterLand commission called for an interactive building that would bring the significance of water, and particularly the hydrological cycles, closer to the visitors, while also relating to a larger environmental project. The island of Neeltje Jans had been constructed as part of a novel and ambitious engineering structure: a permeable storm-surge barrier, itself part of the Oosterscheldekering flood defence program, which allowed for the exchange of saline and fresh water as a means of protecting the ecosystem of the nature area of the Oosterschelde.[26] In light of the history of Dutch water management, which from the early Middle Ages has been fashioned by the threat of tides and rises in the sea level, new notions of interactivity and new technologies were applied to an ecological problem.

Nathalie Bredella

15 Bernhard Franken. Netzstadt ("network city"), 1996. Franken conceptualized hyperlinks and flows of the Internet as virtual structures.

15

16 NOX (Lars Spuybroek). H₂Oexpo, six transversal sections, 1996. AutoCAD file converted to scalable vector graphics format for publication. Original file: 6 2D transversal sections.dwg, 3.5 MB, last modified 22 January 1996. Lars Spuybroek fonds (AP173), CCA. Gift of Lars Spuybroek

17 NOX (Lars Spuybroek). H₂Oexpo, concrete survey axonemtric projections and elevations, 1996. AutoCAD file converted to scalable vector graphics format for publication. Original file: concrete survey axons elevations.dwg, 2.4 MB, last modified 22 January 1996. Lars Spuybroek fonds (AP173), CCA. Gift of Lars Spuybroek

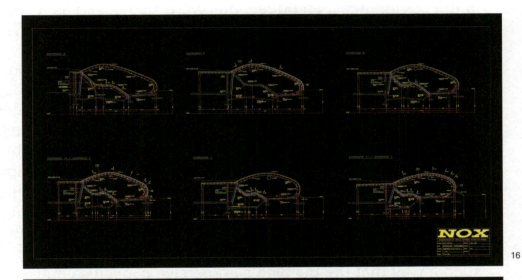

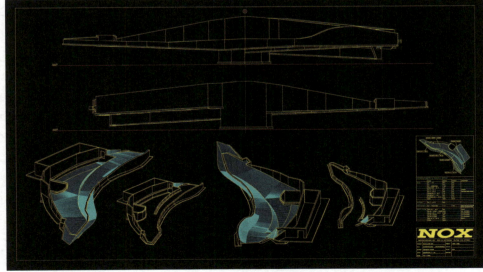

Although issues of media and ecology rarely occupied centre stage in architectural conversations in the 1990s, events like the *ECO-TEC* conferences sponsored by Storefront for Art and Architecture in New York created some interdisciplinary discussion of the relationship between ecology and technology, and also began to raise questions about political control and the environment.[27] Multi-scalar network technologies and their effects on human experience were addressed in the conferences, and questions were also raised as to what extent "ecologization" was related to effects of de-territorialization and contemporary capitalism.[28]

Developed in the context of such questions of technology and the environment, NOX's project for Neeltje Jans, H_2Oexpo, was an opportunity to address the interaction between architecture and electronic media at a specific building site. While other architects focused on the potential of liquidizing architecture in cyberspace—for example, Marcos Novak applied algorithmic techniques to design and thus expanded the definition of architecture into electronic space—the H_2Oexpo pavilion aimed to create experiences in a physical space.[29] In NOX's pavilion, architecture would be combined with information in such a way that the building's immersive capacities could inform the public about the dynamics of water management in the Netherlands. Inter-media relationships were therefore introduced during design and construction.

Early sketches and models of the H_2Oexpo pavilion alluded to a naturally informed shape, tuned by parameters such as wind and dunes that also determined the building's placement in the landscape. A progression of drawings that detailed the shape and structure of the pavilion resulted in a structure resembling a corridor, varying in height and width and passing into the neighbouring saltwater pavilion. Inside NOX's pavilion, visitors could experience water's tactile and auditory qualities by interacting with the space, a possibility facilitated through the installation of EDITSP(L)INE (fig. 18). Typically used in shipbuilding, splines consist of a curve of minimum tension, created through individual fixed points. Spuybroek's design made reference to this method, reiterating it in simulation and within the building itself. EDITSP(L)INE was based on an interactive computer system that controlled sensors; the movements of visitors triggered various events in specific areas of the pavilion corresponding to screen, light and sound projections.[30] This technologically enhanced architecture acted as a media interface, creating events and new experiences. By expanding the visitor's perception, EDITSP(L)INE synchronized different media so that the intake, transfer and processing of information were experienced corporally. A heightened awareness of spatiality was developed through the integration of sound in the pavilion. On a CD-ROM, sound patterns were linked to sensors so that sounds could be distorted and stretched in relation to movement within the space. This could cause noises to move toward or away from visitors, emphasizing the potential of sound to organize space.[31]

The pavilion's geometry and the interaction with water, sound and light involved visitors kinesthetically in the architecture. As Spuybroek suggests, within the building, events were "no longer functions or mechanical actions." They rather arose "from the interaction between a less determined architecture and the body."[32] The relationship between interactive media and design, which was intended to encourage bodily experience of the environment through technologies of sensory extension, also allowed visitors to be more conscious of their position in space and time. Spuybroek considered the pavilion to be a place in which media space and the individual were

Nathalie Bredella

18 NOX (Lars Spuybroek). H$_2$Oexpo, interior installation view, 1997. Original file: intpeople4.jpg, 1.1 MB, last modified 16 August 2003. Lars Spuybroek fonds (AP173), CCA. Gift of Lars Spuybroek

18

integrated. The building, saturated with water but also with information technologies, was meant to remind visitors of their relationship to this dynamic element. As such the pavilion acted as media, while being part of a larger media ecology of water management.

Antecedents to a More Synthetic Approach to Material, Form and Information

Frei Otto's work with materials and construction was significant for architects who addressed inter-media relationships in the 1990s. The Institut für Leichte Flächentragwerke (IL) at the Universität Stuttgart, led by Otto, explored questions of interactivity according to the properties and scale of material, in pursuit of an ecological and economic form of building (figs. 19–22). Otto and his team conducted experiments in order to develop what they saw as a more humane and natural architecture, based on lightweight structures with minimal material and energy requirements.[33] These studies of "natural construction" not only would allow for the cultivation of the well-being of man but were also explicitly conceived as a "light" alternative to "brutal" fascist buildings. In the interdisciplinary context of the institute, architects, engineers, painters, sculptors and philosophers collaborated to develop experimental methods in order to understand structural forces and to represent design parameters visually.[34] Examining the relationship between form, force and mass, Otto and physicist Wolfgang Weidlich suggested that the question of flow should be addressed in experiments in which "the form of a structure can develop without being hindered by the equilibrium of forces as a function of the properties of the material used."[35]

Nathalie Bredella

19 Frei Otto with Marek Kolodziejczyk. Thread model used to determine optimized detour path networks, 1991. Institut für Leichtbau Entwerfen und Konstruieren Bildarchiv, Universität Stuttgart

20 Frei Otto with Marek Kolodziejczyk. Thread model used to determine optimized detour path networks, 1991. Institut für Leichtbau Entwerfen und Konstruieren Bildarchiv, Universität Stuttgart

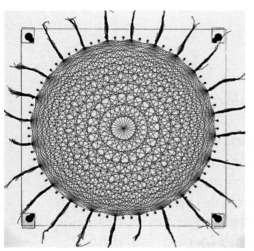

19

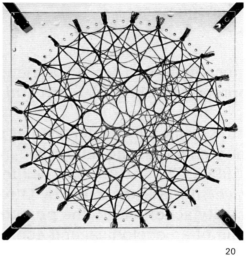

20

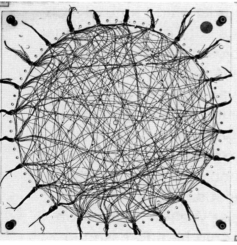

21

21 Frei Otto with Marek Kolodziejczyk. Thread model used to determine optimized detour path networks, 1991. Institut für Leichtbau Entwerfen und Konstruieren Bildarchiv, Universität Stuttgart

22 Frei Otto. Olympic Stadium, Munich, wire net model of the roof, 1:125, 1972. The model was loaded with small weights to simulate snow loads, and the changes in tension were measured with strain gauges (the quarter-circular objects visible on the net). The deformation of the model that results from the load was measured by photographing the net with and without the weights on the same negative. Institut für Leichtbau Entwerfen und Konstruieren Bildarchiv, Universität Stuttgart

Reframing minimum path optimization,[36] one of the classic problems of computer science, Otto had developed an experimental device with which it was possible to determine the lowest cost for the construction and maintenance of infrastructural networks. The experimental set-up of the *optimierten Wegesysteme* ("optimized pathways system") developed as follows: threads were stretched between the nodal start and end points and were then loosened so that they had an excess length of approximately 8 percent. Immersing the threads in water and then removing them caused the threads to bunch up as they were moistened. In the resulting configurations the thread paths were indeed longer than the direct path, but due to their "stickiness" they became interconnected in a "vague order."[37] Otto and architect Bodo Rasch suggested that this had practical implications: "The network of the minimally circuitous route seeks a minimum, namely when applied to the energy for the construction and maintenance of the roads and for traffic in general."[38]

Otto's models were able to assume the function of form-finding instruments; they allowed different elements within a system to interact for a certain period, eventually resulting in a new structure. Through this process, materials attained a degree of freedom of action in the design process.[39] Otto was less concerned with developing general principles than he was with defining parameters in which the materials could find their own forms. According to architect and historian Detlef Mertins, the emergent flexible surfaces of Otto's experiments also blurred the distinction between surface and support, making "construction and structure a function of movement."[40] As a result, design flexibility was understood literally and materially, and the procedural aspect of the form finding led to a coherent language of bending, splitting and curving (fig. 23).[41]

Otto's experiments connected with other instruments and media. At IL's experimental workshop, Otto used optical instruments to construct an apparatus that enabled the observation of a material's behaviour and allowed for the study of organic and inorganic matter at different scales.[42] Processes of mediation between models, photographs and drawings were central to the institute's mode of design, in which information on a material's form was gathered either by optical analysis or by scanning in order to arrive at a mathematical calculation of structural forms.[43] According to engineer Peter Rice, these techniques had from the beginning the aim of developing construction principles. In this way, the analysis of materials took Otto from the initial design concept to the final structure.[44] The design and construction of the German Pavilion at Expo '67 in Montreal (fig. 24)—particularly the roof structure—involved a mediation of modelling techniques. The translation from a series of canvas models to mesh models, used to prove the stress level, was vital in defining the cable lengths of the structure. For architects in the 1990s, the modelling techniques that Otto developed at the institute were of particular interest as they related to a concern with interactivity and with a new role for media and communication in architecture, in which techniques of seeing and mapping converged with the development of design and construction techniques.

At Expo '67, Buckminster Fuller, together with architect Shoji Sadao, realized the Biosphere, a self-supporting structure for the pavilion of the United States. The structural system of the Biosphere portrayed nature and design as a large interconnected system, foregrounding notions derived from ecology. The pavilion presented a vision of environmental and energy control, suggesting that such a system of control would allow for better living conditions and a more equal distribution

Nathalie Bredella

23 Frei Otto. Bic-λ-Diagram, representing the material cost and load-bearing behaviour of artificial and natural objects, humans and animals, 1998. Otto defined the Bic value as the maximum length of a material able to suspend itself. The diagram shows the connection between the mass of an object and the force of the load acting on the object with the transmission distance (relative slenderness: λ), describing the form. Institut für Leichtbau Entwerfen und Konstruieren Bildarchiv, Universität Stuttgart

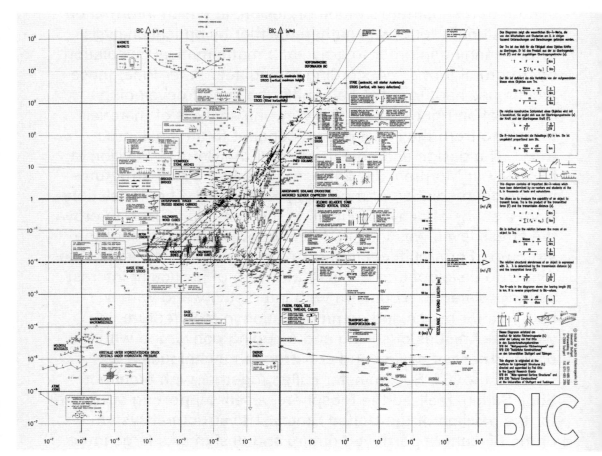

of resources worldwide. Cornelius Borck recounts that Fuller would have liked to use Expo '67, which had as its motto "Man and His World," as a site to exhibit his World Game—a kind of future workshop in which computer simulations provided information on world development to help the game's players make decisions in a series of given scenarios (fig. 25).[45] The game was intended to create the conditions for a more humane world, with reduced poverty and inequality. It was ultimately excluded from Expo '67, a decision that, according to Borck, might well have been provoked by its imitation of Cold War–era war games.[46] The mediation that characterized Fuller's project for Expo '67—a mediation between technocratic gestures of total control and the idea of a global humanity—foreshadowed the 1990s debates on information technology and cultural and political control.[47]

ANY 17: "Forget Fuller? Everything You Always Wanted to Know About Fuller But Were Afraid to Ask," edited by Reinhold Martin and published in 1997, gives historical insight into Fuller's ecological approach to questions of media, economic systems and technology. The issue's contributors reflect on Fuller's utopian models and address in particular his understanding of design as inextricably linked with the social and natural environment. In discussing Fuller's vision of the mediatic qualities of the environment, the authors stress the aesthetic effects of his representations and the role images can play in mediating between architecture and ecology. According to Mark Wigley, giving visibility to interacting phenomena fostered a more ecological way of thinking about design.[48] Fuller's geometric structures therefore acted less as formal systems than as interfaces for gathering and coordinating vast amounts of information. Sanford Kwinter argues that Fuller saw structure as being comprised of energy and information,

Nathalie Bredella

24 Frei Otto. German Pavilion for Expo '67 under construction. Institut für Leichtbau Entwerfen und Konstruieren Bildarchiv, Universität Stuttgart

25 Buckminster Fuller. World Game workshop, 1969

which could be used in production processes. Kwinter describes similar challenges for the twenty-first century, suggesting that the possibilities in society's capital and public goods had yet to be fully realized and concluding that in order to mobilize these resources "we must pass through Fuller."[49] The *ANY 17* contributors frame Fuller's work not as a model to be followed but as a means of advancing a discourse that fostered experimentation, and in which architecture acts "as a form of research," according to Martin, that is constantly "displacing its own boundaries."[50]

Visualization Techniques and Informational Infrastructures

Focusing on the technical as well as the social practices that surround the recording of knowledge, historian and philosopher of science Geoffrey C. Bowker has shown the way informational infrastructures relate to the production of scientific knowledge.[51] Applied to the context of the discussions on media and architecture in the 1990s, Bowker's point offers insight into how values are integrated into information and communications technology, in particular how society and politics influence visualization techniques. By this time, new technologies of sensing, mapping and locating space had become more widespread, thanks in large part to a shift from military application to domestic use of satellites and information networks. In the media art context as well as in architecture, logics of informational space also became the subject of sustained research.

Ars Electronica's 1994 exhibition *Intelligente Ambiente: Intelligent Environment* provides a complementary example of architecture and electronic art in the 1990s. Kathy Rae Huffman and Carole Ann Klonarides co-curated "Intelligent Ambience," a video program that focused on artists' interpretations of architectural and urban space and that dealt with the visualization of space as well as the spatialization of vision. Exploring relationships involved in envisaging urban and architectural environments, Klonarides and Huffman compiled videos organized into four sections entitled "Interim: Within and Beyond Confinement," "Interference: The Invisible Matrix," "Interstitial: Between What Is (Seen)" and "Intervention: The Tactical Tourist." These works shed light on the ability of video technology to make the development of architectural environments perceptible. For example, Branda Miller's music video "Time Squared" (1987) grapples with how the urban renewal program of New York's Times Square risked destroying a lively neighbourhood. By merging sound and images of Times Square, past and present, an intensive visual and auditory experience was contrasted with images of the office of John Burgee Architects, the firm in charge of the area's renovation. Bob Snyder's video "Trim Subdivisions" (1981) uses special effects to manipulate images of suburban houses so that they become a set of interchangeable units. The recurring box form of the architecture enhances the two-dimensionality and redundancy of tract houses, and serves as a metaphor for the regulation of life in the late industrial age. Nancy Buchanan's "American Dream #7: The Price Is Wrong" (1991) uses footage of the Watts riots in Los Angeles in 1965, raising the problems of real-estate speculation and the failure of the American Dream, in which home ownership is no longer a basic right.[52] Reflecting on the exhibition, Huffman argued that multimedia artists could give insight into the social and political formations that are quietly at work in built form.[53]

In response to debates about surveillance strategies and their political consequences for civil society, Thomas Y. Levin curated an exhibition at the ZKM in 2001 entitled *Ctrl [Space]: Rhetorics of Surveillance from Bentham to Big Brother*.[54] The exhibition explored an array of strategies of control, from the eighteenth-century architectural model of the panopticon to forms of surveillance arising from new information technologies, bringing the 1990s activities of media art institutes into the twenty-first century. Among the artists participating in the exhibition, architect Laura Kurgan was invited to produce a piece based on her work with satellite images. For the work, *New York, September 11, 2001, Four Days Later*, Kurgan used a photograph of Manhattan taken by the IKONOS satellite four days after the attack on the World Trade Center. The orbital imager used the register of the transformation of matter —a cloud of smoke—as a means of understanding disaster. By manipulating the pixels of the image Kurgan created an enhanced representation of the attack as a cloud of dust and debris. Enlarged to a size of fifteen by forty-eight feet and printed in section on pre-laminated paper, the image was shown on the floor in one of the gallery spaces at the ZKM. Visitors were encouraged to walk on the image, and from the overhanging balconies above the gallery floor they could view the work from greater distances.[55] Kurgan's piece addresses the relationship of media with geography, and explores how mapping by media distances the viewer from the horror of the event.

In her critical embracing of surveillance technology, Kurgan had previously worked with global positioning systems (GPS) and other mapping technologies as a means of negotiating the concreteness of a place and of locating information. Her work *You Are Here: Information Drift*, exhibited at Storefront for Art and Architecture in 1994, made use of contemporary information and positioning technology in order to map a specific location, in this case the Storefront gallery itself (fig. 26).[56] The work focuses on the interaction between built space and its representation: "Turned into a satellite receiver, the Storefront became both the subject of and the surface on which to register and display the flow of digital mapping with GPS."[57] Kurgan draws attention to the permeability of boundaries usually associated with architecture: inside and outside, or open and closed. Surveillance and mapping technologies created a new awareness of place in relation to global positioning systems, and Kurgan's work uncovers the architectural implications of these technologies in the context of media discourse.

Dedicated to the relationship between architecture, urban culture and electronic media, the *Digital Territories* symposium, which took place at V2_ in 1996, provided a site for theoretical reflection on the social, economic and political formations of virtual networks and the way they connect to physical space. Artists and architects engaged in dialogue with theoreticians, questioning how distributed working processes gave shape to new relations of power and control in virtual environments, and stressing architecture's ability to design and organize new forms of interaction.[58] In her presentation, sociologist and economist Saskia Sassen examined issues of social power and the new hierarchical structures created by electronic networks. Turning her attention to the restructuring of digital space by assertive corporations, Sassen saw the control of information networks, which were increasingly embedded in the development of global cities, as a right held only by those able to afford access. Instead of idealizing connectivity, which is so often characterized as democratic and liberating, Sassen decried the decline in public digital space and called for active contestation.[59]

The financialization of the world economy contributed to the formation of new informational networks, which were

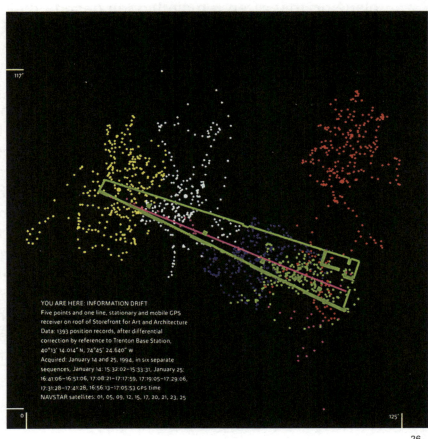

26 Laura Kurgan. *You Are Here: Information Drift*, showing GPS records of Storefront for Art and Architecture, 1994

developing as corollaries of physical networks. Keller Easterling's work in this context was dedicated to the analysis of the changing political landscapes of twentieth-century capitalism. Understanding the strategies by which these networks operated offered, according to Easterling, a way of developing new strategies of action. Working with different media formats such as web installations, games and HyperCard exposed the particularities of specific situations and probed new strategies of action.[60] In her book *American Town Plans: A Comparative Time Line*, published in 1993, Easterling analyzes the organizational protocols and mechanisms that impacted the structuring of landscape and the planning of cities. Using computer technology to record transportation networks, housing types and proposed legislation, Easterling exposes the principles of urban planning that often remain hidden despite their importance in constructing the sprawl that is characteristic of American cities.[61] In this period Easterling was particularly interested in organizational structures and their translation into architectural spaces. In 1994, teaching one of the first paperless studios introduced by Bernard Tschumi at Columbia University's Graduate School of Architecture, Planning and Preservation, Easterling emphasized the spatial consequences of material and immaterial flows of information.[62] Viewing architecture as an "active form," a spatially operating system that shapes society, was central to her work. She asserted, moreover, that computer-aided organizational processes were not limited to the computer itself but were rather conceived as elements of built space. Specifically referencing countercultural programming, Easterling's work implies that architecture could be understood as a site for hacking or disturbing the protocols of networked space, which held the potential to reconfigure existing networks of power. Easterling and Sassen, from their respective disciplinary perspectives, understood architecture as a socio-technological infrastructure that operated within a relational framework.

The Dynamics of a Theory of Architecture

In the essay "The Object of Interactivity," published in *NOX: Machining Architecture* in 2004, the media theorist Arjen Mulder challenges the stability of architecture as a medium characterized by configurations of physical space. Digital technologies in the 1990s had prompted new practices as well as perceptual shifts in the electronic arts and had therefore led to an understanding of architecture as dynamic and responsive rather than static. Writing of an "interactive architecture," Mulder points to the potential of an architecture that could be activated by the user, as well as of a user who could be prompted by the built form to perform certain actions. Interaction was based on the connection between two systems that could change each other reciprocally.[63] Mulder's notion of architecture frames thinking and practice in the terms of the imminent age of ubiquitous computing and digital experimentation.

In the context of media art institutes, architects addressed questions of interaction by looking at technology and how it interacted with politics, economics and society as it produced new spatial conditions. Democratic ideals, often associated with digital technologies, were critically assessed, and practitioners focused on protocols and rules as well as on the aesthetic effects of media technologies. Architecture was thus at the heart of a discourse that uncovered instabilities in technological systems on a global as well as a bodily scale. Architects dealt with epistemic and aesthetic questions of technologically enhanced environments and also focused on the sensory experience of interactive spaces. Through an engagement with visual, auditory and physical processes, projects explicated the media conditions implicit in knowledge production. A more dynamic theory of architecture was developed in response, and new means of augmenting perception and behaviour emphasized the relationship between form and action. This theory fostered design strategies meant to cause disturbances through interaction, in order to reveal the mechanisms by which architecture operates. The projects developed in this context of media art articulate the way architecture worked with other media and, eventually, operated as a form of media itself.

Stan Allen

The beginning of the paperless studios at Columbia University's Graduate School of Architecture, Planning and Preservation in 1992 grew from a convergence of wider debates on theory, technology, media and culture. Intellectual interest in the computer, notably spurred by a popular shift in theoretical emphasis from Derrida's deconstruction and ruptures to Deleuze's difference through continuity, influenced the way computers were adopted by Columbia's experimental studios.

This text is the transcription of a presentation that was given at the CCA in 2013.

STAN ALLEN

1 Greg Lynn. Cardiff Bay Opera House, digital rendering for the competition entry, 1994

THE PAPERLESS STUDIOS IN CONTEXT

1

I certainly don't claim to be a historian or a scholar of the digital. And even though I was involved in the early experiments with the paperless studios at Columbia and in my own practice we're on the computer all day, I'm not an advocate or a partisan of the digital in architecture.

What I have been is an informed observer. I'm going to give a kind of overview, but I don't make any pretence that this is a complete overview. It's a very personal history. It's an anecdotal history. I was—and am—a kind of engaged observer in these early digital experiments, at least to the extent that they occurred around Columbia. I want to give a little bit of context to that, and I'm proposing a periodization, which is sort of up for grabs. For me this is an interesting way to proceed, because I don't really have a dog in this fight.

Stan Allen

I don't necessarily have a strong position one way or another about a lot of these things, so I can recount the history, at least as I observed it.

The first thing I want to say is that I'm very aware that there is a much deeper history to computation than my starting point, which is in the early 1990s. Ivan Sutherland demonstrating Sketchpad, one of the first graphic interfaces, at the Massachusetts Institute of Technology (MIT) in 1963 is an important part of this history. I supervised the PhD dissertation of Ingeborg Rocker and I would send you to her dissertation for details on these developments, especially around Stuttgart in the 1960s. Again, I don't claim a particular expertise there. But you have to remember that early computers were mechanical. There is a kind of on/off logic, which is embedded in Charles Babbage's difference engine or in the Enigma coding machine from the Second World War.

I also want to start off with a terminological distinction, which is not necessarily mine. At Princeton, we've been trained very well by Axel Kilian to refer not to the digital but to computation when we're talking about the computer in architectural terms. I think it's a useful distinction. The digital is a kind of state of being. It's a condition. When you talk about computation, you're talking about active processes.

Especially today, the digital refers to a state that has to do with the World Wide Web, with the digitization of everything, which has turned certain industries on their heads—the recording industry and so on. That to me is quite different than the specific use of the architectural or engineering capacities of the computer, which is what the more narrow category of computation refers to. What the digital has given architecture in the most banal sense, of course, is rendering, which interests me very little. In a crude sense, you could say that if you're dealing with pixels and raster images, you're in a digital world. If you're dealing with vector images, you're in the world of computation. There's an insight that Friedrich Kittler has in *Gramophone, Film, Typewriter*, that at one point there was a medium specificity—records were on vinyl, film was on celluloid. Today, of course, all of that has been collapsed into pixels. So on the one hand the digital is tending toward a kind of single medium that is based on pixels, whereas computation, I think, still retains a certain degree of medium specificity —or at least that's what I would argue.

I'm throwing that terminological distinction out there as a background for a loose and overlapping chronology. I think it is possible to talk about four phases in the digital and computation in architecture. I have quite intentionally not assigned dates to any of them, but in an obvious way, the stages are roughly the 1980s, the 1990s, the early 2000s and the present. But, again, they overlap. There's a lot of fuzziness between these different states.

It's important to pay attention to discussions that were happening around Columbia in the early 1990s when digital technology became available, which provide a kind of backdrop. This was the period of Donna Haraway's "A Manifesto for Cyborgs." The term *cyberspace*, of course, was coined by William Gibson in *Neuromancer*. So this was the texture of what we imagined the digital or the cybernetic to be.

Nobody actually had a computer in the 1980s. Very few people really had access to them. The architecture of the World Wide Web was tested in 1989 and began to be implemented in 1990 and 1991. So there had to be an attempt to imagine what these spaces might be. Of course, the images came from popular culture, from films like *Blade Runner*, and there was this sense of a slippage of identity—certainly feminism and identity politics entered into it through people like Donna Haraway— and a sense that cyberspace, the digital, was a kind of fluid, vertiginous space that allowed all kinds of connectivity, unhampered by the weight of the physical. The book *Cyberspace: First Steps*, for example, edited by Michael Benedikt, came out in 1991 and suggested that this was a space where architects could potentially work. The protocols were not yet established, and this was one of the promises of the digital, at a time when nobody really knew what the digital was going to look like.

Artists and architects were imagining this space as well—spaces of displacement, spaces where identity could be slippery. Bruce Nauman, Vito Acconci and then Diller + Scofidio, in some of their early installations that incorporated video and media, were working in this same territory. They had an installation in the PROJECTS series at the Museum of Modern Art (MoMA) in 1989 (fig. 2), right in the heart of a period when these ideas were being tested, and when architects were trying to understand what their potential role might be within that world.

For me, this is the prehistory to the 1990s, when the early design protocols for these computers were laid out. Clearly, the two people who deserve pride of place in this stage are Greg Lynn and Bernard Cache. The 1992 issue of *Architectural Design* that Greg edited, "Folding in Architecture," is an interesting piece (fig. 3)—though, again, if you look closely at that issue, maybe only a third of the projects used the computer in any way. I think this is an important point, that Greg had theorized smoothness, subtleness and continuity before he was actually working in an intense way with the software.

Another important piece of the emerging aesthetics of the computer at this time came out of an issue of Princeton's journal called *Fetish*. This was also the title of a conference that took place at Princeton in 1989. The journal was edited by Greg, Sarah Whiting and Ed Mitchell, and came out in 1992. *Fetish* very intentionally worked between the Marxist notion of the fetishism of commodities and the Freudian notion of the fetish. There's clearly an aesthetic there that, again, becomes very visible in Greg's work in the 1990s

Stan Allen

388

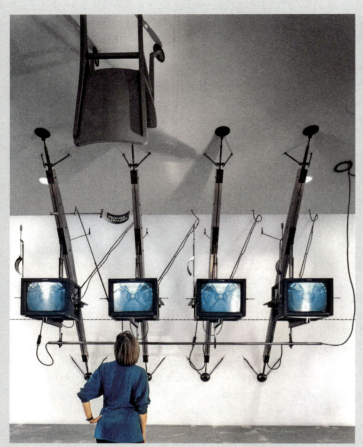

2 Diller + Scofidio. *Para-site*, installation view in MoMA's PROJECTS series, 1989

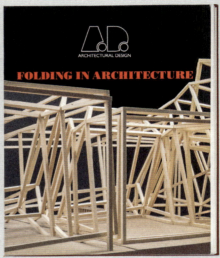

3 Cover of "Folding in Architecture," *Architectural Design* 102 (1993), showing a concept model of Peter Eisenman's Center for the Arts, Emory University, Atlanta, 1991. CCA. W.A755

that predates the actual use of the computer. You'd have a basswood model, but of course it's a wireframe. This phase of work exists in this transition mode in which the notion of a wireframe—a representational strategy that belongs to the computer—would be rendered in this space out of basswood. You probably wouldn't necessarily imagine this kind of model without the use of the computer, yet in 1992 it was still being realized by conventional means.

In Joan Ockman's book on the history of architectural education in North America, I wrote a piece that deals with the period from 1990 to the present. You're given what seems to be a very arbitrary starting point—1990—but it turns out to have been a pretty interesting moment. Of course, the Berlin Wall fell in 1989, so the political landscape was changing. The first George Bush was president. John Major was prime minister in Britain. The Mac Classic was released in 1990, with a massive forty-megabyte hard drive. They had been making Macintosh computers since 1984, so by 1990 they could already call it "classic." But it was really the first widely available desktop computer so, again, it marked a kind of transition.

Nelson Mandela was released from prison in 1990. He'd been in prison for twenty-seven years. The outcry over the Robert Mapplethorpe photographs in Cincinnati was happening in 1990. The first digital cell phone call was made in 1990. In the architecture world, the cover of *Progressive Architecture* announcing the P/A Awards that year was Diller + Scofidio's Slow House. That project was also engaged with media and video technology—not necessarily digital technology—and problems of representation. It's an important marker when you think about the context of the later work. At Columbia, we knew about Bernard Cache mostly through his relationship to Gilles Deleuze. The English translation of *The Fold* came out in 1992. The other point of reference was the MoMA deconstructivism show in 1987, which was the generation of our teachers: Peter Eisenman, Bernard Tschumi, Daniel Libeskind. For Greg Lynn, Hani Rashid, Jesse Reiser, me—these were essentially the father figures. So, to some extent, there was a reaction against deconstructivism.

One of the brilliant things that Greg pointed out was that as stylistically different as Colin Rowe and Michael Graves are, they share a compositional language that is based on fragmentation and discontinuity. So the turn toward continuity, to suppleness, to smoothness, that is, in turn, underwritten by Deleuze and Guattari in general, and specifically by *The Fold*, corresponded also with a turn away from the project of disjunction, fragmentation and discontinuity that had been underwritten by Derrida—at least in the story that was told by Mark Wigley and Philip Johnson in the show at MoMA.

I want to emphasize that there was a sense of moving into a new theoretical territory, a shift from Derrida to Deleuze, a shift away from disjunction, fragmentation and discontinuity to questions of connectivity, smoothness and the supple. This shift was also underwritten to some extent—and this is why the context of the 1980s is important—by an intuition that the emerging world of the web was also about seamless connectivity. So, this formed some of the intellectual backdrop for the experiments that were conducted in those early studios and by people like Bernard Cache and Greg Lynn.

I remember the discussions with Greg. Shoei Yoh had been invited by Bernard Tschumi to teach at Columbia in 1993 or 1994. Greg saw projects like the Odawara sports complex as offering a promise of an architecture that could accommodate difference and maintain continuity (fig. 4). Under the modernist system that Rowe, Graves and the architects of deconstruction were all reacting against, you could only introduce difference into the system by introducing discontinuity. And the idea that you could produce a new sense of the whole, a complex whole—this was a big deal for us at the time. Sanford Kwinter was around, and with his interest in complexity theory, he was leading us through some of these things and their connections to Deleuze. This notion of being able to introduce difference into the system without creating a disjunctive break was a very important underlying thing.

And this was exactly what Greg laid out. I want to point out two things from "Multiplicitous and Inorganic Bodies," an essay that Greg published in *Assemblage* in 1992—again, before the paperless studios had been set up. One is that the model of the Stranded Sears Tower was made by cutting up pieces of foam and bending them and twisting them—again, no computer was involved (fig. 5). Here the supple is a material suppleness. Greg may be the only person to put together Bataille and Wittkower—and Colin Rowe, of course—and then just kind of slide into D'Arcy Wentworth Thompson, and the idea that you can take this regularized grid that's so fundamental to Western architecture and start deforming it.

As opposed to the argument of deconstructivism—that the stability and the hierarchy of conventional classical architecture is something that needs to be violently attacked, head on—Greg's proposition is, no, you accept that as your starting point, and you start pulling it, stretching it and deforming it, and, working from the example of D'Arcy Wentworth Thompson, through an incremental series of deformations you can start to produce difference. Of course, Greg points out that the Sears Tower is also a nine-square grid, as is the internal armature of the Statue of Liberty. That armature supports this complex, supple skin, and there's a whole argument there about the relationship between the kind of stability maintained in the statue while the accommodating, supple skin is facilitated by the armature.

So in these cases, to reiterate, the language and the operations are theorized before the actual use of the com-

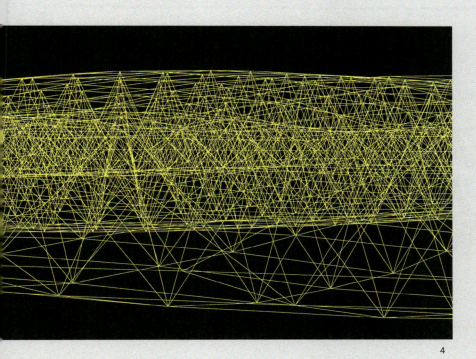

4 Shoei Yoh + Architects. Municipal Sports Complex, Odawara, Kanagawa, Japan, wireframe perspective of the roof structure, 1990–1992. Silk-screened ink on paper mounted on foam board, 109.5 x 79.4 x cm. Shoei Yoh fonds (AP166), CCA. Gift of Shoei Yoh

4

puter. Of course, things were also happening in parallel—the Lewis Residence is the laboratory for this new language in Frank Gehry's work, for example. Frank Gehry has said numerous times that the Lewis Residence was the laboratory that made Bilbao possible. Gehry's own house in Santa Monica was included in the deconstructivism exhibition, but in 1989, he did the Vitra building, where you have a transition from a collage-based language to a language that is all about smoothness and continuity. There's a description of Vitra I like very much, which is that every surface that could potentially get rain has zinc and every other surface is white. Gehry did have access to sophisticated computer technology in the form of CATIA, but there are very similar wireframe drawings from the Lewis Residence, and in a very direct way, what Greg had theorized about that relationship between the armature and the supple skin was being executed at Bilbao (figs. 6–7).

In some sense, all of this is still a kind of prehistory to the paperless stu-

Stan Allen

5   Greg Lynn. The Stranded Sears Tower in "Multiplicitous and Inorganic Bodies," *Assemblage* 19 (1992): 44–45. CCA. W.A8682

6   Frank O. Gehry & Associates. Guggenheim Museum Bilbao under construction, c. 1997

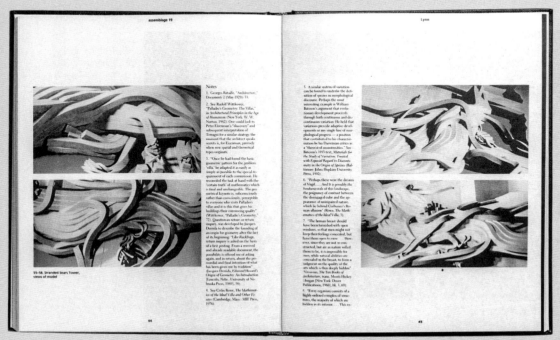

5

6

7 Frédéric Auguste Bartholdi. The Statue of Liberty under construction, 1875

Stan Allen

dios. Greg was working in Eisenman's office from the late 1980s until the early 1990s. I was teaching at Columbia at the time. I would invite Greg up for reviews, and then Greg went out on his own. He was teaching at Columbia and started his own practice, and he got the Korean Presbyterian Church project.

It's important to know that the paperless studios were, at the beginning at least, a relatively small part of what happened at Columbia, even though they became identified very strongly with Columbia. They were initially two of the vertical studios out of twelve or thirteen. They were up on the mezzanine, sort of segregated from the rest of the studios. I designed the space. The model or the norm in schools of architecture was for architectural labs to be in the basement. So it was important for us to bring it from the basement to the attic, up into the light, in a way. We were also taking what up to that point had been mostly a production tool and making it a design tool, and making it part of the studio culture by bringing it up into the studio. Nevertheless, it was incremental at first.

The other thing is that the original paperless studios used Macintosh computers running FormZ. The association with Maya came later. Initially, there were three or four Silicon Graphics machines—which were monopolized by Greg—and the rest were Macintosh. When we had designed the studios, we designated the balconies as model-making spaces, because we thought people would continue to make models. They didn't make models. Pretty soon those balconies were colonized.

I would say that there was a certain amount of tension around the presence of these paperless studios, partly because they were so selective, being only two out of the twelve studios, and also because there were certainly members of the faculty—Kenneth Frampton, Steven Holl, Bob Stern—who were highly suspicious of the computer. I remember some knock-down, drag-out fights at reviews.

Greg and I taught the first two paperless studios that used computers in the fall of 1994, and Greg arrived with a fully formed design agenda. He had a strategy of using the capacities of the computer—at that time, most of the Silicon Graphics machines were running Softimage, a kind of pre-Maya program —to simulate forces. Again, this follows the dictum of D'Arcy Wentworth Thompson that form is a diagram of forces. Greg basically set out to simulate and model those conditions and use that as a way to generate form in architecture. It wasn't a case of looking for biomorphic form; it was really more a question of simulating the procedures of morphogenesis in nature. So if it ended up looking biomorphic, that was not a result of some desired aesthetic end point—although I think Greg knew exactly what he was doing, and he knew what it was going to look like.

I disagree a little bit with the assertion that there was a turn away from theory in the 1990s. Certainly people like Bernard Cache and Greg Lynn were very active as theorists. It is true that once the technology got up and running, there were a lot of people who just jumped on the technology and used it in a very mechanical and sometimes formulaic way, but I think in the early stages it was very much driven by theory. Greg's Cardiff Bay Opera House project is a good example (fig. 1). This is 1994. If two years earlier, when he did the Stranded Sears Tower, he was working with physical models, in a sense simulating the potentials of the computer, by 1994 he got his hands on a Silicon Graphics machine.

I know I'm spending a lot of time on this period. But as much as Greg had an impact in Peter Eisenman's office, he was very much shaped by Peter, and by Peter's notion of form generation as a kind of iterative—one might even say, though actually, I don't think he would say this—recursive process. It's really more additive, where you begin with a geometric primitive and then, through a series of geometrical operations of displacements and slippages, over the course of these different iterations the object gains greater complexity, such that at the end of the process all the information from the previous stages is embedded in the object. You can compare it to House II (fig. 8)—there's an idea of starting with a fixed form that then receives the imprint of all of these geometric operations. Even if you're using the capacity of the computer to model certain forces, I think the approach owes quite a bit to Peter Eisenman's iterative operations. Right from the beginning in Greg's projects you have a series of diagrams that shows the beginning of the project, the running of the series—the animate form in this case is literally animated—and then at a certain point it has to be frozen, and it becomes the index of all of those procedures (fig. 9).

Around Columbia, there was a slightly cultish quality to the digital early on. You either were part of the cult of the digital or you were not. It had its own language; it was slightly mystical and magical, because that's what the computer was in the beginning. It was a kind of magical machine. And if there was a high priest of the cult of the digital it was Karl Chu (fig. 10). There are people like Karl, as a student of Daniel Libeskind, who saw the process of form generation within the virtual world of the computer as an end in itself, as a kind of philosophical and intellectual project. It didn't need to have an existence outside the computer. I think that approach has very much dissipated. But that's one aspect.

The second aspect is aesthetic—and it's hard to see the originality of what Greg, Bernard Cache and other people did in the early 1990s, because it so quickly became accessible to so many people, and became an aesthetic project of smoothness and continuity. I think the degree to which some of that initial work and the intellectual labour of that initial work became simply about smoothness and continuity is something we can be rightly critical of by the end of the 1990s, and it extends right up through the 2000s to the present.

Stan Allen

396

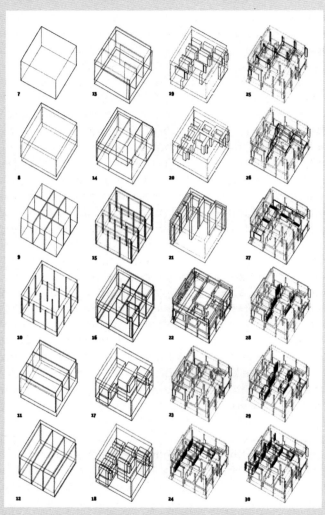

8 Peter Eisenman. House II, analytic diagrams, 1969

9 Greg Lynn. Embryological House, digital rendering, c. 1999. Original file: embryo_EXPLODED_SM.jpeg, 59 KB, last modified 23 December 2015. CCA. Gift of Greg Lynn

10 Metaxy (Karl Chu). X Phylum, Z-rule set lofted splines in perspective (*left*) and frontal elevation (*right*), 1997–1998. Original file: Phylog_1.tif, 58.5 MB, last modified 16 April 1999. Karl Chu X Phylum project records (AP176), CCA. Gift of Karl Chu and Afsheen Rais Rohani

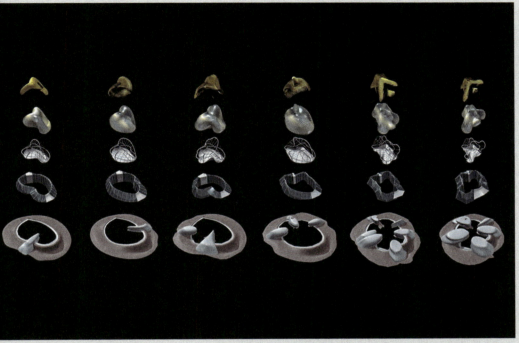

9

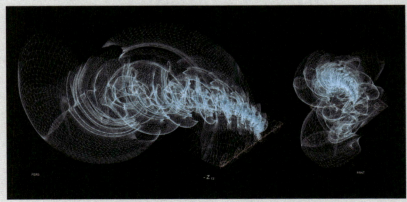

10

Stan Allen

So very quickly after this first phase, which had to do with the emergence of the aesthetics and protocols and theories around early digital or computational design work, the next problem that arose was, how do you actually build this? In that sense, I think it's interesting to look at the project that Greg did with Mark McInturf and Doug Garofalo, the Korean Presbyterian Church. It was, in part, a renovation project; there was an original building from the 1930s there. At the time, the church was criticized because it didn't seem to have any of the smoothness and the supple curvilinearity that had been promised in the drawings. I don't actually find that quite so problematic.

But I also mention this in part because of Gregg Pasquarelli. Gregg was the guy who lived in the trailer on-site and got the church built, and shortly after that, he went out on his own as part of SHoP. The second phase I'm outlining is also this second generation. It's people like Gregg Pasquarelli, who were students of or who worked for Greg Lynn, Hani Rashid or Jesse Reiser. On the one hand, they took this new language as a given. They inherited the language. But I think they also took on the project of fabrication as their own project. How do you actually realize this smooth curvilinear form? What are the tools? How do the protocols of design change?

One thing you see right away in SHoP's Dunescape project at MoMA (fig. 11), for example, is that there are still no curves. It's still approximating curvilinear form through many small sections. This was one of the immediate responses, this MRI section, which you could then translate from one surface to the next. FOA's Yokohama project could be part of this discussion.

There was also an opening up to other industries—to naval architecture, for example. It's not accidental that Bilbao was a centre of the shipbuilding industry—they know how to work with curved surfaces. How you actually build complex form at the scale of a building like Bilbao was really being worked out at this time.

Among the younger generation, the preferred form for experimentation became the pavilion. I want to confess a certain amount of ambivalence about this. The pavilion became the perfect vehicle for a lot of really interesting work that was trying to figure out complex surfaces and questions of joints and so on (fig. 12). I always liked the example of the BOXEL pavilion at the Hochschule Ostwestfalen-Lippe, which was done with beer crates (fig. 13). But the pavilion also became self-limiting, in a way, as a type. There are certain issues that just don't get addressed in a pavilion. I think this was important work that had to be done, and I think that there has been a lot of learning and experimentation as a result, but my concern is that it has a tendency to turn toward the decorative as an end in itself.

This limitation also has to do with the scale of fabrication. I think despite the interest in milling and the advances it

11 SHoP Architects PC. Dunescape, part of the MoMA PS1 Young Architects Program, 2000. David Joseph, photographer

12 Marc Fornes / THEVERYMANY. Labrys Frisae pavilion, installation view at Art Basel Miami, 2011

13 Henri Schweynoch. BOXEL pavilion, 2010. Dirk Schelpmeier, photographer

11

12

13

has made, it is still operating at a fairly small scale. The promise that you could, say, take a form and have a giant 3D printer just print it—I think it was Axel Kilian who pointed out that somebody has actually calculated that milling or 3D printing a normal-size house with current technology would take you something like two and a half years.

The idea of an immediate translation from the file to the object that is somehow run alongside the pavilion is less interesting to me. The experimentation that Gehry Technologies is doing is different. I remember walking by the Lewis Library at Princeton when it was under construction. I know that they're using very sophisticated technology, but there were a couple of guys up on the roof with a sledgehammer knocking a beam into place. Another time there were people with a chalk line getting tangents on the roof. That more mixed condition is still more interesting from my perspective.

I'll end with a snapshot of where I think we are today. From my point of view, we're in a really interesting moment for two reasons. One is the full integration of digital or computational design technology in all architectural offices, where the discussion is no longer about digital design; the discussion is about design, and the computer is a fact of life. Of course, this is partly generational. The kids who are working in our offices today have grown up with a computer—they're much more facile than we are, and they bring a huge reservoir of expertise. There has also been a democratization of the software and the hardware. I mentioned this cult-like aspect to the computer in those early days. The Silicon Graphics machine was very expensive, and it was difficult to learn the software. Now, the software is cheap, readily available and easy to learn.

So you have democratization and widespread accessibility, not only of modelling softwares and production softwares, but also of scripting. You can download physics engines from the Internet, and you can do simulations and form finding in your office without a lot of specialized technology. This is not something I have the capacity to do myself, but I hire someone in the office to write scripts, and we can work with the capacities of computational design in what is not a terribly large and sophisticated office.

That's what I mean by the integration—I should also mention something like how Casey Reas and Ben Fry understand processing, which is as an electronic sketchbook (fig. 14). It's out there, it's available and it's used by artists, architects and designers. And it's changing the protocols of work and design. It doesn't necessarily come with a fixed formal or aesthetic agenda, either. Although I would say that there is certainly a kind of iterative language here that is field-like, serial or working with smaller components. There's a lot of very interesting work done by people like George Legendre. What Greg did in the early 1990s was to take a given software platform and use it against its grain, but he was still working with the

14 Casey Reas. *Network A, a.k.a. Process 4 (Installation 2) (process document)*, 2009. Reas uses custom software to build networks through drawings and digital generative processes.

15 Georg Nees. *Schotter*, 1965. This is an example of Nees's graphic experiments in operationally generating disorder. Kunsthalle Bremen

14

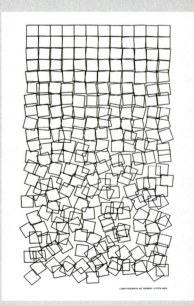

15

architecture of the software as it was given to him, as it was written by someone else. Today there are people writing their own softwares, using some of these widely available platforms, and they're no longer subject to the aesthetic protocols that were written into those early softwares, whether it was Maya, Softimage or FormZ. And I think that is a very positive step, one that is having a fairly widespread impact across the discipline.

At the same time, there is the emergence of highly specialized research by very well-trained people, in which it's almost a given that if you're going to do advanced work in computation that you have the capacity to write code. This feeds into all of the interest in scripting, in robotics and in the integration of sensors into buildings, so that you can begin to think about buildings as a kind of smart technology that is adaptive and reactive, and in the potential of measuring the performative claims that are being made for certain architectures. It's highly specialized research that's not having a widespread impact on the discipline, but I think it's being conducted at a sufficiently high level that it may ultimately filter back into the discipline.

That's the bifurcation I'm getting at: on the one hand, the normalization and democratization of softwares and hardwares, and on the other hand, the emergence of specialized research disciplines that are working in a number of very interesting areas. I'm optimistic about the future. I'm personally not going to be writing code and involved in robotics, but I'm glad there are people who are out there doing it, and I think there's a potential in the future to collaborate with these specialists—but it is also a specialized discourse, in a way.

I'm not in the business of predicting the future, but I want to mention a couple more things. We might go back to someone like Georg Nees (fig. 15). People know about my interest in field conditions, so they will understand why I'm interested in his experiments with computer graphics. I think there's a lot of untapped potential in thinking about the computer in the context of cities and urbanism. If there's a territory that the computer has not yet deeply penetrated or where I think sufficient research and design experimentation hasn't happened yet, it's at the level of cities, and these are perfect tools to think about the complexity of the urban field. That's something that interests me very much.

And then, as we get past the early fascination with this new technology and the need to always be on the cutting edge and working with the most complex, newest and most sophisticated tools, there are artists who are taking a much more hybrid approach. Sanford Kwinter talks about taking an archaic path through the microchip, and this work is in that vein. The artist Michael Golembewski hooked up a scanner and a laptop to a very primitive camera, and he makes photographs that work simultaneously with a nineteenth-century technology and a twenty-first-century technology (fig. 16). By the

16 Michael Golembewski. *The Scanner Photography Project*, c. 2002

17 Photographs of spider webs published in *Spider Communication: Mechanisms and Ecological Significance*, Peter N. Witt and Jerome S. Rovner (Princeton: Princeton University Press, 1982). Constantine Doxiadis used these images in his discussion of ekistics, the science of human settlement.

16

 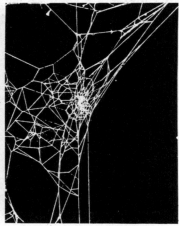

238. a normal spider's web

239. the web spun after the spider had received a dose of dextroamphetamine

way, I know Michael's work because we hired him to write code in the office, and then I discovered that he has this very interesting artistic practice.

For me, these kinds of creative hybrids between the digital and the analog are very interesting for thinking about the future. Because these technologies are more familiar or normative, we can think about them in their hybridized forms. I don't mean that we have to go back to drawing by hand; it's more about understanding where we are in the present and what the potential new hybrids would be moving forward from this point.

I'm also thinking of Constantine Doxiadis and his spider webs (fig. 17). Doxiadis was thinking about the city, but also about the notion that underlying it is a regime of information. The spiders' codes have been messed with. The information has been messed with. The potential moving forward is really thinking at the level of the codes, thinking at the level of information, and not so much the machine itself, or the aesthetics of the machine that we've come to be very familiar with and to associate with the computer.

Bernard Tschumi

05 Conceived <u>in 1992</u>, Columbia University's paperless studios gave a younger group of architects a way to define a language and develop a discourse. The work that resulted quickly started to form an identity, although perhaps not a focus, that established a new set of terms for the ongoing conversation on the role of digital tools in architecture.

This text is the transcription of a presentation that was given at the CCA in 2013.

BERNARD TSCHUMI

1 Paperless studio, Avery Hall,
Columbia University,
c. 1994. David Joseph,
photographer

THE MAKING OF A GENERATION: HOW THE PAPERLESS STUDIOS CAME ABOUT

1

The name *paperless studios* has always been ironic, because we had never produced as much paper as we did once we started using printers and computers. In any case, this story is half the story of a school and half my own story. When I started as dean at Columbia, I had two ambitions. The main one was to try to make a school that had been left behind the locus of a new generation of architects. I had been lucky enough to be at the Architectural Association in the 1970s, at a time when people as diverse as Rem Koolhaas, Léon Krier, Daniel Libeskind, Zaha Hadid and Nigel Coates were there, either as faculty members or as students. They were able to sharpen their own identities in relation to one another. So when I arrived at Columbia in 1988, I wanted to try to "generate the next generation." Although American universities are relatively conservative,

Bernard Tschumi

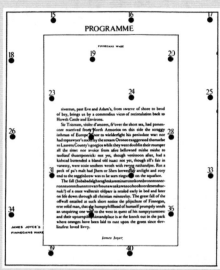

2 Bernard Tschumi. Joyce's Garden, a project using the text of *Finnegans Wake* as an architectural program, 1976–1977

3 Bernard Tschumi. Joyce's Garden, Covent Garden site with point grid, 1976–1977. In an imagined grid over Covent Garden, each student in Tschumi's studio was assigned a point as a site.

with their many tenured faculty members, you can get around this by hiring young, talented adjuncts and giving them the means to develop their own discourse. That was the first ambition.

My second ambition had to do with how you express yourself, knowing that the expression of an architect is generally related to a way of thinking. For example, the argument has often been made that Renaissance architecture was very much related to perspective, a mode of representation. Similarly, Auguste Choisy's invention of a certain form of axonometric in the nineteenth century had an effect on the way architects think about architecture. In this sense, the relationship between the mode of notation and the way of thinking is fundamental to architecture. In the 1970s I tried to find other modes of notation, for example looking at literary texts instead of a program with square metres and rooms. I gave students an excerpt from a text by Edgar Allan Poe, Italo Calvino or James Joyce (figs. 2–4). I did these projects, too, in order to develop a language that would have its own identity in relation to the time we live in.

I was fascinated by modes of notation used in other disciplines, for example the famous score for the film *Alexander Nevsky* (fig. 5), directed by

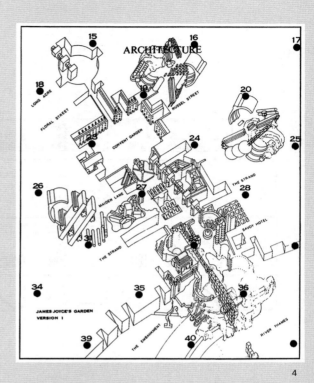

4 Bernard Tschumi. Joyce's Garden, first stage, 1976

Sergei Eisenstein, the Russian avant-garde filmmaker. Eisenstein combined information about the shots, music by Prokofiev, camera angles, the movement of the protagonists and so on. I tried to do the architectural equivalent of this, distinguishing what happens in a space—in other words, the program and the spaces themselves, represented in section, elevation and plan—and the movement of the body in that space (fig. 6). This introduced time and movement into architectural notation, which is not normally done in conventional plans and sections.

Using material from various well-known films, I started to notate the choreography of the movements of bodies in space and to transform them, solidifying them in terms of walls. For example, I approached this with sequences from *Frankenstein*, the 1931 film. Then I developed a tripartite notation that would include program, space and movement. Space Event Movement—SEM—is a form of meaning that architecture would develop, based on a different mode of notation. It led to *The Manhattan Transcripts*, which was about combining space, event and movement in such a way that they would prove to be completely interchangeable, with no hierarchy between them, so that one would not be more important than the

Bernard Tschumi

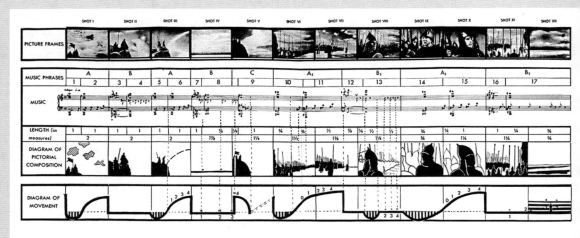

5

other and there would be an intertextuality of program, space and movement. One could then invent various manipulations in which superimposition was a major factor and then edit, cut out and so on. All this was drawn by hand. It was the late 1970s. I always felt one could have multiplied this work to infinity if one had instruments like computers, which came only a bit later.

The axonometric is one of the symbols of the modern movement, but when I started working on the notion of the exploded axonometric—the one that distinguishes between space and movement—I was trying to develop a language that would give an identity to my own work or to the work of other people in my generation. This included things that were done for the fun of it, like the notation of fireworks based on music notation, which eventually became a way to develop architectural projects. For example, in my competition project for the Tokyo Opera House, music notation becomes the starting point for the organization of the building and the mode of thinking about the language —in French, *l'écriture*, the writing— becomes the beginning of a concert.

That's where I was coming from. Arriving at Columbia in 1988, I wanted the school to contribute to a new definition of architecture. In order to

5   Sergei Eisenstein. Score and sequence diagrams for *Alexander Nevsky*, 1938
6   Bernard Tschumi. Joyce's Garden Notation: Homage to Eisenstein, 1977

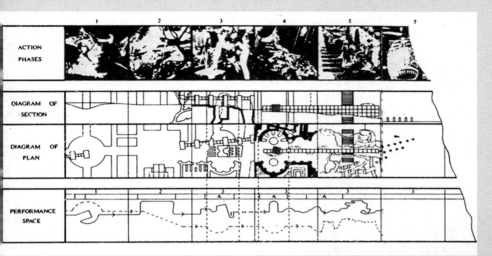

find out what the new generation would do, I hired people like Hani Rashid, Greg Lynn and Jesse Reiser. The idea was that the school would make it possible for them to develop their own language, even though I didn't really know how that language would express itself.

In 1992 I was already using computers in my office, but not in the same creative way that this new generation would come to use them. My work with computers at the time was based on the idea of superimposed layers. In the same way that there are the layers of space, event and movement in *The Manhattan Transcripts*, a computer program would address layers of material—the layer of concrete, glass, steel and so forth. This approach took some of the characteristics of the computer language, of software, in order to reinterpret architecture itself.

At this time, in 1992 and 1993, I started talking to the university to try to get funding to bring computers into the school, so we could find out how an architect can think with computers in the creative process. We prepared a proposal asking for $1 million. The university looked at it, had us present it in front of experts and a few weeks later came back to us, saying, "Oh, very well, but it's not enough. You really want $1.5 million." Within a few months

Bernard Tschumi

7 Work from a studio led by Wiel Arets, fall 1992

412

8 Work from a studio led by Hani Rashid, fall 1992
9 Work from a studio led by Amy Anderson, spring 1993

8

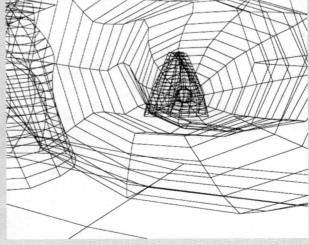

9

Bernard Tschumi

—this is now the summer of 1994—we had the equipment. This had an effect on the school over a five- or six-year period.

I brought in people to try to activate the new tools—there is no question that Bob Stern and Kenneth Frampton were key members of the faculty, but they were not necessarily the ones who would be the inventors of a new language. Wiel Arets was using film and photographs (fig. 7), and Hani Rashid made installations (fig. 8). This was fall 1992 and spring 1993, and we see the use of photographic devices, models and inversions. Amy Anderson's wireframe drawings (fig. 9) and models by Zaha Hadid with Patrik Schumacher (fig. 10) are further examples. Computers weren't being used yet. But look at the language; it's not quite the language of standard architectural work. Greg Lynn was working without a computer, making cardboard models. In the spring of 1994, you could start to see in his work a vast horizon in front of him. I mostly brought in Americans, but I also involved many people from the Netherlands—Ben van Berkel, Wiel Arets and, later, Winy Maas and the NOX group.

That summer of 1994, once we had the machines, we put together a group of people who were the first to experiment in teaching in the computer studios, the "paperless" studios. The

10

10 Work from a studio led by Zaha Hadid with Patrik Schumacher, spring 1993

11 Work from a studio led by Greg Lynn, fall 1994

11

first four were Stan Allen, Keller Easterling, Greg Lynn and Scott Marble. The computers were all in the attic of Avery Hall (fig. 1). Within a few weeks, when you walked into the room, just by looking at the screens and without knowing who the faculty member was, you were able to immediately identify which work was by Greg Lynn, which by Stan Allen, which by Scott Marble and which by Hani Rashid. Scott Marble used fly-through. Stan Allen used datascapes. Hani did a lot of collage—Photoshop used in a sort of crypto-Surrealist manner—and Greg Lynn was already experimenting with models from other fields like fluid mechanics (fig. 11). It immediately became possible to identify the work in relation to each person's past concerns and investigations. There was no unified software available; people had to improvise. Some faculty members, including me, didn't know how to use the new machines. So we needed a DA, a digital assistant: a young, smart kid who knew how to use computers.

Bernard Tschumi

416

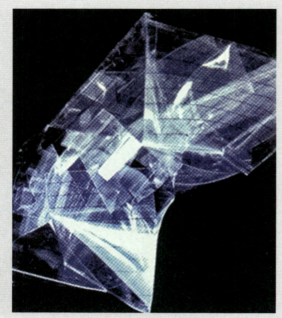

12

13

12 Work from a studio led by Bill
	Mac Donald with Sulan Kolatan,
	summer 1996
13 Work from a studio led by Hani
	Rashid, summer 1996
14 Work from a studio led by Stan
	Allen, spring 1997

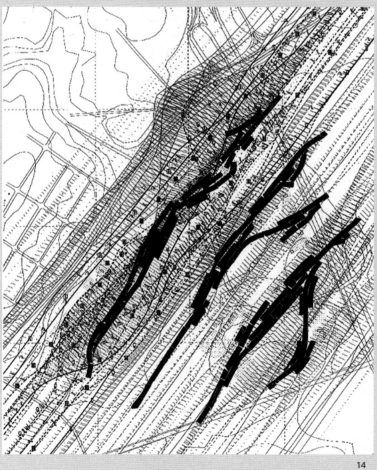

Bernard Tschumi

The paperless studio enterprise was very much testing without a plan, without really knowing what would come out of it. During the fifteen years of my deanship at Columbia, I rarely taught because I was trying to juggle my architectural practice and the deanship, but at the same time I felt that teaching a paperless studio was essential in order to understand the relationship between computers and architectural education. Not that I got a definite answer at the end of that semester. I probably still don't have it.

That first year was very much an experiment. Soon everybody in the school wanted to join in, including people you never would have expected. Even Steven Holl, with his watercolours, started to investigate with the computer. Little by little, but at an incredible speed—it all happened in three to five years—the language in the school completely changed. But it didn't change radically; it simply accelerated things that were already in the works. You could make the analogy of the elevator in the nineteenth century. All architects had designed towers before and had built some, but the invention of the elevator accelerated the making of towers, and hence Manhattan emerged. In the same way, the arrival of the computer accelerated a number of things for that particular generation. That generation developed its own language, just as previous ones had. The work immediately began to have an incredible effect on the architectural culture around us. Historically, what happened in architectural offices—in the profession, so to speak—influenced what was being taught in the schools. In the early 1990s, it went the other way; what was happening in the schools began to have an influence on what was happening in architectural offices.

The work done at Columbia started to have an identity and very much of an influence on other schools, but not necessarily a focus (figs. 12–14). That leads to a question: to what extent did the computer enable architecture to develop new concepts? Or did it simply allow for an internal logic to the mode of notation that architecture was taking, without necessarily discovering a new conceptual approach?

The reason I raise this question is that I ask myself whether what one calls the "diagram" or the "conceptual sketch" is something that the computer cannot do. There is an issue of speed, as well as of transformation. Diagrams done by hand, which are fundamental to architectural concept thinking, are much quicker than the computer (fig. 15). What does this mean today? To what extent does it allow us to say that the digital tool we use is more than a formal device that has a fantastic ability to be translated in construction terms? Does it necessarily allow us to renew the conceptual thinking of what architecture is?

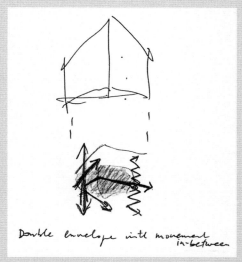

15 Bernard Tschumi. Electronic Media Performing Arts Center, diagram for the competition entry, 2001

Phil Bernstein

Building information modelling (BIM) was first proposed by Autodesk <u>in 2002</u>. Using this tool, architects can generate a highly accurate digital version of a building, to investigate structure, test energy consumption and carry out lighting studies before construction. With BIM, architects have rejected the traditional relationship between client, architect and builder that was carried through in smooth continuity from the era of Alberti through to the end of the twentieth century, and that was only superficially changed by increasingly sophisticated technologies. The information contained in the digital model gives the architect more control of the processes of design and construction, reducing risk and creating the potential for a new collaborative arena for the architect and the construction contractor.

This text is the transcription of a presentation that was given at the CCA in 2016.

PHIL BERNSTEIN

1 Robert Smythson. Design for a rose window, 1599. Ink on paper. British Architectural Library, Royal Institute of British Architects. SD38/II/33

SOUND ADVICE AND CLEAR DRAWINGS: DESIGN AND COMPUTATION IN THE SECOND MACHINE AGE

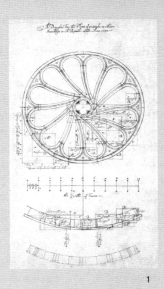

1

I want to talk about the implications of technology on the architect's working process, roles and responsibilities, and on how we practice architecture accordingly. In *The Architecture of Neoliberalism*, Douglas Spencer writes: "Swarm-modelled figures dispersed across smooth space. Steered between buildings. Channelled along elevated walkways. The architecture is fluid. Its forms materialize out of thin air or extrude themselves into existence. The pleats, grilles and apertures patterning their surfaces seemingly subject to the same unseen forces. There are no signs of labour. Threaded between the buildings and pathways, sometimes woven into the architectural envelope, are the green spaces that signal sustainability, deference to the laws of nature. The trajectory of the virtual camera as elegantly choreographed as that of the environment it records as it spirals around the site, tracking pathways, banking over structures and hovering, momentarily, over details. The scenography of contemporary architecture. The friction-free space supposed to liberate the subject from the strictures of both modernism and modernity, to re-unite it with nature, to liberate its nomadic, social and creative dispositions, to re-enchant its sensory experience of the world, to conjoin it with a technology itself now operating in accord with the very laws of the material universe, with emergence, self-organization and complexity."

Spencer is describing much of the aspiration of technology as it has been applied to the problem of architectural design for the last twenty years. In general, architects consider technology to be instruments that give us freedom and provide techniques by which we can create a different set of expressive ideas. It's clear that a whole different genre of form making has emerged with digital tools. I'm interested not in the implication of formal questions, but in process and in the implications for process. At Yale, Bob Stern referred to the work of people who used computation to make complex forms as the Blobmeisters, and I'll stipulate that the Blobmeisters are actually interrogating and extrapolating technology in different ways, and in doing so, creating a particular set of opportunities. I want to suggest that form optimization, or the use of different kinds of computational techniques to explore form, is just the very beginning and one of the least important implications of the evolution of digital technologies. There are large questions of the role of the architect in the overall design process, and technology remediates the role of the architect in a number of different ways.

In his Embryological House project of 1999, Greg Lynn created twenty thousand variations on a house. He used two technologies that have become pre-eminent in form generation today: animation software (made by Autodesk), and scripting—sets of rules. Technology in this case was used to explore a certain limited set of formal questions. More recently, computation is beginning to provide a different set of opportunities. The Embryological House anticipated those opportunities, but they are now leading us in a different direction. There are new possibilities for simulation, prediction and the understanding of the outcomes of the design process, beyond formal questions. I want to argue that there are profound implications for what we do as architects, and that these are perhaps as profound as the re-definitions of the role of the architect that occurred in the Renaissance.

Two of the most important turning points in the definition of the practice of architecture happened simultaneously at the end of the Enlightenment. The first, of course, came with Brunelleschi, who articulated the very romantic notion that design, expression, control of construction and understanding of the building enterprise were completely conflated in a single entity called the master builder. A story about Brunelleschi told by Mario Carpo gives some insight here. As Brunelleschi was designing and managing the construction of the dome of the Florence cathedral, he would make study models out of radishes. He would be out in the field talking to the construction workers and would make a sketch in three dimensions by carving a radish. He would show the radish to the construction worker, and then eat the radish, so that he would be the only one who had any memory of that transaction. Brunelleschi took the traditional means of transmitting information and destroyed it in each construction transaction.

We know that Brunelleschi fiercely controlled all the details of construction, but at the same time that Brunelleschi was working, Alberti was writing his seminal treatise, which defined the profession of architecture. Alberti asserted that models—intellectual models, ideas—are separate from building. Until then, the ideation of the building and the construction of the building were considered to be one phenomenon. Alberti argued that the ideas were actually the more important of the two and that the architect should conceive of the building with clarity and instructive descriptions, so that when construction began, it would adhere slavishly, without deviation, to the instructions of the architect. In Mario's translation, Alberti insists that the only responsibility of the architect is to provide "sound advice and clear drawings," which would be sufficient to actualize the construction of a building. All at once, Alberti created the profession of architecture and, without realizing it, professional liability insurance companies. With that definition of the practice of architecture, I want to unpack the way digital technology has influenced the process by which buildings are delivered.

In every building project today, there is an attempt to reconcile three strong roles. The client aspires to have a building, but has neither the technical nor the financial ability to organize forces in a way that makes that building possible. The designers, the architects, are responsible for defining what has become known as design intent. This is a legal concept that holds that the architect is responsible for articulating the expression of the building in its final state, without any responsibility for how the final built state is actually achieved. In the United States, the architect is prohibited from being involved in the means and methods of construction by contract and insurance. The architect is responsible for describing the end state. The contractor, who is responsible for building the building, is the executer. This relationship, in which architects are responsible for thinking and contractors for building, creates an odd asymmetry.

Technology has profound effects on the business structure and therefore on the terms of this working relationship. Technology changes the instruments of service, the way the architect delivers ideas to the client. In the building industry over the past fifty years, there have been attempts to remediate questions of risk and reward, the allocation of information and value propositions by creating different kinds of relationships between the client, the architect and the contractor. There are four distinct periods of time in which representational technologies played a part in the construct of this relationship.

The first period is what I will call the era of drawing. This was before computers were available for any representational processes. For hundreds of years, we used drawing techniques to hone a specific set of strategies for expressing the design intent of a building, for creating sound advice and clear drawings. An example is a drawing by Robert Smythson from 1599 that is labelled "a rounde windowe Standinge in A Rounde walle" (fig. 1). In it, Smythson expresses a fairly complex idea. It's essentially a complex curve, a shape that is curving in two directions. The drawing includes all the instructions that the stone mason needs to make the window by rotating the pre-fabricated parts in a circle: the way the proportions work, the plan and the plan without notation. The shop drawings for this window in a twenty-first-century project would probably be three hundred pages long.

In 2000, when I first joined Autodesk, I asked my software engineering teams why two drawings, with about twelve dimensions and five notes, provided enough information for a competent carpenter to build a small one-car garage. I could have very easily had a garage built with one 8.5 x 11 sheet of paper. This is something that Mario Carpo characterizes as "the incredible CPU challenge of architecture." The challenge in architectural representation lies in central processing unit (CPU) cycles. You're trying to represent this enormously complex thing and you have to abstract it. You have to use all kinds of abstraction strategies because you can't draw it in three dimensions, you can't draw it at full scale and you can't represent it at a detailed, material, almost molecular level. Every element of a building's representation must be made using these kinds of notational characteristics. For hundreds of years the CPU constraint is what defined the process of creating the information that bridged the gap between design and construction. And even complex pre-Blobmeister forms could be represented using these kinds of strategies. Drawings for Eero Saarinen's TWA Terminal contain all the necessary geometry that the concrete subcontractor needed to lay out these kinds of concrete forms (fig. 2). The drawings were done with compasses, scales and dividers, and maybe slide rules. The advent of scripting was not a necessary predicate to making complex forms.

In the second era of representation, the CAD revolution of the early 1990s, we used computers to attack the CPU problem. We translated beautiful drawings like Saarinen's into less beautiful drawings on the surface of a monitor (fig. 3). It felt like a deeply important change at the time, but it really wasn't. We were simply using techniques that

2   Eero Saarinen Associates. Trans World Airlines terminal, John F. Kennedy Airport, New York, plan and section of the concrete overhang, 1963. 37.8 x 28.6 cm. Eero Saarinen collection, Manuscripts & Archives, Yale University

3   Van Berkel & Bos Architectuurbureau. Erasmus Bridge, Rotterdam, section of the second pier, 1996. AutoCAD file, converted to scalable vector graphics format for publication. Original file: WEB-28.dwg, 86 KB, last modified 16 June 1996. UNStudio Erasmus Bridge project records (AP175), CCA. Gift of UNStudio

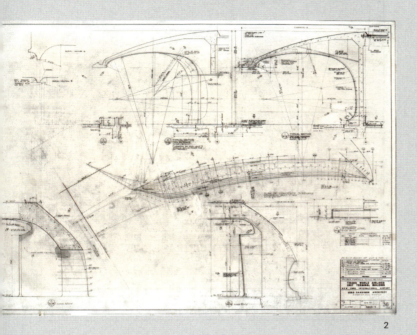

2

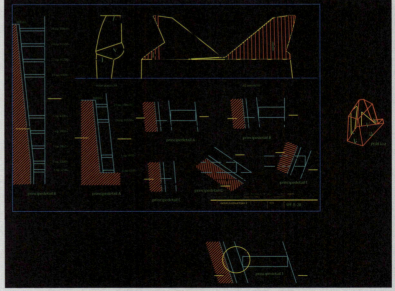

3

Phil Bernstein

428

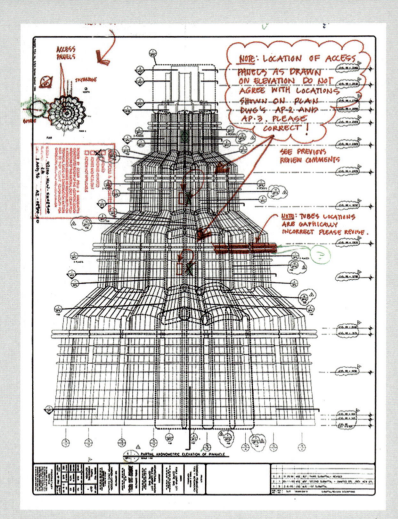

4 Pelli Clarke Pelli Architects. Petronas Towers, Kuala Lumpur, partial axonometric elevation of the pinnacle, 1996

were well understood—drafting and CPU preservation—and making them electronic. So instead of compasses and dividers and scales, we were using line commands and, later, mice and more robust computers. An example is a shop drawing, one of hundreds, of the stainless steel at the top of the Petronas Towers in Kuala Lumpur (fig. 4). This building was designed by César Pelli in New Haven. I was working in Pelli's office at the time. The technical architect was in Kuala Lumpur and the stainless steel fabricator was in Sheffield, England. The stainless steel fabricator made this drawing by copying, in AutoCAD, a construction document that the technical architect in Kuala Lumpur had made by copying plots of drawings of the top of the building that we made in New Haven using AutoCAD. We made a drawing in AutoCAD, plotted it on a piece of paper, rolled this into a tube, sent it via FedEx across the world, and someone would roll it out and draw it again in AutoCAD, plot it and then send it to someone else. So by the time the circuit is complete and the drawing came back to us, there were notes on the drawing like "location of access panels on elevation do not agree with locations shown on plan drawings." Obviously. This drawing, this set of information, had been represented and re-represented and sent around the world. As the design architects, we would stamp the drawing with a block of text, which essentially says, "We reviewed this drawing, but we take absolutely no responsibility for it whatsoever. You use any information that we have marked on this drawing with red felt-tip pen at your own risk."

The year after I joined Autodesk our then-CEO Carol Bartz said to me, "I want to know why Federal Express makes more money shipping drawings made by our software than we make selling the software itself. I want you to try to explain that to me." One of the reasons was that FedEx allowed us to do things more accurately and quickly using existing drawing techniques. And so the CAD era, as much as it felt interesting, didn't create any tools that were particularly profound for the working relationship. Much more influential was the third era, which is the transition from CAD drafting to building information modelling (BIM), beginning around 2002.

It's true that we now have higher-resolution screens and we can apply more storage and bandwidth—more CPU power, a precondition for the more robust computation demanded by BIM. But what building information modelling really allows us to do is to make a behaviourally correct, parametrically constructed simulation of the building that is being proposed. The designer can create a three-dimensional mock-up of the actual phenomenon that is occurring. When Greg Lynn used Maya to create the Embryological House, he was creating three-dimensional, unintelligent geometric shapes. They had no inherent awareness of themselves as buildings, whereas, in a building information model, a column knows it is a column and it knows its relationship to the wall.

Phil Bernstein

The pipes know that they are pipes and that they can't go through columns.

The shift from CAD to BIM created a new set of opportunities. It is possible to interrogate a digital version of the building prior to creating the physical version of the building. That interrogation might be about something simple, such as how much concrete to use, or it might be about something more complicated like energy consumption or lighting conditions. These are not particularly profound design ideas but they do create a different kind of context for the design process. The quality of this kind of information creates opportunities for the architect to have a much deeper understanding of the implications of a design before it is built in the real world. The architect can make a digital prototype. This information is also very useful for the contractor. The building information model contains data about all the different kinds of things that the contractor has to do in order to build the building. The question is: will the architect enter into the kind of relationship with the contractor in which that data can be properly leveraged?

This is a mechanical system for a hospital (fig. 5). The building is represented with a high degree of precision —the construction company has much more insight about this building than they had when they would get two-dimensional routing diagrams from a mechanical engineer, whose fee had been cut so severely that the drawings were not coordinated. When the construction company tried to follow the two-dimensional drawings, it was a nightmare. So, there is a low degree of profundity in terms of the philosophical implications, but a high degree of profundity in terms of the process implications. The process implications have to do with the magnetic force of this information as a link between the designers and the builders. Traditionally, architects render their judgement, and builders make things. There are terrible liability problems if this distinction collapses. But, with BIM, the designer is in possession of powerful information concerning how to put the building together. There can be a new, closer relationship between the client, the architect and the contractor.

The means of representation through these eras of drawing, CAD and BIM are directly correlated to the evolution of business models in the building industry. In 1970, everything was done through hard-bid projects, and the means of representation were tracing paper and pin-register drafting. No one sued each other, drawings were meant to be beautiful things and architects and contractors got along nicely. Then, in the United States, interest rates were raised, energy prices became very high and people started suing each other. At the same time, computers became cheap enough for architects to use and suddenly a new set of ideas emerged around the figure of the construction manager. Architects produced precise drawings in large quantities in order to prove that they understood the

31

5 Autodesk. Prototype design for a hospital, rendering of the building information model, 2014

5

building. Drafting sets became more complicated and people were drawing things in multiple scales, in response to the presence of the construction manager.

During the liability crisis of the 1980s, the client decided that it would be simpler to sue one party, rather than suing the architect and the contractor separately. So the design–build model emerged, which conflated the roles of the architect and the contractor. Meanwhile, CAD software was becoming more sophisticated, as computers became faster. You no longer had to draw two lines and an arc and call it a door; you could call up a door object and drop it in your drawing. The door object knows, from a drafting perspective, that it is a door. It knows how to cut the lines, make the space and enter itself on a door schedule, so it was the kind of primordial ooze out of which building information modelling came.

Design–build was prevalent in the 1990s, and then there was an economic downturn and, around 2000, people started to become interested in sustainability. Building information modelling emerged, and with it came a realization that perhaps various kinds of restructured business models that tinker with the roles of the designers and builders, but leave the essential challenges intact, were not, in fact, the solution to the larger problem. There was a desire to experiment with new kinds of project delivery in which everyone is locked together under a single contract and information and risks are shared. This is what has now become known as the integrated project delivery movement.

We can now already see the end of the BIM phenomenon, because the technological infrastructure has profoundly changed. Cloud computing —infinite processing and storage speed— has unbound the computational limit. Computation has always been constrained for architects because we can only achieve as much CPU power as we can afford, usually on our desktop. Now with your credit card, you have access to the same cloud infrastructure through Amazon S2 that Autodesk uses to build its software. Complex models can be stored at essentially any size and information can be delivered through all sorts of Internet-connected devices to any point of work. The constraints of the desktop are essentially eliminated. In this fourth age, beyond BIM, enormous amounts of interconnected information and processing power make it possible for us to extend this idea of the predictive power of building information models into an entirely new realm of possibility for simulation.

A good example is agent-based modelling, in which the behaviour of individual agents can be programmed to do something distinct. A virtual fire can be set in a model and the agents will exit individually (fig. 6). This is much closer to a video game than an energy simulation, because each one of the agents has a personality and behaves in a context, providing a more realistic simulation of human activity during this emergency. It is also possible to collect large amounts

6   Autodesk. Kynapse AI-based evacuation scenario planning, 2016

7   Autodesk. Structural analytical model of the United States Air Force Academy Cadet Chapel, Colorado Springs, 1959–1962, by Walter Netsch (Skidmore, Owings & Merrill), 2015

6

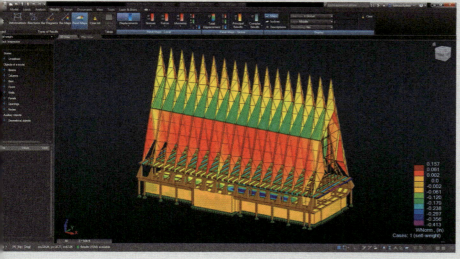

7

Phil Bernstein

of information from the environment and then apply analytical reasoning to it. This is a project that Autodesk is working on at Walter Netsch's Air Force Academy Cadet Chapel (fig. 7). We laser-scanned the entire building, extrapolated a structural model from the laser scan and did a series of analyses of the effect of wind and water on the model that we collected from the actual environmental conditions. This creates a high degree of fluidity of insight from design to construction. In another example, a series of algorithms can take a building information model and test whether that project could be built as a pre-cast concrete building. It's a banal idea, but it used to require the judgement of a structural engineer in the early part of the project. This architect has articulated a building conceptually in concrete, and we can use a series of algorithms to decide how this building should work at the level of rebar and decide whether it should be done in pre-cast concrete. All this insight is completely free—we didn't have to pay anyone to do this. Deep construction insight is now available algorithmically to the designer at the beginning of the design process rather than at the end, and this insight is no longer dependent upon a third-party consultant.

Thus the idea of design intent versus execution is under attack from all sides. The contractor is very interested in the information that comes from the designer, and the contractor's insight, because of the technology, is now moving forward in the process. When scripting is used with building information modelling, it is possible to manipulate geometry, to access the underlying behavioural representation of the design. The designer can systematically explore design alternatives in a much broader way, and the knowledge created with that script is permanently memorialized and usable in another context. There is a permanent record of the insight recorded when the design process resulted in an algorithm instead of the traditional direct manipulation of geometry and data to describe a building.

We are long past the time of using a compass to draw a line on a piece of paper to represent a building, and we are even past using a mouse to draw a three-dimensional wall in a building information modeller to represent that wall. We are now making the rules to create the wall itself. An Autodesk team working on a research centre in the MaRS District in Toronto is generating and evaluating the design, rather than creating it in a traditional way (fig. 8). That team has identified what they consider to be eight design constraints varying from adjacencies to access to daylight and to something they call equality, which refers to equal access to all the amenities in the building. They are using a series of algorithms to represent their insight about these relationships to generate a series of options for how to solve the planning of the floor plates.

But this approach can create a dilemma. In Pelli's office, we were so proud of ourselves when we bought our first computers and plotters in 1989.

8 Autodesk. MaRS Discovery District research centre, Toronto, design alternatives for the plan configuration, 2015

One day, César came into a design review, and we had plastered a wall with many alternatives: the A series and the B series, and option 15, 16, 17, 18, 19, 20. César was horrified. He said, "You are using these computers for the systematic generation of useless alternatives. That's not what I pay you for. I pay you to exercise your judgment, and I want you to edit these things."

So, computational generation of many alternatives is not sufficient. You have to apply a series of rules that address trade-offs between various kinds of problems so you can make a choice. You can correlate an algorithmic understanding of different characteristics of a project and then begin to generate solutions that you would not have been able to generate otherwise. As a designer, you still have to make a choice, but the algorithms create a new set of options. This is a convergence of a set of traditions that began with the CPU-constrained representational strategies that we used as architects for hundreds of years, which became electronically enabled through CAD and then behaviourally enabled through building information modelling, but which have now entered the realm of big data, optimization and the ability to examine and predict the outcomes of projects. The problem of design becomes one of correctly defining the problem, generating a series of answers about the problem and then choosing the right answer using your judgment.

For a long time, technology supported a design process or a digital fabrication process. You extract the geometry from the Embryological House and use it to drive a computer-controlled machine that lets you vary the geometry. But now the technological platform is starting to expand to create new potential for the entire supply chain of the building industry, which creates a different set of obligations for the players in the industry itself. The ability to predict what will happen, to systematically explore a problem and use the interaction of the relationships of the outcomes creates an interesting possibility for architects. The current business model of architecture, put simply, is as follows: The client wants a building. The client gives the architect a certain fixed amount of money that is often not correlated to the amount of money necessary to do the work. The architect starts working and hopes that when the project is done, there will be some money left over, but frequently that turns out not to be the case. So you pour money in the top and hope that there will be money left at the bottom, and the results are largely uncorrelated with the value of the artifact that is being produced. That artifact has value because of the way it behaves and the kinds of things that it does, and we are now starting to see the emergence of technologies that allow you to predict that. So why not leverage that prediction to change the risk, reward and value proposition of practice? The architect can say to clients, "Not only am I going to accomplish certain philosophical and aesthetic aims, but I'm also going to accomplish certain kinds of performative aims. If those aims are met, I'd like to get paid for them because they create value for you. If your hospital uses fewer nurses, for example, that's valuable." Performance creates an interlock between the responsibilities of the client, the architect and the contractor. It is possible to change the commoditized, fixed-fee business model based on low profit margins to one built on relationships that have more to do with values outcomes rather than commoditized interactions. And with connected systems of data, we can work together based on measured performance outcomes.

Architecture practice over the next ten or fifteen years will largely rely on design process options. The efficacy of information and the predictive value of large amounts of data will affect almost everything that we do. If we, as architects, want to maintain control of the design process, we must take advantage of big data, machine learning, modelling, simulation and analysis, and convert these tools into proper propositions that accurately reflect the real value of what we do.

Wolfgang Ernst
TOWARD A MUSEOLOGY OF ALGORITHMIC ARCHITECTURES FROM WITHIN

1. Matthew G. Kirschenbaum, *Mechanisms: New Media and the Forensic Imagination* (Cambridge, MA: MIT Press, 2008).

2. Derek J. de Solla Price, "An Ancient Greek Computer," *Scientific American* 200 (June 1959): 60–67; Derek J. de Solla Price, *Gears from the Greeks: The Antikythera Mechanism, a Calendar Computer from c. 80 BC* (Philadelphia: American Philosophical Society, 1974).

3. Achim Menges and Sean Ahlquist, eds., *Computational Design Thinking* (Chichester, UK: John Wiley & Sons, 2011).

4. In his analysis of Internet protocols, Christoph Neubert explicitly refers to the *arché* ("origin") and *téktôn* ("fabric") of OSI architecture. Christoph Neubert, "Elektronische Adressordnung," in *Die Adresse des Mediums*, eds. Stefan Andriopoulos, Gabriele Schabacher and Eckhard Schabacher. (Cologne: DuMont, 2001), 36–63.

5. Friedrich Kittler, "Museums on the Digital Frontier," in *The End(s) of the Museum*, ed. Thomas Keenan (Barcelona: Fondació Antoni Tápies, 1996), 77.

6. For an example of a virtually viable two-bit CPU made in Minecraft that can read and write four memory banks, see Lucas Fraser's YouTube video "2 Bit CPU In Minecraft," 19 December 2011, http://www.youtube.com/watch?v=MvCJcMPWQiw.

7. See the exhibition catalogue *Daniel Libeskind: One to the Other, Arbeiten 1983–1987* (Berlin: Aedes Galerie für Architektur und Raum, 1987).

8. The purpose of classical machines is to transform energy, while "trans-classical machines" process information, as defined by Gotthard Günther, *Das Bewußtsein der Maschinen. Eine Metaphysik der Kybernetik* (Krefeld: Agis-Verlag, 1963), in Supplement IV ("Die 'zweite' Maschine"), 179–203.

9. First published in French as "Notions sur la machine analytique de M. Charles Babbage" in *Bibliothèque Universelle de Genève* (October 1842): 352–376.

10. Lovelace's translation was first published in 1843 as "Sketch of the Analytical Engine invented by Charles Babbage, Esq. By L. F. Menabrea, of Turin, Officer of the Military Engineers" in the third volume of *Scientific Memoirs, Selected from the Transactions of Foreign Academies of Science and Learned Societies*, edited by Richard Taylor.

11. Sybille Krämer, "Operative Schriften als Geistestechnik. Zur Vorgeschichte der Informatik," in *Informatik und Philosophie*, eds. Margaret A. Boden and Peter Schefe (Mannheim: BI Wissenschaftsverlag, 1993), 69–84.

12. This is an argument made by Kittler in "Museums on the Digital Frontier," referring explicitly to the computer project of rendering the ruins of the abbey church of Cluny in virtual reality. See *Cluny: Architektur als Vision*, eds. Horst Cramer et al. (Heidelberg: Edition Braus, 1993).

13. Kittler, "Museums on the Digital Frontier," 73.

14. See "Fun with Masked ROMs – Atmel MARC4," Adam Laurie, 27 January 2013, http://adamsblog.aperturelabs.com/2013/01/fun-with-masked-roms.html.

15. Kittler, "Museums on the Digital Frontier," 78.

16. Doron Swade, "Collecting Software: Preserving Information in an Object-Centred Culture," *History and Computing* 4, no. 3 (1992): 206–210; Doron Swade, "Virtual Objects: Threat or Salvation?," in *Museums of Modern Science*, eds. Svante Lindqvist, Marika Hedin and Ulf Larsson (Canton, MA: Science History Publications, 2000), 139–147.

17. On Alberti's "digital" tradition of architectural urban memory through its radical sampling and quantifying into numbers in a Cartesian grid, see Mario Carpo, "*Descriptio urbis Romae*. Ekphrasis geografica e cultura visuale all'alba della rivoluzione tipografica," *Albertiana* 1 (1998): 111–132.

18. Frederik Stjernfelt, *Diagrammatology: An Investigation on the Borderlines of Phenomenology, Ontology, and Semiotics* (Dordrecht and London: Springer, 2007).

19. Abraham A. Moles, "Introduction to the Colloquy Computers and Visual Research, Center for Culture and Information, August 3–4, 1968, Zagreb," in *A Little-Known Story About a Movement, a Magazine, and the Computer's Arrival in Arts: New Tendencies and Bit International, 1961–1973*, ed. Margit Rosen (Karlsruhe: ZKM and Cambridge, MA: MIT Press, 2011), 264.

20. See the catalogue of the exhibition *Inventaire* (Paris: Editions du Centre Georges Pompidou, 1985).

21. Jean-François Lytoard, "After Six Months of Work ... (1984)," in *30 Years after Les Immatériaux: Art, Science, Theory,* eds. Yuk Hui and Andreas Broeckmann (Lüneburg: Meson Press, 2015), 26. The English translation of this text is based on the transcription of a talk given by Jean-François Lyotard in 1984.

22. Paul Virilio, "The Overexposed City," *Zone* 1–2 (1986): 545.

23. "Glossary," Swiss Federal Archives, https://www.bar.admin.ch/bar/en/home/research/searching/glossary.html.

24. On the neologism *chronopoetics*, see Wolfgang Ernst, *Sonic Time Machines: Explicit Sound, Sirenic Voices and Implicit Sonicity in Terms of Media Knowledge* (Amsterdam: Amsterdam University Press, 2016).

25 See "Z1 der erste Computer der Welt gebaut von Konrad Zuse - gesehen von Thilo," Thilo-W. Finger, 16 October 2011, https://www.youtube.com/watch?v=Pchhg-ffy6Q. For another example of virtually viable computer architecture, see "D1–Z1 [22,686,575:1]," Troughworks, 22 July 2010, http://vimeo.com/13543943.

26 See the 2011 installation *Voice of Sisyphus* by George Legrady, with software development by Ryan McGee and Joshua Dickinson.

27 Shintaro Miyazaki, *Algorythmisiert. Eine Medienarchäologie digitaler Signale und (un)erhörter Zeiteffekte* (Berlin: Kadmos, 2013); Shintaro Miyazaki, "Algorhythmics: Understanding Micro-Temporality in Computational Cultures," *Computational Culture 2* (2012), http://computationalculture.net/article/algorhythmics-understanding-micro-temporality-in-computational-cultures.

Orit Halpern
ARCHITECTURE AS MACHINE: THE SMART CITY DECONSTRUCTED

1 Nicholas Negroponte, *The Architecture Machine: Toward a More Human Environment* (Cambridge, MA: MIT Press, 1970); Tristan d'Estrée Sterk, "Building Upon Negroponte: A Hybridized Model of Control Suitable for Responsive Architecture," in *Digital Design: 21st eCAADe Conference Proceedings* (Graz: eCAADe, 2003), 407.

2 For excerpts of the map, see "Aspen Interactive Movie Map," Stefan Marti, 25 October 2006, https://www.youtube.com/watch?v=Hf6LkqgXPMU.

3 Andrew Lippman, interviewed by the author, 25 November 2014. See also Michael Naimark, "Aspen the Verb: Musings on Heritage and Virtuality," *Presence* 15, no. 3 (June 2006): 330–335.

4 *Software—Information Technology: Its New Meaning for Art* (New York: Jewish Museum, 1970); Nicholas Negroponte, *Soft Architecture Machines* (Cambridge, MA: MIT Press, 1975); Marisa Renee Brandt, "War, Trauma, and Technologies of the Self: The Making of Virtual Reality Exposure Therapy" (PhD dissertation, University of California, San Diego, 2013).

5 Jennifer Light, *From Warfare to Welfare: Defense Intellectuals and Urban Problems in Cold War America* (Baltimore and London: Johns Hopkins University Press, 2003).

6 Aubrey Anable, "The Architecture Machine Group's Aspen Movie Map: Techno-Paranoia and Urban Crisis in the 1970s," *Television & New Media* 13, no. 6 (November 2012): 512–514.

7 Kevin Lynch, *The Image of the City* (Cambridge, MA: MIT Press, 1960); Jay Forrester, *Industrial Dynamics* (New York: MIT Press and John Wiley and Sons, 1961); Orit Halpern, *Beautiful Data: A History of Vision and Reason Since 1945* (Durham, NC and London: Duke University Press, 2014), 79–199.

8 Jay Forrester, *Urban Dynamics* (Cambridge, MA: MIT Press, 1969), 1.

9 Ibid., ix–x, 14–18, 107–115.

10 Ibid., ix–x, 12–17.

11 Jonathan Massey, "Risk and Regulation in the Financial Architecture of American Houses," in *Governing by Design: Architecture, Politics, and Economy in the Twentieth Century,* eds. Daniel Abramson et al. (Pittsburgh: University of Pittsburgh Press, 2012), 21–46; Daniel Abramson, "Boston's West End: Urban Obsolescence in Mid-Twentieth-Century America," in Daniel Abramson et al., eds. *Governing by Design: Architecture, Politics, and Economy in the Twentieth Century* (Pittsburgh: University of Pittsburgh Press, 2012), 47–69.

Notes

12. Robert Fishman, *Urban Utopias in the Twentieth Century: Ebenezer Howard, Frank Lloyd Wright, and Le Corbusier* (Cambridge, MA: MIT Press, 1982).

13. Shannon Mattern, "Methodolatry and the Art of Measure," *Places Journal* (November 2013), https://placesjournal.org/article/methodolatry-and-the-art-of-measure.

14. Molly Wright Steenson, "Architectures of Information: Christopher Alexander, Cedric Price, and Nicholas Negroponte & MIT's Architecture Machine Group" (PhD dissertation, Princeton University, 2014).

15. Negroponte, *The Architecture Machine*, i.

16. Ibid., 5.

17. Ibid., 3.

18. Steenson, "Architectures of Information."

19. Negroponte, *The Architecture Machine*, 74–76.

20. Ibid., 7.

21. In 1967, The New Urban League of Greater Boston, led by Mel King, began a series of protests against Boston Redevelopment Authority (BRA)'s eminent domain practices that were clearing mostly African American residents out of the South End in the interest of relocating highways (Route 93), overhead rail systems and shopping centres to the neighbourhood. Initial protests started at a site called "tent city" (today a public–private housing project adjacent to Copley Place, one of the most luxurious shopping centres in the United States, as assessed by cost of retail per square foot), and were successful in stalling BRA's plans. These protests gave birth to a movement titled "the Rainbow Coalition" that was later adopted by Jesse Jackson in his bid for presidency in the 1980s. Today there is a set of community gardens and public housing on sites initially planned for transport that would divide the neighbourhood and cut off the primarily African American area of Roxbury from business and luxury retail downtown, and from the suburbs. Riots over the issue of school buses occurred in the mid-1970s as the city attempted to desegregate its public school system.

    Mel King went on to start the Community Fellows Program in the Department of Urban Studies and Planning at MIT. He later started the South End Technology Center@Tent City, a still-existing partnership between MIT and the Tent City Corporation, providing low-cost access and training to computer-related technology. King also ran a nearly successful mayoral campaign against Raymond Flynn in 1983.

22. Between 1950, when Boston's population peaked at 801,444, and 1970, when it dipped to 641,071, the city shed much manufacturing and replaced it with finance, insurance, real estate and high technology. At the same time, Boston's suburbs saw marked growth, going from a population of 1.6 million to 2.3 million, encouraged by the construction of the Massachusetts Turnpike, Route 93 and I-495. This was a remarkably rapid transformation fueled by changes in the legal regulation of securities and the construction of new office spaces over older neighbourhoods in the city centre, starting with the Prudential Center in 1965.

23. Negroponte, *The Architecture Machine*, 1.

24. Peter Galison, "The Ontology of the Enemy: Norbert Wiener and the Cybernetic Vision," *Critical Inquiry* 21 (1994): 228–266; Paul Edwards, *The Closed World: Computers and the Politics of Discourse in Cold War America* (Cambridge, MA: MIT Press, 1997); Tara Abraham, "(Physio)Logical Circuits: The Intellectual Origins of the McCulloch-Pitts Neural Networks," *Journal of the History of the Behavioral Sciences* 38, no. 1 (Winter 2002): 3–25; Lily E. Kay, "From Logical Neurons to Poetic Embodiments of Mind: Warren S. McCulloch's Project in Neuroscience," *Science in Context* 14, no. 4 (2001): 591–614.

25. Steve Heims, *The Cybernetics Group* (Cambridge, MA: MIT Press, 1991); Galison, "The Ontology of the Enemy."

26. Norbert Wiener, *Cybernetics; Or, Control and Communication in the Animal and the Machine* (New York: MIT Press, 1961).

27. The pair would go to MIT in 1952 at Wiener's behest.

28. Kay, "From Logical Neurons to Poetic Embodiments of Mind."

29. Warren McCulloch and Walter Pitts, "A Logical Calculus of Ideas Immanent in Nervous Activity," in *Embodiments of Mind*, ed. Warren McCulloch (Cambridge, MA: MIT Press, 1970), 19–39. Originally published in 1943.

30. Frank Rosenblatt, "The Perceptron: A Probabilistic Model for Information Storage and Organization in the Brain," *Psychological Review* 65 (November 1958): 386.

31. Ibid., 387.

32. Ibid., 388.

33. Oliver Selfridge, "Pandemonium: A Paradigm for Learning," in *Mechanisation of Thought Processes; Proceedings of a Symposium Held at the National Physical Laboratory on 24th, 25th, 26th and 27th November 1958* (London: Her Majesty's Stationery Office, 1959). AMG also worked with people such as Marvin Minsky, Warren McCulloch and W. Ross Ashby.

34. Branden Hookway, *Pandemonium: The Rise of Predatory Locales in the Post-War World* (Cambridge, MA: MIT Press, 1999).

35. Selfridge, "Pandemonium," 513.

Notes

36 Hookway, *Pandemonium*.

37 Negroponte, *Soft Architecture Machines*, 129.

38 Theodora Vardouli, "Nicholas Negroponte: An Interview," *Open Architectures* (27 October 2011), https://openarchitectures.com/2011/10/27/an-interview-with-nicholas-negroponte/.

39 Thomas Hess, "Gerbils Ex Machina," *Art News* (December 1970): 23.

40 Edward Shanken, "The House That Jack Built: Jack Burnham's Concept of 'Software' as a Metaphor for Art," *Leonardo Electronic Almanac* 6, no. 10 (November 1998), http://www.artexetra.com/House.html.

41 Negroponte, *Soft Architecture Machines*, viii.

42 Mohsen Mostafavi, conversation with Nicholas Negroponte, 29 October 2013, http://archinect.com/lian/liveblog-mosen-mostafavi-in-conversation-with-nicholas-negroponte.

43 Michael Naimark, "Aspen the Verb"; Michael Naimark, interviewed by the author, 12 August 2013.

44 Michael Naimark and Andrew Lippman, interviewed by the author, 12 August 2013. Both Naimark and Lippman informed me that they went out at the same times every day to record footage.

45 Mostafavi, conversation.

46 Felicity Scott, "Aspen Proving Grounds" (lecture, *Technics and Art: Architecture, Cities, and History after Mumford*, The Temple Hoyne Buell Center for the Study of American Architecture, Columbia University, 14 April 2012).

47 Sterk, "Building Upon Negroponte."

Andrew Witt
THE MACHINIC ANIMAL: AUTONOMOUS NETWORKS AND BEHAVIOURAL COMPUTATION

1 Sigfried Giedion, *Space, Time and Architecture: The Growth of a New Tradition* (Cambridge, MA: Harvard University Press, 1982), 166.

2 Murray Milne, "From Pencil Points to Computer Graphics," *Progressive Architecture* 51 (June 1970): 168–177.

3 Nicholas Negroponte, "Toward a Theory of Architecture Machines," *Journal of Architectural Education* (1947–1974) 23, no. 2 (March 1969): 9–12.

4 Yona Friedman, *Toward a Scientific Architecture* (Cambridge, MA: MIT Press, 1975), 53.

5 Ibid., 27.

6 Ibid., 81.

7 Ibid., 8.

8 Ibid., 72.

9 Ibid., 59.

10 Stefano Converso and Fabrizio Bonatti, "Parametric Model for Architectural Design," in *Game Set and Match: On Computer Games, Advanced Geometries, and Digital Technologies*, eds. Kas Oosterhuis and Lukas Feireiss (Rotterdam: Episode Publishers, 2006), 243.

11 Luigi Moretti, *Exhibition of Parametric Architecture and of Mathematical and Operational Research in Town-Planning* (Rome: Istituto nazionale di Ricerca Matematica e Operativa per l'Urbanistica, 1960), 5.

12 Helmut Emde, "Development of Spatial Lattice Frameorks," in *Architect and Computer: A Man-Machine-System*, ed. Helmut Emde (n.p., 1976), 16, 17.

13 Joachim Luther, "RES (Grid-Oriented Design System)," in *Architect and Computer: A Man-Machine-System*, ed. Helmut Emde (n.p., 1976), 4.

14 Cornelie Leopold, "Precise Experiments: Relations between Mathematics, Philosophy and Design at Ulm School of Design," *Nexus Network Journal* 15, no. 2 (August 2013): 375.

15 Kenneth Frampton, "Apropos Ulm: Curriculum and Critical Theory," *Oppositions* 3 (May 1974): 23.

16 Leopold, "Precise Experiments," 371; René Spitz, *HfG Ulm: The View Behind the Foreground. The Political History of the Ulm School of Design, 1953–1968*, trans. Ilze Klavina (Stuttgart and London: Edition Axel Menges, 2002), 219.

17 Frampton, "Apropos Ulm," 25.

18 Tomás Maldonado and Gui Bonsiepe, "Science and Design," *Ulm* 10/11 (May 1964): 14.

19 Martin Krampen, "Computers and Design: A Survey," *Ulm* 19/20 (August 1967): 2–3.

20 C. West Churchman, Jean-Pierre Protzen and Melvin M. Webber, "Horst W. J. Rittel, Architecture: Berkeley," in *University of California: In Memoriam*, ed. David Krogh (n.p., 1992), 146–147.

21 Horst Rittel, quoted in Jean-Pierre Protzen and David J. Harris, *The Universe of Design: Horst Rittel's Theories of Design and Planning* (Oxford and New York: Routledge, 2010), 1.

22 Max Bill, "The Mathematical Approach in Contemporary Art," trans. Morton Shand, *Arts and Architecture* 71, no. 8 (1954): 20–21.

23 Ronald D. Resch, "The Topological Design of Sculptural and Architectural Systems," in *National Computer Conference and Exposition* (Montvale, NJ: AFIPS Press, 1973), 643.

24 Ibid., 650.

25 Ibid., 645.

Nathalie Bredella
IN THE MIDST OF THINGS: ARCHITECTURE'S ENCOUNTER WITH DIGITAL TECHNOLOGY, MEDIA THEORY AND MATERIAL CULTURE

1 Ars Electronica was launched in 1979 in Linz as a festival dedicated to the relational network of art, technology and society, and it expanded its activities with the introduction of the Prix Ars Electronica in 1987 and the Ars Electronica Center and Future Lab in 1996. The Institut für Neue Medien at the Städelschule in Frankfurt was founded as an experimental laboratory for interactive new media art in 1989 by Kaspar König, and since 1994 it has been organized as an autonomous platform in the field of new media research. The ZKM in Karlsruhe was founded in 1989, and works at the intersection of art and science. The Frac Centre in Orléans, founded in 1982, has hosted exhibitions and conferences on experimental architecture since the 1990s. On the Frac, see *Archilab: Radical Experiments in Global Architecture*, eds. Frédéric Migayrou and Marie-Ange Brayer (London: Thames & Hudson, 2001). On Storefront for Art and Architecture, founded in 1982 as an experimental forum and exhibition space in New York, see *Storefront Newsprints: 1982–2009*, ed. Joseph Grima (New York: Storefront for Art and Architecture, 2009).

2 The relationship between media studies and architecture can be traced to Marshall McLuhan's work in the postwar period. McLuhan's exchange with architectural historian Sigfried Giedion and modernist town planner Jaqueline Tyrwhitt informed interdisciplinary media research. On the collaborative environment of the Explorations Group, founded by Tyrwhitt, Giedion, McLuhan and others at the University of Toronto in 1951, see Mark Wigley, "Network Fever," *Grey Room* 4 (Summer 2001): 82–122. On Tyrwhitt's work bridging the fields of architecture, urbanism and media theory, see Michael Darroch, "Bridging Urban and Media Studies: Jaqueline Tyrwhitt and the Explorations Group, 1951–1957," *Canadian Journal of Communication* 33, no. 2 (2008): 147–169.

3 On the history of V2_, see http://v2.nl/organization/history. With the opening of the V2_Lab as an interdisciplinary workspace in 1998, V2_ expanded its activities to include research and practice.

4 Paul Virilio, "The Law of Proximity," in *Book for the Unstable Media*, eds. Alex Adriaansens et al. ('s-Hertogenbosch: Stichting V2_, 1992), 121–127. V2_ also showed Stefaan Decostere's documentary *Why We Men Love Technology That Much* (1985), which focused on the relationship between war and technology, in the context of a conversation with Virilio. On Virilio's writing and work in the context of architecture and urbanism see John Armitage, *Virilio for Architects* (London and New York: Routledge, 2015).

5 Alex Adriaansens, "Introduction," in *Book for the Unstable Media*, eds. Alex Adriaansens et al., 12.

Notes

6. Hannes Leopoldseder, "Foreword," in *Ars Electronica: Facing the Future: A Survey of Two Decades*, ed. Timothy Druckrey (Cambridge, MA: MIT Press, 1999), 2–13, 8ff.

7. On the development of Ars Electronica's festival, its prize, its centre and the Future Lab, see "About," Ars Electronica, http://www.aec.at/about/de/.

8. The manifesto was published as an advertisement in the Dutch national newspaper *de Volkskrant*. "Manifest," V2_ Lab for the Unstable Media, http://v2.nl/events/manifest/?searchterm=Manifesto.

9. Among the theoreticians participating in the events during the 1990s were philosophers Brian Massumi, architectural theorist Bart Lootsma and historian N. Katherine Hayles. See "DEAF98 Symposium," V2_ Lab for the Unstable Media, http://v2.nl/events/deaf98-symposium/?searchterm=lootsma; *The Art of the Accident*, eds. Andreas Broeckmann et al. (Rotterdam: NAI Publishers and V2_ Organisatie, 1998).

10. "Manifestation for the Unstable Media 4," V2_ Lab for the Unstable Media, http://v2.nl/archive/events/manifestation-for-the-unstable-media-4.

11. "The Legible City," V2_ Lab for the Unstable Media, http://v2.nl/archive/works/the-legible-city.

12. The manifestation was moderated by architectural theorist Wim Nijenhuis, and participants included architects Kees Christiaanse, Daniel Libeskind and Lebbeus Woods, and theorists Florian Rötzer and Derrick de Kerckhove. See "Manifestation 4 – Symposium," V2_ Lab for the Unstable Media, http://v2.nl/events/manifestation-4-symposium/?searchterm=Manifestation%204%20Symposium.

13. Woods's project One Berlin (1990) for Berlin's Mitte after the fall of the Wall—in opposition to real-estate projects intended to mask the gaps between city parts—introduced a loosely knit network of spaces, where new forms of experimental living could be explored. See Lebbeus Woods, "Taking on Risk: Nine Experimental Scenarios," in *Lebbeus Woods: Experimental Architecture*, ed. Tracy Myers (Pittsburgh: Carnegie Museum of Art, The Heinz Architectural Center, 2004), 24

14. On Woods's presentation "The Secret of the White Box," see "Manifestation 4 – Symposium," V2_ Lab for the Unstable Media.

15. Greg Lynn, ed., *Lars Spuybroek, H₂Oexpo* (Montreal: Canadian Centre for Architecture, 2015). E-publication.

16. Elizabeth Diller and Ricardo Scofidio, *Flesh: Architectural Probes* (New York: Princeton Architectural Press, 1993), 252.

17. The lecture also made reference to the installation *Bad Press* by Diller + Scofidio (1993), which featured eighteen unconventionally ironed shirts and dealt with questions of domesticity. On the lecture at V2_, see "Designing in Architecture and Industry," V2_ Lab for the Unstable Media, http://v2.nl/events/designing-in-architecture-and-industry/.

18. The group of German-Swiss artists was formed in 1991. See their website, http://www.krcf.org.

19. Knowbotic Research, "IO_Dencies_Questioning Urbanity," in *The Art of the Accident*, eds. Andreas Broeckmann et al. (Rotterdam: NAI Publishers and V2_ Organisatie, 1998), 186–192.

20. On the work of the institute see F. A. Bechthold and Michael Klein, *Profiles: INM; Institut für Neue Medien* (Frankfurt am Main: Institut für Neue Medien Selbstverlag, 1996).

21. Bernhard Franken, "From Architecture to Hypertecture," in *Profiles: INM; Institut für Neue Medien* vol. 1, *1994/95*, F. A. Bechthold and Michael Klein (Frankfurt am Main: Institut für Neue Medien Selbstverlag, 1996), 36ff.

22. On projects dealing with virtual cities conducted at the INM, see Gabriele Gramelsberger, "Die Stadt im Spiel der Winde. Skylink: Ein Projekt des Instituts für Neue Medien," *Leonardo: Magazin für Architektur* 6 (1996): 52–55.

23. In the 1990s, William J. Mitchell developed his ideas on the "city of bits" at the Massachusetts Institute of Technology, addressing an understanding of the city based on telecommunications systems and electronic infrastructures. William J. Mitchell, *City of Bits: Space, Place, and the Infobahn* (Cambridge, MA: MIT Press, 1995).

24. Vilém Flusser, "Entwurf von Relationen," *Arch+* 111 (March 1992): 49.

25. On the saltwater pavilion and Kas Oosterhuis's concept of an interactive architecture, see *Kas Oosterhuis and Ilona Lénárd, Kas Oosterhuis: Programmable Architecture* (Milan: L'Arca edizioni, 2002).

26. "Deltawerken Online," Delta Works Online Foundation, http://www.deltawerken.com/English/10.html?setlanguage=en.

27. Amerigo Marras, ed., *ECO-TEC: Architecture of the In-Between* (New York: Princeton Architectural Press, 1999). On more recent studies on media and environment, see Jussi Parikka, *A Geology of Media* (Minneapolis and London: University of Minnesota Press, 2015).

28. See for example Félix Guattari, "The Object of Ecosophy," in *ECO-TEC*, ed. Amerigo Marras, 10–21.

Notes

29. On the concept of a "liquid architecture" see Marcos Novak, "Liquid Architectures in Cyberspace," in *Cyberspace: First Steps*, ed. Michael Benedikt (Cambridge, MA and London: MIT Press, 1991), 225–254.

30. Lars Spuybroek, *NOX: Machining Architecture* (London: Thames & Hudson, 2004), 20.

31. Marshall McLuhan writes on the social organization of city spaces, arguing for the concept of "acoustic space," in which the translation of audible forms would become central to the spatial planning of a city. See Darroch, "Bridging Urban and Media Studies," 158ff. On the role of sound in multimedia environments in the emerging American and European counterculture during the postwar period, see Fred Turner, *The Democratic Surround: Multimedia & American Liberalism from World War II to the Psychedelic Sixties* (Chicago: University of Chicago Press, 2013).

32. Spuybroek, *NOX*, 38.

33. The *Institut für Leichte Flächentragwerke* (IL) at the Universität Stuttgart was founded by Frei Otto in 1964 and ran until 1991. In collaboration with other institutes, biologists, physicians and mathematicians at IL developed structures derived from an analysis of pneumatic and biological design principles. Collaborative research projects such as the SFB 64 *Weitgespannte Flächentragwerke* and SFB 230 *Natürliche Konstruktionen*, funded by the Deutsche *Forschungsgemeinschaft*, were based on interdisciplinary research. Projects such as the German Pavilion at Expo '67 in Montreal and the buildings for the Olympic Games in Munich in 1972 grew out of the institute. In 2001, IL became part of the newly formed Institut für Leichtbau Entwerfen und Konstruieren (ILEK) at the Universität Stuttgart. See the website of the Verein zur Förderung des Leichtbaus e.V., http://www.leichtbauverein.de. On the SFB 230 see Klaus Teichmann and Joachim Wilke, *Prozeß und Form: "Natürliche Konstruktionen": Der Sonderforschungsbereich 230* (Berlin: Ernst & Sohn, 1996).

34. Frei Otto and Wolfgang Weidlich, "Vorwort," in *Experimente*, Siegfried Gaß (Stuttgart: Institut für leichte Flächentragwerke, 1990), 14.

35. Ibid.

36. See William Thomas, *Rational Action: The Sciences of Policy in Britain and America, 1940–1960* (Cambridge, MA and London: MIT Press, 2015).

37. The model-making method was developed by Otto in 1958, refined with students at Yale University during the 1960s and finalized at Atelier Warmbronn. For a detailed description, see Frei Otto and Bodo Rasch, *Gestalt Finden. Auf dem Weg zu einer Baukunst des Minimalen* (Stuttgart: Edition Axel Menges, 1995), 68ff.

38. Translated from the original: "Das Netz der 'minimalen Umwege' strebt einem Minimum zu und zwar in Bezug auf die für Bau und Unterhaltung der Wege und für den Verkehr insgesamt aufgebrachte Energie." Ibid., 68.

39. Ibid., 352–359.

40. Detlef Mertens, "Bioconstructivism," in Lars Spuybroek, *NOX: Machining Architecture* (London: Thames & Hudson, 2004), 360.

41. Ibid.

42. In 1965, a test model for the German Pavilion at Expo '67 was built on the university campus. Theo Crosby et al., "Frei Otto at Work," *Architectural Design* 41 (1971): 140.

43. On the inter-media processes in Otto's work, see Daniela Fabricius's PhD dissertation, "Calculation and Risk: The Rational Turn in West German Architecture 1965–1985" (Princeton University, forthcoming) and her essay "Material Models, Photography, and the Threshold of Calculation," forthcoming.

44. Crosby et al., "Frei Otto at Work," 150.

45. Cornelius Borck, "Der Transhumanismus der Kontrollmaschine: Die Expo '67 als Vision einer kybernetischen Versöhnung von Mensch und Welt," in *Die Transformationen des Humanen: Beiträge zur Kulturgeschichte der Kybernetik*, eds. Michael Hagner and Erich Hörl (Frankfurt am Main: Suhrkamp, 2008), 125–162, 151.

46. Ibid., 152.

47. On Fuller's rejection of politics in favour of a "revolution by design," see Felicity Scott, "Fluid Geographies: Politics and the Revolution by Design," in *New Views on R. Buckminster Fuller*, eds. Hsiao-Yun Chu and Robert G. Trujillo (Stanford, CA: Stanford University Press, 2009), 160–217.

48. Mark Wigley, "Planetary Homeboy," in "Forget Fuller? Everything You Always Wanted to Know About Fuller But Were Afraid to Ask," ed. Reinhold Martin, *ANY* 17 (1997): 16–23.

49. Sanford Kwinter, "FFE: Fuller Themselves," in "Forget Fuller? Everything You Always Wanted to Know About Fuller But Were Afraid to Ask," ed. Reinhold Martin, *ANY* 17 (1997): 62.

50. Reinhold Martin, "Fuller? Why Fuller? Why Now?," in "Forget Fuller? Everything You Always Wanted to Know About Fuller But Were Afraid to Ask," ed. Reinhold Martin, *ANY* 17 (1997): 15.

51. Geoffrey C. Bowker, *Memory Practices in the Sciences* (Cambridge, MA: MIT Press, 2005).

52. The video program curated by Kathy Rae Huffman and Carole Ann Klonarides is available here: http://archive.aec.at/media/archive/1994/183063/File_02924_AEC_FE_1994.pdf.

53. Kathy Rae Huffmann, "Video and Architecture: Beyond the Screen", in *Ars Electronica*, ed. Druckrey, 135–139.

Notes

54. Thomas Y. Levin, Ursula Frohne and Peter Weibel, eds., *Ctrl [Space]: Rhetorics of Surveillance from Bentham to Big Brother* (Karlsuhe: ZKM Center for Art and Media; Cambridge, MA: MIT Press, 2002), 10.

55. See Michael J. Dear, ed., *Geohumanities: Art, History, Text at the Edge of Place* (London: Routledge, 2011).

56. "You Are Here: Information Drift," Storefront for Art and Architecture, http://storefrontnews.org/archive/1990s/you-are-here-information-drift.

57. Laura Kurgan, *Close Up at a Distance: Mapping, Technology & Politics* (New York: Zone Books, 2013), 80.

58. On the *Digital Territories* symposium, see Andreas Broeckmann, "Digital Territories—The Symposium," http://v2.nl/archive/articles/digital-territories-the-symposium.

59. Sassen's presentation was entitled "The Topoi of E-Space: Global Cities and Global Value Chains." See "DEAF96 Symposium," V2_ Lab for the Unstable Media, http://v2.nl/events/deaf96-symposium; Saskia Sassen, *The Global City: New York, London, Tokyo* (Princeton: Princeton University Press, 1991); Saskia Sassen, *Losing Control?: Sovereignty in the Age of Globalization* (New York: Columbia University Press, 1996).

60. See the installation "Wildcards: A Game of Orgman," http://kellereasterling.com/tags/tag:Wildcards.

61. Keller Easterling, *American Town Plans: A Comparative Time Line* (New York: Princeton Architectural Press, 1996); Keller Easterling, *Organization Space: Landscapes, Highways, and Houses in America* (Cambridge, MA: MIT Press, 2001).

62. On Easterling's paperless studios, see Nathalie Bredella, "The Knowledge Practices of the Paperless Studio," in "Intuition and the Machine," *Grazer Architecture Magazine* 10 (2014): 112–127.

63. Arjen Mulder, "The Object of Interactivity," in Lars Spuybroek, *NOX: Machining Architecture* (London: Thames & Hudson, 2004), 333.

Bibliography

Abraham, Tara. "(Physio)Logical Circuits: The Intellectual Origins of the McCulloch-Pitts Neural Networks." *Journal of the History of the Behavioral Sciences* 38, no. 1 (Winter 2002): 3–25.

Abramson, Daniel. "Boston's West End: Urban Obsolescence in Mid-Twentieth-Century America." In *Governing by Design: Architecture, Politics, and Economy in the Twentieth Century*, edited by Daniel Abramson, Lucia Allais, Arindam Dutta, John Harwood, Timothy Hyde, Jonathan Massey, Pamela Karimi, M. Ijlal Muzaffar, Michael Osman and Meredith TenHoor, 47–69. Pittsburgh: University of Pittsburgh Press, 2012.

Adriaansens, Alex. "Introduction." In *Book for the Unstable Media*, edited by Alex Adriaansens, Joke Brouwer, Rik Delhaas and Eugenie den Uyl, 12. 's-Hertogenbosch: Stichting V2_, 1992.

Alberti, Leon Battista. *Libri De re ædificatoria dece....* Paris: B. Rembolt et L. Hornken, 1512.

Alexander, Christopher. "A City Is Not a Tree, Part I." *Architectural Forum* 122, no. 1 (April 1965): 58–62.

———. "A City Is Not a Tree, Part II." *Architectural Forum* 122, no. 2 (May 1965): 58–62.

———. *Notes on the Synthesis of Form.* Cambridge, MA: Harvard University Press, 1964.

———. *The Timeless Way of Building.* New York: Oxford University Press, 1979.

Alexander, Christopher, Sara Ishikawa and Murray Silverstein. *A Pattern Language: Towns, Buildings, Construction.* New York: Oxford University Press, 1977.

Allen, Stan. "The Future That Is Now." In *Architecture School: Three Centuries of Educating Architects in North America*, edited by Joan Ockman with Rebecca Williamson, 202–229. Cambridge, MA: MIT Press, 2012.

Anable, Aubrey. "The Architecture Machine Group's Aspen Move Map: Techno-Paranoia and Urban Crisis in the 1970s." *Television and New Media* 13, no. 6 (November 2012): 498–519.

Anderson, Carl David. "The Positive Electron." *Physical Review* 43 (March 1933): 491–494.

Armitage, John. *Virilio for Architects.* London and New York: Routledge, 2015.

Ballard, J. G. "De Duizend Dromen van Stellavista" ["The Thousand Dreams of Stellavista"]. In *NOX: Chloroform*, 55–87. Amsterdam: Stichting Highbrow, 1993. Reprinted from Ballard, J. G. *De zingende beeleden*. Amsterdam: De Bezige Bij, 1973.

Baudrillard, Jean. "Please Follow Me." Translated by Maurice Nio. In *NOX: Actiones in distans*, 147–157. Amsterdam: Stichting Highbrow, 1991.

Beck, Ulrich. *Risk Society: Towards a New Modernity.* London: Sage Publications, 1992.

Bechtold, F. A. and Michael Klein. *Profiles: INM; Institut für Neue Medien.* Frankfurt am Main: Institut für Neue Medien Selbstverlag, 1996.

Benedikt, Michael, ed. *Cyberspace: First Steps.* Cambridge, MA: MIT Press, 1992.

Bill, Max. "The Mathematical Approach in Contemporary Art." Translated by Morton Shand. *Arts and Architecture* 71, no. 8 (1954): 20–21.

Borck, Cornelius. "Der Transhumanismus der Kontrollmaschine: Die Expo '67 als Vision einer kybernetischen Versöhnung von Mensch und Welt." In *Die Transformationen des Humanen: Beiträge zur Kulturgeschichte der Kybernetik*, edited by Michael Hagner and Erich Hörl, 125–162. Frankfurt am Main: Suhrkamp, 2008.

Bowker, Geoffrey C. *Memory Practices in the Sciences.* Cambridge, MA: MIT Press, 2005.

Brandt, Marisa Renee. "War, Trauma, and Technologies of the Self: The Making of Virtual Reality Exposure Therapy." PhD diss., University of California, San Diego, 2013.

Bredella, Nathalie. "The Knowledge Practices of the Paperless Studio." In "Intuition and the Machine." *Grazer Architecture Magazine* 10 (2014): 112–127.

Broeckmann, Andreas, Joke Brouwer, Bart Lootsma, Arjen Mulder and Lars Spuybroek, eds. *The Art of the Accident.* Rotterdam: NAI Publishers and V2_ Organisatie, 1998.

Cache, Bernard. *Earth Moves: The Furnishing of Territories.* Translated by Anne Boyman. Edited by Michael Speaks. Cambridge, MA: MIT Press, 1995.

Carpo, Mario. "*Descriptio urbis Romae.* Ekphrasis geografica e cultura visuale all'alba della rivoluzione tipografica." *Albertiana* 1 (1998): 111–132.

———. "Ten Years of Folding." In "Folding in Architecture," edited by Greg Lynn. *Architectural Design* 102 (1993): 14–19. Revised edition, 2004.

Cennini, Cennino. *Il libro dell'arte, o Trattato della pittura.* Florence: F. Le Monnier, 1859.

Centre Georges Pompidou. *Inventaire.* Paris: Editions du Centre Georges Pompidou, 1985.

Cesariano, Cesare, trans. *Di Lucio Vitruuio Pollione De architectura libri dece....* Como: Gotardus de Ponte, 1521.

Churchman, C. West, Jean-Pierre Protzen and Melvin M. Webber. "Horst W. J. Rittel, Architecture: Berkeley." In *University of California: In Memoriam*, edited by David Krogh, 146–148. n.p., 1992.

Converso, Stefano, and Fabrizio Bonatti. "Parametric Model for Architectural Design." In *Game Set and Match: On Computer Games, Advanced Geometries, and Digital Technologies*, edited by Kas Oosterhuis and Lukas Feireiss, 242–247. Rotterdam: Episode Publishers, 2006.

Cramer, Horst, Manfred Koob, Ulrich Best and Werner Richner, eds. *Cluny: Architektur als Vision.* Heidelberg: Edition Braus, 1993.

Crosby, Theo, Berthold Burkhardt, Hermann Kendel and Koji Kamiya. "Frei Otto at Work." *Architectural Design* 41 (1971): 137–167.

Daniell, Thomas. "Bug Eyes and Blockhead." *Log* 36 (Winter 2016): 34–47.

Darroch, Michael. "Bridging Urban and Media Studies: Jaqueline Tyrwhitt and the Explorations Group, 1951–1957." *Canadian Journal of Communication* 33, no. 2 (2008): 147–169.

Dear, Michael J., ed. *Geohumanities: Art, History, Text at the Edge of Place.* London: Routledge, 2011.

Bibliography

Deleuze, Gilles. *The Fold: Leibniz and the Baroque.* Translated by Tom Conley. Minneapolis: University of Minnesota Press, 1992.

Diller, Elizabeth, and Ricardo Scofidio. *Flesh: Architectural Probes.* New York: Princeton Architectural Press, 1993.

Easterling, Keller. *American Town Plans: A Comparative Time Line.* New York: Princeton Architectural Press, 1996.

———. *Organization Space: Landscapes, Highways, and Houses in America.* Cambridge, MA: MIT Press, 2001.

Edwards, Paul. *The Closed World of Computers and the Politics of Discourse in Cold War America.* Cambridge, MA: MIT Press, 1997.

Emde, Helmut, ed. *Architect and Computer: A Man-Machine-System.* n.p., 1976.

———."Development of Spatial Lattice Frameworks." In *Architect and Computer: A Man-Machine-System,* edited by Helmut Emde, 16–24. n.p., 1976.

Ernst, Wolfgang. *Sonic Time Machines: Explicit Sound, Sirenic Voices and Implicit Sonicity in Terms of Media Knowledge.* Amsterdam: Amsterdam University Press, 2016.

Evans, Robin. *The Projective Cast: Architecture and Its Three Geometries.* Cambridge, MA: MIT Press, 2000.

Fabricius, Daniela. "Calculation and Risk: The Rational Turn in West German Architecture 1965–1985." PhD diss., Princeton University (forthcoming).

———. "Material Models, Photography, and the Threshold of Calculation" (forthcoming).

Finger, Thilo-W. "Z1 der erste Computer der Welt gebaut von Konrad Zuse - gesehen von Thilo." 16 October 2011. https://www.youtube.com/watch?v=Pchhg-ffy6Q.

Fishman, Robert. *Urban Utopias in the Twentieth Century: Ebenezer Howard, Frank Lloyd Wright, and Le Corbusier.* Cambridge, MA: MIT Press, 1982.

Flusser, Vilém. "Entwurf von Relationen." *Arch+* 111 (March 1992): 49–52.

Forrester, Jay. *Industrial Dynamics.* New York: MIT Press and John Wiley and Sons, 1961.

———. *Urban Dynamics.* Cambridge, MA: MIT Press, 1969.

Frampton, Kenneth. "Apropos Ulm: Curriculum and Critical Theory." *Oppositions* 3 (May 1974): 17–36.

Franken, Bernhard. "From Architecture to Hyperstructure." In *Profiles: INM; Institut for Neue Medien.* Vol. 1, 1994/95, edited by F. A. Bechtold and Michael Klein. Frankfurt am Main: Institut für Neue Medien Selbstverlag, 1996.

Fraser, Lucas. "2 Bit CPU In Minecraft." 19 December 2011. http://www.youtube.com/watch?v=MvCJcMPWQiw.

Friedman, Yona. "The Flatwriter: Choice by Computer." *Progressive Architecture* 52 (March 1970): 98–101.

———. *Pro Domo.* Barcelona: Actar, 2006.

———. *Toward a Scientific Architecture.* Cambridge, MA: MIT Press, 1975.

Galison, Peter. "The Ontology of the Enemy: Norbert Wiener and the Cybernetic Vision." *Critical Inquiry* 21, no. 1 (1994): 228–266.

Gibson, William. *Neuromancer.* New York: Ace Books, 1984.

Giedion, Sigfried. *Space, Time and Architecture: The Growth of a New Tradition.* Cambridge, MA: Harvard University Press, 1982.

Goos, R. "The ASKA Finite Element System." In *Finite Element Systems: A Handbook,* edited by C. A. Brebbia, 55–79. (Berlin: Springer-Verlag, 1985).

Gramelsberger, Gabriele. "Die Stadt im Spiel der Winde. Skylink: Ein Projekt des Instituts für Neue Medien." *Leonardo: Magazin für Architektur* 6 (1996): 52–55.

Grima, Joseph, ed. *Storefront Newsprints: 1982–2009.* New York: Storefront for Art and Architecture, 2009.

Guattari, Félix. "The Object of Ecosophy." In *ECO-TEC: Architecture of the In-Between,* edited by Amerigo Marras, 10–21. New York: Princeton Architectural Press, 1999.

Günther, Gotthard. *Das Bewußtsein der Maschinen. Eine Metaphysik der Kybernetik.* Krefeld: Agis-Verlag, 1963.

Halpern, Orit. *Beautiful Data: A History of Vision and Reason Since 1945.* Durham, NC and London: Duke University Press, 2014.

Haraway, Donna. "A Manifesto for Cyborgs: Science, Technology, and Socialist Feminism in the 1980s." *Socialist Review* 15, no. 2 (1985): 65–107.

Harwood, John. *The Interface: IBM and the Transformation of Corporate Design, 1945–1976.* Minneapolis: University of Minnesota Press, 2011.

Heims, Steve. *The Cybernetics Group.* Cambridge, MA: MIT Press, 1991.

Hess, Thomas. "Gerbils Ex Machina." *Art News* (December 1970): 23.

Hookway, Branden. *Pandemonium: The Rise of Predatory Locales in the Post-War World.* Cambridge, MA: MIT Press, 1999.

Huffman, Kathy Rae. "Video and Architecture: Beyond the Screen." In *Ars Electronica: Facing the Future: A Survey of Two Decades,* edited by Timothy Druckrey, 135–139. Cambridge, MA: MIT Press, 1999.

Jewish Museum. *Software—Information Technology: Its New Meaning for Art.* New York: Jewish Museum, 1970.

Kay, Lily E. "From Logical Neurons to Poetic Embodiments of Mind: Warren S. McCulloch's Project in Neuroscience." *Science in Context* 14, no. 4 (2001): 591–614.

King, Augusta Ada, Countess of Lovelace, trans. "Sketch of the Analytical Engine invented by Charles Babbage, Esq. By L. F. Menabrea, of Turin, Officer of the Military Engineers." In *Scientific Memoirs, Selected from the Transactions of Foreign Academies of Science and Learned Societies,* edited by Richard Taylor. Vol. 3, 666–731. London: Richard and John E. Taylor, 1843.

Kirschenbaum, Matthew G. *Mechanisms: New Media and the Forensic Imagination.* Cambridge, MA: MIT Press, 2008.

Kittler, Friedrich. *Gramophone, Film, Typewriter.* Stanford, CA: Stanford University Press, 1999.

———. "Museums on the Digital Frontier." In *The End(s) of the Museum,* edited by Thomas Keenan, 67–80. Barcelona: Fondació Antoni Tápies, 1996.

Bibliography

Knowbotic Research. "IO_Dencies_ Questioning Urbanity." In *The Art of the Accident*, edited by Andreas Broeckmann, Joke Brouwer, Bart Lootsma, Arjen Mulder and Lars Spuybroek, 186–192. Rotterdam: NAI Publishers and V2_ Organisatie, 1998.

Krämer, Sybille. "Operative Schriften als Geistestechnik. Zur Vorgeschichte der Informatik." In *Informatik und Philosophie*, edited by Margaret A. Boden and Peter Schefe, 69–84. Mannheim: BI Wissenschaftsverlag, 1993.

Krampen, Martin. "Computers and Design: A Survey." *Ulm* 19/20 (August 1967): 2–8.

Kwinter, Sanford. "FFE: Fuller Themselves." In "Forget Fuller? Everything You Always Wanted to Know About Fuller But Were Afraid to Ask," edited by Reinhold Martin. *ANY* 17 (1997): 62.

Laurie, Adam. "Fun with Masked ROMs – Atmel MARC4." 27 January 2013. http://adamsblog.aperturelabs.com/2013/01/fun-with-masked-roms.html.

Leopold, Cornelie. "Precise Experiments: Relations Between Mathematics, Philosophy and Design at Ulm School of Design." *Nexus Network Journal* 15, no. 2 (August 2013): 363–380.

Leopoldseder, Hannes. "Foreword." In *Ars Electronica: Facing the Future: A Survey of Two Decades*, edited by Timothey Druckrey, 2–13. Cambridge, MA: MIT Press, 1999.

Levin, Thomas Y., Ursula Frohne and Peter Weibel, eds. *Ctrl [Space]: Rhetorics of Surveillance from Bentham to Big Brother*. Karlsruhe: ZKM; Cambridge, MA: MIT Press, 2002.

Libeskind, Daniel. *Daniel Libeskind: One to the Other, Arbeiten 1983–1987*. Berlin: Aedes Galerie für Architecktur und Raum, 1987.

Light, Jennifer S. *From Warfare to Welfare: Defense Intellectuals and Urban Problems in Cold War America*. Baltimore and London: Johns Hopkins University Press, 2003.

———. *The Nature of Cities: Ecological Visions and the American Urban Professions, 1920–1960*. Baltimore: Johns Hopkins University Press, 2009.

Luther, Joachim. "RES (Grid-Oriented Design System)." In *Architect and Computer: A Man-Machine-System*, edited by Helmut Emde, 4–13. n.p., 1976.

Lynch, Kevin. *The Image of the City*. Cambridge, MA: MIT Press, 1960.

Lynn, Greg. *Animate Form*. New York: Princeton Architectural Press, 1999.

———. "Multiplicitous and Inorganic Bodies." *Assemblage* 19 (1992): 32–49.

Lynn, Greg, ed. *Archaeology of the Digital*. Montreal: Canadian Centre for Architecture; Berlin: Sternberg Press, 2013.

———. *Archaeology of the Digital* e-publications, 25 vols. Montreal: Canadian Centre for Architecture, 2014–2017.

———. "Folding in Architecture." *Architectural Design* 102 (1993).

Lynn, Greg, Edward Mitchell and Sarah Whiting, eds. *Fetish: The Princeton Architectural Journal* 4 (1992).

Lyotard, Jean-François. "After Six Months of Work… (1984)." In *30 Years after Les Immatériaux: Art, Science, Theory*, edited by Yuk Hui and Andreas Broeckmann, 25–66. Lüneburg: Meson Press, 2015.

Maldonado, Tomás, and Gui Bonsiepe. "Science and Design." *Ulm* 10/11 (May 1964): 10–29.

Marras, Amerigo, ed. *ECO-TEC: Architecture of the In-Between*. New York: Princeton Architectural Press, 1999.

Marti, Stefan. "Aspen Interactive Movie Map." 25 October 2006. https://www.youtube.com/watch?v=Hf6LkqgXPMU.

Martin, Reinhold. "Fuller? Why Fuller? Why Now?" In "Forget Fuller? Everything You Always Wanted to Know About Fuller But Were Afraid to Ask," edited by Reinhold Martin. *ANY* 17 (1997): 15.

———. *The Organizational Complex: Architecture, Media, and Corporate Space*. Cambridge, MA: MIT Press, 2003.

Martin, William R. *Network Planning for Building Construction*. London: Heinemann, 1969.

Massey, Jonathan. "Risk and Regulation in the Financial Architecture of American Houses." In *Governing by Design: Architecture, Politics, and Economy in the Twentieth Century*, edited by Daniel Abramson, Lucia Allais, Arindam Dutta, John Harwood, Timothy Hyde, Jonathan Massey, Pamela Karimi, M. Ijlal Muzaffar, Michael Osman and Meredith TenHoor, 21–46. Pittsburgh: University of Pittsburgh Press, 2012.

Mattern, Shannon. "Methodolatry and the Art of Measure." *Places Journal* (November 2013). https://placesjournal.org/article/methodolatry-and-the-art-of-measure.

McCulloch, Warren, and Walter Pitts. "A Logical Calculus of Ideas Immanent in Nervous Activity." In *Embodiments of Mind*, edited by Warren McCulloch, 19–39. Cambridge, MA: MIT Press, 1965. Originally published in 1943.

Menabrea, Luigi Federico. "Notions sur la machine analytique de M. Charles Babbage." *Bibliothèque Universelle de Genève* (October 1842): 352–376.

Menges, Achim, and Sean Ahlquist, eds. *Computational Design Thinking*. Chichester, UK: John Wiley and Sons, 2011.

Mertins, Detlef. "Bioconstructivisms." In *NOX: Machining Architecture*, Lars Spuybroek, 360–369. London: Thames and Hudson, 2004.

Migayrou, Frédéric, and Marie-Ange Brayer, eds. *Archilab: Radical Experiments in Global Architecture*. London: Thames and Hudson, 2001.

Milne, Murray. "From Pencil Points to Computer Graphics." *Progressive Architecture* 51 (June 1970): 168–177.

Mitchell, William J. *City of Bits: Space, Place, and the Infobahn*. Cambridge, MA: MIT Press, 1995.

Miyazaki, Shintaro. "Algorhythmics: Understanding Micro-Temporality in Computational Cultures." *Computational Culture* 2 (2012). http://computationalculture.net/article/algorhythmics-understanding-micro-temporality-in-computational-cultures.

———. *Algorythmisiert. Eine Medienarchäologie digitaler Signale und (un)erhörter Zeiteffekte*. Berlin: Kadmos, 2013.

Bibliography

Moles, Abraham A. "Introduction to the Colloquy Computers and Visual Research, Center for Culture and Information, August 3–4, 1968, Zagreb." In *A Little-Known Story About a Movement, a Magazine, and the Computer's Arrival in Arts: New Tendencies and Bit International, 1961–1973*, edited by Margit Rosen, 263–266. Karlsruhe: ZKM; Cambridge, MA: MIT Press, 2011.

Moretti, Luigi. *Exhibition of Parametric Architecture and of Mathematical and Operational Research in Town-Planning*. Rome: Istituto nazionale di Ricerca Matematica e Operativa per l'Urbanistica, 1960.

Mulder, Arjen. "The Object of Interactivity." In *NOX: Machining Architecture*, Lars Spuybroek, 332–341. London: Thames and Hudson, 2004.

Naimark, Michael. "Aspen the Verb: Musings on Heritage and Virtuality." *Presence* 15, no. 3 (June 2006): 330–335.

Negroponte, Nicholas. *The Architecture Machine: Toward a More Human Environment*. Cambridge, MA: MIT Press, 1970.

———. *Being Digital*. New York: Knopf, 1995.

———. *Soft Architecture Machines*. Cambridge, MA: MIT Press, 1975.

———. "Toward a Theory of Architecture Machines." *Journal of Architectural Education* 23, no. 2 (March 1969): 9–12.

Neubert, Christoph. "Elektronische Adressordnung." In *Die Adresse des Mediums*, edited by Stefan Andriopoulos, Gabriele Schabacher and Eckhard Schabacher, 34–63. Cologne: DuMont, 2001.

Novak, Marcos. "Liquid Architectures in Cyberspace." In *Cyberspace: First Steps*, edited by Michael Benedikt, 225–254. Cambridge, MA and London: MIT Press, 1991.

Ockman, Joan, with Rebecca Williamson, eds. *Architecture School: Three Centuries of Educating Architects in North America*. Cambridge, MA: MIT Press, 2012.

Onwuka, Chidi. "Ik Ben de Hemelpoort." Translated by Eggheads Inc. Vertaalburo. In *NOX: Djihad*, 14, 16–18, 20–22. Amsterdam: Stichting Highbrow, 1995.

Oosterhuis, Kas, and Ilona Lénárd. *Kas Oosterhuis: Programmable Architecture*. Milan L'Arca edizioni, 2002.

Otto, Frei, and Wolfgang Weidlich. "Vorwort." In *Experimente*, edited by Siegfried Gaß, 14. Stuttgart: Institut für leichte Flächentragwerke, 1990.

Otto, Frei, and Bodo Rasch. *Gestalt Finden. Auf dem Weg zu einer Baukunst des Minimalen*. Stuttgart: Edition Axel Menges, 1995.

Palladio, Andrea. *I quattro libri dell'architettura…*. Venice: Appresso Dominico de Franceschi, 1570.

Parikka, Jussi. *A Geology of Media*. Minneapolis and London: University of Minnesota Press, 2015.

Phocas, Marios C. "John Argyris and His Decisive Contribution in the Development of Light-Weight Structures: Form Follows Force." Lecture at the *5th Greek Association of Computational Mechanics*, Limassol, Cyprus, 29 June–1 July 2005.

Picon, Antoine. *Ornament: The Politics of Architecture and Subjectivity*. Chichester, UK: Wiley, 2013.

———. *La ville territoire des cyborgs*. Besançon: Les Editions de l'Imprimeur, 1998.

Protzen, Jean-Pierre, and David J. Harris. *The Universe of Design: Horst Rittel's Theories of Design and Planning*. Oxford and New York: Routledge, 2010.

Resch, Ronald D. "The Topological Design of Sculptural and Architectural Systems." In *National Computer Conference and Exposition*, 643–650. Montvale, NJ: AFIPS Press, 1973.

Rosenblatt, Frank. "The Perceptron: A Probabilistic Model for Information Storage and Organization in the Brain." *Psychological Review* 65 (November 1958): 386–408.

Sassen, Saskia. *The Global City: New York, London, Tokyo*. Princeton: Princeton University Press 1991.

———. *Losing Control?: Sovereignty in the Age of Globalization*. New York: Columbia University Press, 1996.

Scamozzi, Vincenzo. *L'idea della architettura universale*. Venice: printed by the author, 1615.

———. *Tutte l'opere d'architettura et prrospetiva [sic] di Sebastiano Serlio…*. Venice: Presso gli heredi di Francesco de' Franceschi, 1600.

Scott, Felicity. "Aspen Proving Grounds." Lecture at the conference *Technics and Art: Architecture, Cities, and History after Mumford*, The Temple Hoyne Buell Center for the Study of American Architecture, Columbia University, 14 April 2012.

———. "Fluid Geographies: Politics and the Revolution by Design." In *New Views on R. Buckminster Fuller*, edited by Hsiao-Yun Chu and Robert G. Trujillo, 160–217. Stanford, CA: Stanford University Press, 2009.

Selfridge, Oliver. "Pandemonium: A Paradigm for Learning." In *Mechanisation of Thought Processes: Proceedings of a Symposium Held at the National Physical Laboratory on the 24th, 25th, 26th and 27th November 1958*, 513–531. London: Her Majesty's Stationery Office, 1959.

Shannon, Claude, and Warren Weaver. *The Mathematical Theory of Communication*. Urbana, IL: University of Illinois Press, 1963.

Shanken, Edward. "The House That Jack Built: Jack Burnham's Concept of 'Software' as a Metaphor for Art." *Leonardo Electronic Almanac* 6, no. 10 (November 1998). http://www.artexetra.com/House.html.

de Solla Price, Derek J. "An Ancient Greek Computer." *Scientific American* 200 (June 1959): 60–67.

———. *Gears from the Greeks: The Antikythera Mechanism, a Calendar Computer from c. 80 BC*. Philadelphia: American Philosophical Society, 1974.

Spencer, Douglas. *The Architecture of Neoliberalism*. London and New York: Bloomsbury, 2016.

Spitz, René. *HfG Ulm: The View Behind the Foreground. The Political History of the Ulm School of Design, 1953–1968*. Translated by Ilze Klavina. Stuttgart and London: Edition Axel Menges, 2002.

Spuybroek, Lars. "De Zwarte Secties." In *NOX: Actiones in distans*, 107–111. Amsterdam: Stichting Highbrow, 1991.

———. *NOX: Biotech*. Amsterdam: Stichting Highbrow, 1992.

———. *NOX: Machining Architecture*. London: Thames and Hudson, 2004.

Bibliography

———. *The Sympathy of Things: Ruskin and the Ecology of Design*. Rotterdam and New York: NAI Publishers and V2_ Organisatie, 2011.

Steenson, Molly Wright. "Architectures of Information: Christopher Alexander, Cedric Price, and Nicholas Negroponte and MIT's Architecture Machine Group." PhD diss., Princeton University, 2014.

Sterk, Tristan d'Estrée. "Building Upon Negroponte: A Hybridized Model of Control Suitable for Responsive Architecture." In *Digital Design: 21st eCAADe Conference Proceedings*, 407–414. Graz: eCAADe, 2003.

Steyerl, Hito. "Too Much World: Is the Internet Dead?" In *The Internet Does Not Exist*, edited by Julieta Aranda, Brian Kuan Wood and Anton Vidokle, 10–26. Berlin: Sternberg Press, 2015.

Stjernfeldt, Frederik. *Diagrammatology: An Investigation on the Borderlines of Phenomenology, Ontology, and Semiotics*. Dordrecht, and London: Springer, 2007.

Swade, Doron. "Collecting Software: Preserving Information in an Object-Centred Culture." *History and Computing* 4, no. 3 (1992): 206–210.

———. "Virtual Objects: Threat or Salvation?" In *Museums of Modern Science*, edited by Svante Lindqvist, Marika Hedin and Ulf Larsson, 139–147. Canton, MA: Science History Publications, 2000.

Swiss Federal Archives. "Glossary." https://www.bar.admin.ch/bar/en/home/research/searching/glossary.html.

Tafuri, Manfredo. *Architecture and Utopia: Design and Capitalist Development*. Translated by Barbara Luigia La Penta. Cambridge, MA: MIT Press, 1976.

Talbot, William Henry Fox. *The Pencil of Nature*. London: Longman, Brown, Green and Longmans, 1844.

Tschumi, Bernard. *The Manhattan Transcripts*. London: Academy Editions, 1994.

Thomas, William. *Rational Action: The Sciences of Policy in Britain and America, 1940–1960*. Cambridge, MA and London: MIT Press, 2015.

Thompson, D'Arcy Wentworth. *On Growth and Form*. Cambridge: Cambridge University Press, 1917.

Troughworks. "D1–Z1 [22,686,575:1." 22 July 2010. http://vimeo.com/13543943.

Turner, Fred. *The Democratic Surround: Multimedia and American Liberalism from World War II to the Psychedelic Sixties*. Chicago: University of Chicago Press, 2013.

Vardouli, Theodora. "Nicholas Negroponte: An Interview." *Open Architectures* (27 October 2011). https://openarchitectures.com/2011/10/27/an-interview-with-nicholas-negroponte/.

da Vignola, Giacomo Barozzi. *Regola delli cinque ordini d'architettura*. Rome: Si Stampa da Gio. Batta de Rossi, 1617.

Virilio, Paul. "The Law of Proximity." In *Book for the Unstable Media*, edited by Alex Adriaansens, Joke Brouwer, Rik Delhaas and Eugenie den Uyl, 121–127. 's-Hertogenbosch: Stichting V2_, 1992.

———. "The Overexposed City." *Zone* 1–2 (1986): 540–550.

Weiser, Mark. "The Computer for the 21st Century." In "Communications, Computers, and Networks," *Scientific American* 265, no. 3 (September 1991): 94–104.

Wheeler, Mortimer. *Archaeology from the Earth*. Oxford: Clarendon Press, 1954.

Wiener, Norbert. *Cybernetics; Or, Control and Communication in the Animal and the Machine*. New York: MIT Press, 1961.

Wigley, Mark. "Network Fever." *Grey Room* 4 (Summer 2001): 82–122.

———. "Planetary Homeboy." In "Forget Fuller? Everything You Always Wanted to Know About Fuller But Were Afraid to Ask," edited by Reinhold Martin. *ANY* 17 (1997): 16–23.

Wilke, Joachim. *Prozeß und Form: "Natürliche Konstruktionen": Der Sonderforschungsbereich 230*. Berlin: Ernst und Sohn, 1996.

Woods, Lebbeus. "Taking on Risk: Nine Experimental Scenarios." In *Lebbeus Woods: Experimental Architecture*, edited by Tracy Myers, 24–37. Pittsburgh: Carnegie Museum of Art, The Heinz Architectural Center, 2004.

Projects selected as part of the Archaeology of the Digital research program

Peter Eisenman,
  Eisenman/Robertson Architects.
  Biozentrum, Goethe-Universität,
  Frankfurt am Main, 1987.
  Peter Eisenman fonds (AP143).
  © CCA

Chuck Hoberman,
  Hoberman Associates.
  Expanding Sphere, 1988–1992;
  Iris Dome, 1990–1994.
  Chuck Hoberman fonds (AP165).
  Gift of Chuck Hoberman.
  © Hoberman Associates

Frank O. Gehry & Associates.
  Lewis Residence, Lyndhurst,
  Ohio, United States, 1989–1995.
  Images courtesy of Frank O.
  Gehry & Associates.
  © Frank O. Gehry & Associates

Shoei Yoh + Architects.
  Municipal Sports Complex,
  Odawara, Kanagawa, Japan,
  1990–1991;
  Galaxy Toyama Gymnasium,
  Imizu, Toyama, Japan,
  1990–1992.
  Shoei Yoh fonds (AP166).
  Gift of Shoei Yoh.
  © Shoei Yoh + Architects

NOX (Lars Spuybroek).
  H$_2$Oexpo, Neeltje Jans,
  the Netherlands, 1993–1997.
  Lars Spuyboek fonds (AP173).
  Gift of Lars Spuybroek.
  © NOX

Metaxy (Karl Chu).
  Catastrophe Machine,
  1994–1998;
  X Phylum, 1997–1998.
  Karl Chu X Phylum and Catastrophe Machine project records (AP176).
  Gifts of Karl Chu and Afsheen Rais Rohani.
  © Karl S. Chu

Objectile (Bernard Cache,
  Patrick Beaucé).
  Objectile panels, 1995–2013.
  Objectile fonds (AP169).
  Gift of Bernard Cache.
  © Bernard Cache

dECOi Architects (Mark Goulthorpe).
  Hyposurface, 1997–.
  Mark Goulthorpe Hyposurface project records (AP170).
  Gift of Mark Goulthorpe.
  © Mark Goulthorpe

Asymptote Architecture
  (Hani Rashid, Lise Anne Couture).
  New York Stock Exchange Virtual Trading Floor, 1997–1998;
  New York Stock Exchange Command Center. 1998–1999.
  Asymptote Architecture New York Stock Exchange Virtual Trading Floor and Command Center project records AP184).
  Gift of Asymptote.
  © Asymptote

ONL [Oosterhuis__énárd]
  (Kas Oosterhuis, Ilona Lénárd).
  NSA Muscle, 2003–2004.
  ONL [Oosterhuis_Lénárd] NSA Muscle project records (AP167).
  Gift of Kas Oosterhuis.
  © Kas Oosterhuis

Van Berkel & Bos Architectuurbureau.
  Erasmus Bridge, Rotterdam,
  1990–1996.
  UNStudio Erasmus Bridge project records (AP175).
  Gift of UNStudio.
  © UNStudio

Peter Kulka with Ulrich Königs.
  Chemnitz Stadium, 1995.
  Ulrich Königs Chemnitz Stadium project records (AP183).
  Gift of Ulrich Königs.
  © Peter Kulka with Ulrich Königs

Kolatan/Mac Donald Studio.
  O/K Apartment, New York,
  1995–1997
  KOL/MAC project records (AP185).
  Gift of KOL/MAC.
  © KOL/MAC

Foreign Office Architects.
  Yokohama International Port Terminal, 1995–2002.
  Foreign Office Architects fonds (AP171).
  Gift of Farshid Moussavi and Alejandro Zaera-Polo.
  © Farshid Moussavi and Alejandro Zaera-Polo

Neil M. Denari Architects.
  Interrupted Projections, Tokyo, 1996.
  Neil Denari *Interrupted Projections* project records (AP168).
  Gifts of Neil Denari and Mr. Koz.
  © Neil Denari

Reiser + Umemoto. Kansai-kan,
  National Diet Library, Kyoto, 1996.
  RUR Architecture Kansai-kan, National Diet Library project records (AP177).
  Gift of RUR Architecture.
  © RUR Architecture

Morphosis. Hypo Alpe-Adria Center,
  Klagenfurt, Austria, 1996–2002.
  Morphosis Hypo Alpe-Adria Center project records (AP192).
  Gift of Morphosis.
  © Morphosis

OCEAN North.
  Jyväskylä Music and Arts Centre,
  Jyväskylä, Finland, 1997.
  Johan Bettum OCEAN North project records (AP194).
  Gift of Johan Bettum.
  © OCEAN North.
  Kivi Sotamaa OCEAN North project records (AP198).
  Gift of Kivi Sotamaa.
  © OCEAN North

Office dA.
  Witte Arts Center, Green Bay, United States, 2000.
  Office dA project records (AP179).
  Gift of Mónica Ponce de León and Nader Tehrani.
  © Office dA

Zaha Hadid Architects.
  Phaeno Science Centre, Wolfsburg, Germany, 2000–2005.
  Zaha Hadid Architects Phaeno Science Centre project records (AP195).
  Gift of Zaha Hadid Foundation.
  © Zaha Hadid Foundation

Cloud 9.
  Villa Nurbs, Empuriabrava, Spain, 2000–2015.
  Cloud 9 Villa Nurbs project records (AP186).
  Gift of Enric Ruiz Geli.
  © Enric Ruiz Geli/Cloud 9

Projects selected as part of the Archaeology of the Digital research program

Testa & Weiser. Carbon Tower, 2001.
    Testa & Weiser project records (AP174).
    Gift of Peter Testa and Devyn Weiser.
    © Peter Testa and Devyn Weiser

Preston Scott Cohen.
    Eyebeam Atelier Museum, New York, 2001.
    Preston Scott Cohen Eyebeam project records (AP190).
    Gift of Preston Scott Cohen.
    © Preston Scott Cohen

COOP HIMMELB(L)AU.
    BMW Welt, Munich, 2001–2007.
    COOP HIMMELB(L)AU BMW Welt project records (AP181).
    Gift of COOP HIMMELB(L)AU.
    © COOP HIMMELB(L)AU

R&Sie(n).
    Water Flux, Évolène, Switzerland, 2002–2010.
    R&Sie(n) project records (AP193).
    Gift of New-Territories/R&Sie(n) by François Roche and Stéphanie Lavaux. © New-Territories/R&Sie(n) by François Roche and Stéphanie Lavaux

Index

Page numbers in italics refer to images.

Alberti, Leon Battista, 36, *37*, 39, 44, 425, 439n17

Alexander, Christopher, 87, 196–202, *197*, *199*, 261

Anderson, Amy, *413*, 414

Anderson, Carl David, *103*, 106, 115

Archaeology of the Digital, 281–334

Archigram, *86*, 87, *88*, 89, *179*, *184*

Architecture Machine Group, *123*, 125–176, *140*, *141*, *162*, 206–209, 248, 285; transition to Media Lab, 126, 136, 168, 206, 209. *See also* Aspen Movie Map

Arets, Wiel, *412*, 414, 415

Argyris, John, *267*, *268*, 269–270

Ars Electronica, 290, *337*, 339–341, *342*, 345, *376*

Ashby, W. Ross, 196, *197*, 441n33

Aspen Movie Map, *128–129*, 131–132, 142, 168–174, *169*, *171*, *172*, 207

Asymptote Architecture (Hani Rashid and Lise Anne Couture), *60–61*, 63, 70, 300, *302*, 303

Babbage, Charles, 51–53, *53*, *54*, 62–63, 386

Balmond, Cecil, 323, *328*

Baran, Paul, *200*, 201

Behnisch, Günther, 236, 263, *264–265*

Benjamin, Walter, 44, 170

Berkeley, University of California, *116*, 118

Bernal, J. D., 260

Bertillon, Jacques, *94*, 95

Bill, Max, 259, 271

BIM (building information modelling), 316, 423–437

Branch, Melville, 95, *96*

Brunelleschi, Filippo, 424–425

Cache, Bernard, 90, 308, 387, 390, 395; Objectile panels, 287–289, *288*, 300, 309–314, *311*, *313*

Cennini, Cennino, 30–31

Cesariano, Cesare, *27*, 28–29

Chu, Karl, 90, 395; Catastrophe Machine and X Phylum, 287, 300, 308–309, *310*, *311*, *397*

Cloud 9, 315, *329*, 330, *332*

Cohen, Preston Scott, 92, 287, 315, 323, *327*

Columbia University. *See* paperless studios

computer numerical control (CNC), 84, *85*, 275, 287, 289, 299, 312–314, 315, 316, 330, 398

Coop Himmelb(l)au, 315, 322, 323, *324*, *329*

Corbusier, Le (Charles-Édouard Jeanneret), 42, 95, 136

cybernetics, 84, 87, 95, 125–175, 223–224, 261

Deleuze, Gilles, 90, 312, 389–390

Demers, Pierre, 115

Denari, Neil, 315, 322, *325*

Derrida, Jacques, 389

digital fabrication. *See* computer numerical control (CNC)

Diller + Scofidio (Elizabeth Diller and Ricardo Scofidio), 354–355, *358*, 387, *388*, 389

Doxiadis, Constantine, *403*, 404

Eames, Charles and Ray, 87, *190*, 207

Easterling, Keller, 380–381, 415

Eisenman, Peter, 89, 90, 202, *388*, 389, 395, *396*; Biozentrum, *281*, 289–290, 293, 294, *296*, 299

Eisenstein, Sergei, 409, *410*

Emde, Helmut, 235–236, 246–256, *251*, 262–263

exhibitions, 73, 161–167, 286–287, 300. *See also* Archaeology of the Digital; Ars Electronica; Emde, Helmut; Expo '67; Expo '70; Museum of Modern Art (MoMA); Storefront for Art and Architecture; V2_Institute for the Unstable Media; Venice Biennale

Experiments in Art and Technology (EAT), 205, 227–231, *233*

Index

Expo '67, 371–373, *374*, 445n33, 445n42

Expo '70, *215*, 227–231, *228–229*, *230*, *232*, *233*, 241

FedEx, 97, 429

Flusser, Vilém, 361

Foreign Office Architects, *35*, 315, *321*, 322, 398

Forrester, Jay, 132–134, *135*, 137

Foucault, Michel, 49, 58, 70

Franken, Bernhard, 359, *362*

Frazer, John, 205–206

Friedman, Yona: the Flatwriter, 87, 220–222, 235–246, *237*, *241*, 262, 269, 275; *la ville spatiale*, *185*, 187

Fuller, Buckminster, 89, 221, 259, 348, 371–375, *374*

Galvani, Luigi, 222

Gehry, Frank, 270, 295, *296*, *297*, 391, *392*

Glaser, Donald Arthur, 106, *116*, 118

Golembewski, Michael, 402–404, *403*

Goulthorpe, Mark, *306*, 307–308

Greene, David, *181*, 183, *184*, 187. *See also* Archigram

Hadid, Zaha, 95, 315, 323, *326*; involvement in paperless studios, 407, 414, *415*

Harvard University, 118, 133, 196, 248

Hoberman, Chuck, *288,* 289, *298*, 299, 304

Huffman, Kathy Rae, 376–377

IBM: control rooms, 95, 125–126, *127*; research and machines, 25, 83, 87, *181*, 182, 196, 202

Institut für Neue Medien, 339, 359

Internet, 25, 31, 55, 83, 359, 386–387; impact on architecture practice, 84, 97, 312, 432

Isozaki, Arata, *215*, 227, *230*, *231*, *232*

Jaquet-Droz, Pierre, 224, *225*

Kahn, Louis, 31, 221

Kiesler, Frederick, 191

Klonarides, Carole Ann, 376

Knowbotic Research, 355–359, *360*

Kolatan/Mac Donald Studio, 315, *317*, 318, 322–323, *326*

Königs, Ulrich, 315, 323, *328*

Koolhaas, Rem, 92, 407

Krampen, Martin, 261–262

Kuhn, Thomas, 102–104

Kulka, Peter, 315, 323, *328*

Kurgan, Laura, 377–378, *379*

Kwinter, Sanford, 375, 390, 402

Leibniz, Gottfried Wilhelm, 51

Leonidov, Ivan, *186*, 187

Libeskind, Daniel, 58–62, 389, 395, 407, 444n12

Llull, Ramon, 51, *52*

Lovelace, Augusta Ada King, Countess of, 62. *See also* Babbage, Charles

Luther, Joachim, *247*, *252*, 253

Lynch, Kevin, 132–133

Lynn, Greg: Embryological House, 283–284, 309, *397*, 424, 429, 436; involvement in paperless studios, 394, 410–411, 414–415, *415*; theoretical work, 42, 89–90, 387, *388*, 389–391, *392*. *See also* Archaeology of the Digital

Mac Donald, Bill, *416*. *See also* Kolatan/Mac Donald Studio

Maldonado, Tomás, 224–225, 256–259, *257*

March, Lionel, *86*, 87, 221

Marey, Étienne-Jules, 90, *91*

Martin, Leslie, 87, 221

Martin, Reinhold, 87, 373–375

Martin, William R., *203*, 205

Massachusetts Institute of Technology: research labs, 87, 118, 119, 182, 196, 207, 386; urbanism research, 133–134, 234, 441n21. *See also* Architecture Machine Group; Sutherland, Ivan; Wiener, Norbert

McCulloch, Warren, 150–158, *154*

McLuhan, Marshall, 76, 188, 443n2, 445n31

Media Lab. *See* Architecture Machine Group

Menabrea, Luigi Federico, 62

Mies van der Rohe, Ludwig, 44, 187

military: funding and sponsorship of research, 113–115, 119–120, 131, 151–153, 158, 182, 206; technology used by, 85, 207–209, 386. *See also* simulation

Millikan, Robert, *105,* 106, 112

Milne, Murray, 227, 234

Moretti, Luigi, 221, 242–246, *243*, *244*

Mulder, Arjen, 381

Museum of Modern Art (MoMA): *Deconstructivist Architecture*, 389, 391; definition of drawing, 180–183

Muybridge, Eadweard, 90, *91*

Nees, Georg, *401*, 402

Negroponte, Nicholas: *The Architecture Machine* and machine intelligence, 136–151, *138–139*, *143*, *144–145*, *148–149*, 224–226, 234–235, 242; *Being Digital*, 83; *Soft Architecture Machines* and responsive environments, 126–130, 161–174, *164–165*. *See also* Architecture Machine Group

Novak, Marcos, 364

NOX (firm), 354, 415; H$_2$Oexpo, 300–303, *301*, 348, 361–367, *363*, *366*

NOX (magazine), *352*, *353*, 354, *356*, 357

Noyes, Eliot, 87

Index

OCEAN North, 315, 318, *320*

Office dA, 315, 330, *331*

ONL (Kas Oosterhuis and Ilona Lénárd), 285, 287, 300, 304–307, *305*, 361

Otto, Frei: Olympic Stadium in Munich, 236, 262–270, *264–265*, 272, *369*; research at the Institut für Leichtbau Entwerfen und Konstruiren, 367–375, *368*, *372*

Palladio, Andrea, *38*, 39–40

paper: material condition, 55–56, 70, 97, 407; paper machines, 51, 58–63; as a support for drawing, 25–31, 35–44, 179–180, 191, 426–429, 430–432

paperless studios, 28, 89, 97, 289, 380–381, 385–404, 407–419

Pasquarelli, Gregg. *See* SHoP Architects

photographs: 90, 187–191, 303, 322, 402–404, 414; and image analysis, 104–106, 111–115, 118, 269–270, 367–371

Pitts, Walter, 153–156, *154*

Powell, C. F., 112–113, *114*

Price, Cedric, 87, 183, *183*, *195*, 196, 202–206, *203*, *204*

Rashid, Hani, 89, 389, 398; involvement in paperless studios, 411–415, *413*, *416*. *See also* Asymptote Architecture

Reas, Casey, 400, *401*

Reiser + Umemoto, 315, 318, *319*

Resch, Ron, 272–276, *273*, *274*

Rittel, Horst, 261–262

Roche, François, 92, *93*, 315–316, *317*

Rosenblatt, Frank, *155*, 156–157

Rutherford, Ernest, *108*, 111

Saarinen, Eero, 87, 426, *427*

Sassen, Saskia, 378–381

Scamozzi, Vincenzo, 30, *37*

Scarpa, Carlo, *30*, 31

Schumacher, Patrik, 309, 323; involvement in paperless studios, 414, *414*

Second World War, 69, 113–120, 151, 245, 386

Selfridge, Oliver, *155*, 158–160

Serlio, Sebastiano, 39, 42

Shannon, Claude, 217–224, *218*, *220*, 262

SHoP Architects, 338, *399*

simulation: behavioural, 130–134, 235, 270–271; of forces, 222, 263–270, 292–294, 315, 323, 394, 429–430; military and war games, 131, 261–262, 373

software: animation, 309, 322, 359, 424; CAD, 55, 182, 295, 426–432; coding and customization, 219, 235–242, 246–256, 262–277, 287–289, 294, 299, 307–314, 402; FormZ, 289, 318, 394, 402; Maya, 309, 394, 402, 429; Softimage, 303, 309, 394, 402; in terms of media archaeology, 51–55, 70

Spuybroek, Lars, 89. *See also* NOX (firm) and *NOX* (magazine)

Storefront for Art and Architecture, 364, 378, *379*, 443n1

Sutherland, Ivan, *181*, 182, 206, 386

Talbot, William Henry Fox, 188

Tange, Kenzo, 201, 227, *228–229*, *230*, *232*

Teicholz, Eric, 248, 253, *254*

Testa & Weiser, 315, 322, *327*

Thompson, D'Arcy Wentworth, 196, *198*, 390, 394

Tschumi, Bernard, 92, 195, 389, 390, *408*, *409*, *411*, *418*. *See also* paperless studios

Turing, Alan, 62, 70, 146, 153

Ulm, Hochschule für Gestaltung, 87, 220–221, 224, 256–262

V2_ Institute for the Unstable Media, 303, 339–355, *343*, *344*, *346*, *347*, 378

Van Berkel & Bos Architectuurbureau, 315, 316, *317*, *427*

Venice Biennale, 58–62, 286, 307

Vignola, Giacomo Barozzi da, *38*, 39–40, *41*, *43*

Virilio, Paul, 73, 341–345, 354

virtual reality: and archiving the immaterial, 56, 63–70; and interactivity, 303–307, 337, 345, 349–351, 359, 378; and the "real," 131, 173, 209

Vitruvius, 36–39

Wiener, Norbert, 152, 221, 223–224, 259, 262

Wilson, C. T. R., *109*, 110–112, 115

Woods, Lebbeus, *346*, 351, 354

Xenakis, Iannis, *74*, 76

Yoh, Shoei, 290–294, *291*, *293*, 390, *391*

Zentrum für Kunst und Medientechnologie, 339, 377

Biographies

Stan Allen
is an architect and George Dutton '27 Professor of Architecture at the School of Architecture, Princeton University, where he directs the Center for Architecture, Urbanism, and Infrastructure. He taught at Columbia University's Graduate School of Architecture, Planning and Preservation from 1989 until 2002, and served as dean of the School of Architecture at Princeton from 2002 until 2012.

Phil Bernstein
is an architect and is a lecturer in professional practice at the Yale School of Architecture. From 2000 through 2016 he was Vice President, Strategic Industry Relations at Autodesk, where he set the company's vision and strategy for technology and cultivated and sustained relationships with industry leaders and associations. Before joining Autodesk, Bernstein was a principal at Pelli Clarke Pelli Architects.

Nathalie Bredella
is a visiting professor of architectural history, with a focus on media and gender studies, at the Universität der Künste Berlin, where she previously led the research project Architecture and New Media, funded by the Deutsche Forschungsgemeinschaft (DFG).

Mario Carpo
is Reyner Banham Professor of Architectural History and Theory, The Bartlett, University College London. His work addresses the Vitruvian tradition in the early modern period, as well as contemporary digital design theory. He was head of the Study Centre at the Canadian Centre for Architecture from 2002 until 2005. He is the author of *Architecture in the Age of Printing* (MIT Press, 2001), *The Alphabet and the Algorithm* (MIT Press, 2011) and other books.

Wolfgang Ernst
is a professor of media theories at the Institut für Musikwissenschaft und Medienwissenschaft at the Humboldt-Universität zu Berlin. Trained as a historian and a classicist, he works on media archaeology, archival theory and museology. His current research is concerned with technologies of cultural transmission, micro-temporal media aesthetics and sound analysis. Most recently, he is the author of *Sonic Time Machines: Explicit Sound, Sirenic Voices and Implicit Sonicity in Terms of Media Knowledge* (University of Amsterdam Press, 2016) and *Chronopoetics: The Temporal Being and Operativity of Technological Media* (Rowman and Littlefield, 2016).

Marco Frascari
(1945–2013) was an architect and theorist of architecture. He was director of the Azrieli School of Architecture and Urbanism at Carleton University. His work addresses architectural representation, tectonics, food and architecture, storytelling, and architectural thinking. He is the author of *Monsters of Architecture: Anthropomorphism in Architectural Theory* (Rowman and Littlefield, 1991) and *Eleven Exercises in the Art of Architectural Drawing: Slow Food for the Architect's Imagination* (Routledge, 2011).

Peter Galison
is Joseph Pellegrino University Professor at Harvard University. He is a historian of science, and his research principally concerns twentieth-century microphysics. He is the author of *Image and Logic: A Material Culture of Microphysics* (University of Chicago Press, 1997), *Objectivity* (with Lorraine Daston, Zone Books, 2007) and other books. With Robb Moss, he directed the film *Containment* (2015), which addresses the need to guard radioactive materials for the next ten thousand years. His forthcoming book *Building Crashing Thinking* concerns the back and forth between the self and modern technologies.

Andrew Goodhouse
is an editor at the Canadian Centre for Architecture. He is a graduate of the master of arts program at the Bard Graduate Center: Decorative Arts, Design History, Material Culture.

Orit Halpern
is an associate professor of anthropology and sociology at Concordia University. Her work bridges the histories of science, computing and cybernetics with design and art practice. She is also co-director of the Speculative Life research lab, a design research cluster at the intersection of art, the life sciences, architecture and computational media that is part of the Milieux Institute for Arts, Culture and Technology at Concordia. She is the author of *Beautiful Data: A History of Vision and Reason Since 1945* (Duke University Press, 2014).

Greg Lynn
is an architect working from Los Angeles. He taught at Columbia University's Graduate School of Architecture, Planning and Preservation from 1992 until 1999. He is currently Ordentlicher University Professor at the Universität für angewandte Kunst Wien and a studio professor at the School of Architecture and Urban Design at the University of California, Los Angeles, where he developed an experimental robotics research laboratory.

Antoine Picon
is G. Ware Travelstead Professor of the History of Architecture and Technology and the director of research at Harvard University's Graduate School of Design. His research concerns the history of architectural and urban technologies from the eighteenth century to the present. He is the author, most recently, of *Smart Cities: A Spatialised Intelligence* (Wiley, 2015).

Molly Wright Steenson
is an associate professor at Carnegie Mellon School of Design. Her research looks at the intersection of technology, architecture and communication in the 1960s and 1970s. Her book *Architecting Interactivity* will be published by MIT Press in 2017.

Biographies

Bernard Tschumi
is an architect with offices in New York and Paris. Between 1976 and 1981 he developed the Manhattan Transcripts, a theoretical project that proposed a reading of architecture through the relationships between space, event and movement. He currently teaches at Columbia University's Graduate School of Architecture, Planning and Preservation, where he was dean from 1988 until 2003.

Mark Wigley
is a professor of architecture at Columbia University's Graduate School of Architecture, Planning and Preservation, where he was dean from 2004 until 2014. He is a historian and theorist who explores the intersection of architecture, art, philosophy, culture and technology. His latest books include *Buckminster Fuller Inc.: Architecture in the Age of Radio* (Lars Müller Publishers, 2015) and, with Beatriz Colomina, *Are We Human?: Notes on an Archaeology of Design* (Lars Müller Publishers, 2016). He has curated numerous exhibitions. Most recently, he co-curated the 3rd Istanbul Design Biennial with Beatriz Colomina, titled *Are We Human?: The Design of the Species: 2 seconds, 2 days, 2 years, 200 years, 200,000 years.*

Andrew Witt
is an assistant professor in practice in architecture at Harvard University's Graduate School of Design. His work addresses the relationship of geometry to perception, construction, automation and culture. He is trained as an architect and a mathematician and is a co-founder of Certain Measures, a design and technology incubator with offices in Boston and Berlin that applies systemic and scalable approaches to spatial problems.

Mirko Zardini
is an architect, author and curator, and has been director of the Canadian Centre for Architecture since 2005. His research engages the transformation of contemporary architecture and its relationship with the city and the environment by questioning and re-examining assumptions on which architects operate today. *It's All Happening So Fast*, his exhibition at the CCA in 2016 and 2017, is a reflection on our often conflicting ideas about human relationships to the environment.

Image and copyright credits

Every reasonable attempt has been made to appropriately credit material appearing in this publication. Errors and omissions will be corrected in subsequent reprints.

Marco Frascari
AN AGE OF PAPER

2 Photograph by Jörg P. Anders. Courtesy of Art Resource

Mario Carpo
BUILDING WITH GEOMETRY, DRAWING WITH NUMBERS

1 © Farshid Moussavi and Alejandro Zaera-Polo

2 Courtesy of Mario Carpo

Wolfgang Ernst
TOWARD A MUSEOLOGY OF ALGORITHMIC ARCHITECTURES FROM WITHIN

1 Image produced by the New Materialities research team at the Institut für Physik, Humboldt-Universität zu Berlin, led by Prof. Dr. Saskia F. Fischer, with special thanks to Jürgen Solle

2 Courtesy of the Institut für Physik, Humboldt-Universität zu Berlin. Photograph by Benjamin Renter

3 Courtesy of the National Archaeological Museum, Athens. Photograph by Kostas Xenikakis. © Hellenic Ministry of Culture and Sports/Archaeological Receipts Fund

5, 6 Courtesy of the Science Museum/Science & Society Picture Library

7 Courtesy of the Deutsches Museum, München

9 © Asymptote

10 Stiftung Frauenkirche Dresden, made by Jörg Lauterbach, architect, 1997–2005

11 Courtesy of the Medienarchäologischer Fundus, Humboldt-Universität zu Berlin. Photograph by Benjamin Renter

12 Courtesy of Adam Laurie, Aperture Labs Ltd.

13 Courtesy of Nikita Braguinski

14 Courtesy of the Bibliothèque nationale de France. © Collection Famille Xenakis

Antoine Picon
HISTORIES OF THE DIGITAL: INFORMATION, COMPUTER AND COMMUNICATION

1 Courtesy of the Friedrich-Wilhelm-Murnau-Stiftung

4, 6 Image courtesy of Archigram Archives. © Archigram

5 Courtesy of Lionel March

9 © New-Territories/R&Sie(n) by François Roche and Stéphanie Lavaux

Peter Galison
EPISTEMIC MACHINES: IMAGE AND LOGIC

1 Courtesy of the British Geological Survey

3 Courtesy of CERN. © CERN

6 Photograph by Pascal Faligot. © Musée des arts et métiers-Cnam, Paris

9 Courtesy of the University of Glasgow Archive Services

10 Courtesy of Science Photo Library

11, 12 Courtesy of Lawrence Berkeley Laboratory Archives

13 Courtesy of the Fermi National Accelerator Laboratory

Image and copyright credits

Orit Halpern
ARCHITECTURE AS MACHINE: THE SMART CITY DECONSTRUCTED

1, 11   Courtesy of the MIT Museum

2   Photograph by Orit Halpern

3, 5, 6, 7, 8, 9, 10, 17, 18, 19, 20
Courtesy of the MIT Media Lab

15, 16
Courtesy of Nicholas Negroponte

Mark Wigley
BLACK SCREENS: THE ARCHITECT'S VISION IN A DIGITAL AGE

1, 5   Courtesy of Archigram Archives. © Archigram.

3   Courtesy of General Motors Media Archive. © General Motors

4   © CCA

6, 7   © Yona Friedman

9   Courtesy of Antique Home Style

10   © 2016 Eames Office, LLC

Molly Wright Steenson
INFORMATION ARCHAEOLOGIES

1, 10, 12   © CCA

2, 3, 6, 7   © 1964 by the President and Fellows of Harvard College. © renewed 1992 by Christopher Alexander

8   Courtesy of the Rand Corporation

9   Courtesy of the Science Museum/ Science & Society Picture Library

13, 14
Courtesy of Nicholas Negroponte

15   Courtesy of Mark Dorf. © Mark Dorf

Andrew Witt
THE MACHINIC ANIMAL: AUTONOMIC NETWORKS AND BEHAVIOURAL COMPUTATION

1, 8, 9,
Courtesy of Arata Isozaki & Associates.
© Arata Isozaki & Associates

2   Courtesy of Keystone/Stringer/ Getty Images

6, 7, 10   © Bill Cotter

11   © J. Paul Getty Trust

12, 13   © Yona Friedman

16, 17, 18, 19, 20, 21, 22
Courtesy of the Goethe-Institut.
© 1976 Goethe-Institut

23   Photograph by Hans G. Conrad. © René Spitz

25   © Meunierd/Shutterstock.com

26   © Marios C. Phocas

27   © Springer-Verlag Berlin Heidelberg

28   © Douglas Trumbull

29   Photograph by Myke Waddy

Greg Lynn
GOING NATIVE: NOTES ON SELECTED ARTIFACTS FROM DIGITAL ARCHITECTURE AT THE END OF THE TWENTIETH CENTURY

1, 6, 7   © CCA

2, 11, 12   © Hoberman Associates

3, 22, 23   © Bernard Cache

4, 5   © Shoei Yoh + Architects

8, 9, 10
Courtesy of Frank O. Gehry & Associates. © Frank O. Gehry & Associates

13, 14   © NOX

15   © Asymptote

16, 17   © Kas Oosterhuis

18, 19   © Mark Goulthorpe

20, 21   © Karl S. Chu

24   © UNStudio

25   © New-Territories/R&Sie(n) by François Roche and Stéphanie Lavaux

26   © KOL/MAC

27, 28   © RUR Architecture

29   © Morphosis

30   © OCEAN North

31, 32   © Farshid Moussavi and Alejandro Zaera-Polo

33, 42   © COOP HIMMELB(L)AU

34, 35   © Neil Denari

36   © Michael Moran / OTTO

37   Courtesy of Zaha Hadid Foundation. © Zaha Hadid Foundation

38   © Preston Scott Cohen

39   © Peter Testa and Devyn Weiser

40   © Peter Kulka with Ulrich Königs

41   Courtesy of Cecil Balmond. © Cecil Balmond

43, 45   © Enric Ruiz Geli/Cloud 9

44   © Office dA

Image and copyright credits

Nathalie Bredella
IN THE MIDST OF THINGS: ARCHITECTURE'S ENCOUNTER WITH DIGITAL TECHNOLOGY, MEDIA THEORY AND MATERIAL CULTURE

1, 8 Courtesy of Jeffrey Shaw. © Jeffrey Shaw

2 Courtesy of Getty Images

3 Courtesy of Christine Meierhofer. © Christine Meierhofer

4, 5, 6, 7, 14 © V2_ Lab for the Unstable Media

9, 10, 11, 12, 16, 17, 18 © NOX

13 Courtesy of Jan Sprij. © Jan Sprij

15 Courtesy of Franken Architekten. © Franken Architekten

19, 20, 21, 22, 23, 24 © Institut für Leichtbau Entwerfen und Konstruieren Universität Stuttgart

25 Courtesy of The Estate of R. Buckminster Fuller

26 © Laura Kurgan

Stan Allen
THE PAPERLESS STUDIOS IN CONTEXT

1 Courtesy of Greg Lynn. © Greg Lynn

2 Courtesy of Diller Scofidio + Renfro

4 © Shoei Yoh + Architects

6 Photograph by Stan Allen

8 © Eisenman Architects

9 © Greg Lynn

10 © Karl S. Chu

11 © SHoP Architects PC

12 © Marc Fornes / THEVERYMANY

13 © Hochschule Ostwestfalen-Lippe

14 Courtesy of Casey Reas and bitforms gallery, New York. © Casey Reas

15 Courtesy of Kunsthalle Bremen. © Estate of Georg Nees

16 © Michael Golembewski

17 © Estate of Peter N. Witt

Bernard Tschumi
THE MAKING OF A GENERATION: HOW THE PAPERLESS STUDIOS CAME ABOUT

1 © David Joseph Photography

2, 3, 4, 6, 15 © Bernard Tschumi

7, 8, 9, 10, 11, 12, 13, 14 © The Trustees of Columbia University in the City of New York

Phil Bernstein
SOUND ADVICE AND CLEAR DRAWINGS: DESIGN AND COMPUTATION IN THE SECOND MACHINE AGE

1 Courtesy of RIBA

2 Courtesy of Manuscripts and Archives, Yale University Library

3 © UNStudio

4 © Pelli Clarke Pelli Architects

5, 6, 7, 8 © Autodesk

Credits

Edited by Andrew Goodhouse

Editorial assistance:
Annie Breton, Irene Chin, Jayne Kelley

Design:
Studio Katja Gretzinger, Berlin

Transcription:
Christiane Côté, Jay Watts

Rights and reproductions:
Elspeth Cowell, Pierre-Alexis Jasmin, Marc Pitre, Yan Romanesky

CCA photography:
Michel Boulet, Denis Farley, Mélissa Pilon

Special thanks to Dennis Crompton, Paola Frascari, Federica Goffi, Stefan Kloo, Andrew Lippman and Gabriela Metzger.

The CCA is an international research centre and museum founded on the conviction that architecture is a public concern. Based on its extensive collection, exhibitions, programs and research opportunities the CCA is a leading voice in advancing knowledge, promoting public understanding and widening thought and debate on architecture, its history, theory, practice and role in society today.

CCA Board of Trustees
Phyllis Lambert, Founding Director Emeritus; Bruce Kuwabara, Chair; Pierre-André Themens, Vice-Chair; Guido Beltramini; Stephen R. Bronfman; Barry Campbell; Michael Conforti; Timur Galen; Normand Grégoire; Isabelle Jomphe; Sylvia Lavin; Frederick Lowy; Gerald Sheff; Mirko Zardini. Honorary members: Serge Joyal, Warren Simpson

This publication received the generous support of the Graham Foundation for Advanced Studies in the Fine Arts. The CCA gratefully acknowledges the additional support of the Ministère de la Culture et des Communications, the Canada Council for the Arts and the Conseil des arts de Montréal.

This is a companion volume to *Archaeology of the Digital*, edited by Greg Lynn and published by the CCA and Sternberg Press in 2013. It is also issued in French under the title *Quand le numérique marque-t-il l'architecture?*

For more information on CCA Publications, please visit cca.qc.ca/publications.

Canadian Centre for Architecture
1920, rue Baile
Montréal, Québec
Canada H3H 2S6
www.cca.qc.ca

Sternberg Press
Caroline Schneider
Karl-Marx-Allee 78
D-10243 Berlin
www.sternberg-press.com

All rights reserved under international copyright conventions

Legal deposit: April 2017

Printed and bound by
DZA Druckerei zu Altenburg

Bibliothèque et Archives nationales du Québec and Library and Archives Canada cataloguing in publication

Main entry under title :
When is the digital in architecture?
Co-published by Sternberg Press.
Issued also in French under title :
Quand le numérique marque-t-il l'architecture?
Includes bibliographical references and index.

ISBN 978-2-927071-46-5

1. Architectural design - Data processing. 2. Architecture - Technological innovations. I. Goodhouse, Andrew, 1989- . II. Canadian Centre for Architecture.

NA2728.W43 2016   720.285
C2016-941878-2